SUDAN

4.⁰⁰

DR RICHARD COCKETT has reported from Latin America, Africa and Asia for *The Economist*. He was South-East Asia correspondent from 2010–14. Before joining *The Economist* he was a senior lecturer in history and politics at the University of London. He is the author of several books, including *Blood, Dreams and Gold: The Changing Face of Burma* (Yale, 2015). He lives in London.

SUDAN

THE FAILURE AND DIVISION OF AN AFRICAN STATE

RICHARD COCKETT

YALE UNIVERSITY PRESS
NEW HAVEN AND LONDON

For information about this and other Yale University Press publications, please contact:

U.S. Office: sales.press@yale.edu   yalebooks.com
Europe Office: sales@yaleup.co.uk   yalebooks.co.uk

Set in Janson Text by IDSUK (DataConnection) Ltd

Maps by Peter Winfield

Printed in Great Britain by Hobbs the Printers Ltd, Totton, Hampshire

Library of Congress Control Number: 2016950450

A catalogue record for this book is available from the British Library.

ISBN 978-0-300-21531-1 (pbk)

10 9 8 7 6 5 4 3 2 1

CONTENTS

ACKNOWLEDGEMENTS

Just like the various international peacekeeping forces that have tried to bring some sort of order to Sudan, this book is also something of a 'hybrid'. It is part journalism and part history, reflecting my two chosen careers (to date).

Sudan: Darfur and the Failure of an African State is mainly the product of six trips to Sudan undertaken between 2005 and 2010 for *The Economist* while I was Africa editor of the paper. Yet the book should also, I hope, be rooted in the academic discipline of history. For before joining *The Economist* I was a lecturer in history, politics and political thought for ten years or so at the University of London, principally at Royal Holloway and Bedford New College, where I gained a PhD in history in 1988.

I thus have two sets of intellectual and professional debts to record here. I owe my enduring love of history to my two schoolmasters, Dr Peter Carter and Oliver Ramsbotham; their classes continue to inspire everyone who was lucky enough to be present, even if it is now thirty-odd years ago. And at *The Economist*, Gideon Rachman and Emma Duncan showed me how to be a journalist, in as far as what we do at the paper can be described as such. Peter David brought me into the Foreign Department and let me loose in Africa, while Xan Smiley accepted my frequent absences in the deserts and marshes of Sudan with good grace. The editor, John Micklethwait, generously gave me a substantial amount of time off to research and write the book; this also allowed me time to travel to America, France and Chad to do some extra interviews. It's one of the paper's better intellectual traditions that journalists are positively encouraged to explore their favourite subjects at greater length. Also at *The Economist*, Peter Winfield helped with the maps; Bagehot and the famous author provided the cheer and good company. I am grateful to them all. Nonetheless, all the views expressed in this book are my own, independent of the editorial position of *The Economist*.

I must also thank several people who have guided me, both intellectually and sometimes physically, around the country and its rich history. Some of them are also victims of a similar obsession with Sudan – some of them are actually Sudanese. They have been my companions throughout this project, often intervening to help and sharpen my thinking at crucial moments. They are Aicha Elbasri, Blake Evans-Pritchard, Richard Gowan, Mo Ibrahim, Hadeel Ibrahim, Laura James, Jonathan Ledgard and Athanasios and George Pagoulatos, the proprietors of the Acropole Hotel in Khartoum, the best establishment of its kind in Africa and reason alone to keep coming back to the country. I am also indebted to Alex de Waal for reading part of the manuscript, and to Juliana Barrett for sharing her insights on southern Sudanese place-names and for doing the index. In the end though, all the judgements in this book are mine, as are the misjudgements.

At Yale University Press Phoebe Clapham snapped the book up encouragingly quickly and has guided the whole process through firmly and efficiently. Thanks to her, and to my agent Araminta Whitley.

I spoke to scores of Sudanese people, in all walks of life, for the book. Some of them feature by name in the following pages. However, I would also like to thank those below who agreed to do more formal interviews with me, often on several occasions and sometimes over the course of a couple of days:

ACKNOWLEDGEMENTS

Ali Abdulrahman Abbas; Al Tayib Zein al-Abdin; Jimmy Abirigo; Ahmed Hussein Adam; Malik Agar; Saif Ahmad; Ali Abdalla Ali; Pa'gan Amum; Elthar Bashery Ali; Ghazi Atabani; Omer Abdel Ati; Cage Banseka; Sajoh Bar; Saif Adeen al-Bashir; Ahmed Bedawi; Oliver Bercault; Sam Brownback; Margie Buchanan-Smith; Jack Christofides; Yu Chunhua; Luigi Cignolini; Richard Cizik; Ian Cliff; Orla Clinton; Baroness Caroline Cox; Gillian Cull; Francis Deng; Nick Donovan; Jan Egeland; John Eibner; Aicha Elbasri; Abduljabbar Abdellah Fadul; Mia Farrow; Alberto Fernandez; Michael Gerson; Alan Goulty; Lise Grande; David Gressly; Diane de Guzman; Jonah Fisher; Jerry Fowler; Mark Hanis; Simon Haselock; AbuZeid el-Hassan; Randa Hassan; Michael Hoare; Nathan Holt; Mo Ibrahim; Amira Idris; Margunn Indreboe; Ronald Isaacson; Omer Ismail; Chris Johnson; Hassan Kambal; Dr Mukesh Kapila; Asha el-Karib; Sayid el-Khatib; Monyluak Kuol; Ring Kuol; Patricia Lane; Osama Latif; Ian Levine; Gill Lusk; Riek Machar; Adam Madibu; Abda al-Mahdi; Sadiq al-Mahdi; Mubarak A.F. al-Mahdi; Bona Malwal; Rosalind Marsden; Andrew Marshall; Kuol Athian Mawien; Opheera McDoom; Ruth Messinger; Hafiz Mohamed; Abdul Mohammed; Stephen Morrison; Osman Mudawi; Albaqir Alafif Mukhtar; Theo Murphy; Robert Muwanga; Deborah Mwania; Andrew Natsios; Caroline Nursey; David Nyuma; Michael O'Neil; Salih M. Osman; Athanasios Pagoulatos; George Pagoulatos; Sarah Pantuliano; Donald Payne; Andrew Pendleton; Sir Derek Plumbly; Sir Kieran Prendergast; Bashir Adam Rahma; Philip Rowe; Salim A. Salim; Jago Salmon; Mario Samja: Jill Savitt; Michael Scheuer; Amy Scott; Derk Segaar; David Shinn; Clare Short; Amal Sidahmed; Jerzy Skuratowicz; Hugo Slim; Gayle Smith; Charles Snyder; Eythan Sontag; Lazarus Sumbeiywo; Peter Sweetnam; Elias Taban; Khalid Tigani; David, Lord Triesman; Hassan al-Turabi; Oliver Ulich; Gloria White-Hammond; Frank Wolf; Amin Salih Yasin.

I have tried to make this book as transparent and accessible as possible, thus attributing all the quotes in the book to the people who gave them to me at the appropriate point in the text. Only very occasionally have I been obliged to hide the identity of a source; this is usually because naming him or her in relation to a particular incident or point of view would jeopardize their current employment or adversely affect their residency in Sudan. Similarly, where it is appropriate, references indicate the sources I used for other information; there is also a selected bibliography at the end. In terms of the Arabic translation of words, I have chosen to be inconsistent. People's names are given in English as they chose to give their names to me, for instance, rather than adhering to some notional set of rules which does not really exist in Arabic. Likewise, place names in Arabic are given as they are most commonly rendered in the English-language literature on Sudan; they may not be spelt the same in all books on Sudan.

Finally, I happily thank my wife Harriet not only for living with Sudan at one remove for a couple of years but also for volunteering to read the text and for suggesting improvements. It can't have been too much of a burden, because in the middle of it all we had a child, Joe. He illuminates our lives immeasurably and spurred us all towards the finishing line when otherwise we might have flagged.

Richard Cockett
Hammersmith, London, 2016

LIST OF ILLUSTRATIONS

MAPS

PHOTOGRAPHS

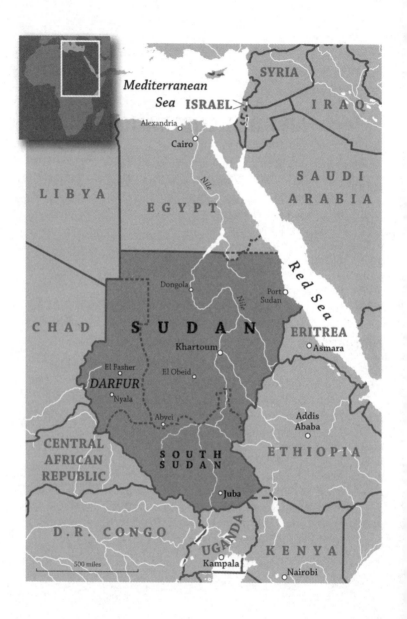

INTRODUCTION

This book is about one of the greatest humanitarian and political disasters of our age: Sudan. Why it came about, and how it became so bad. And why, despite the prolonged involvement of almost every major country and humanitarian agency in the world, conflict still rages across most of South Sudan and Sudan.

The scale of suffering across lands home to about 40 million people is daunting. The killings and destruction in the western region of Darfur, described as a 'genocide' by US Secretary of State Colin Powell in 2004, have become synonymous with Sudan in the eyes of most Westerners. Yet Darfur, where as many as 300,000 have died and about three million have been made homeless, constitutes only a small proportion of the total suffering and misery.

An on-off fifty-year civil war between the Islamist government in Khartoum and secessionist Christians and animists in the south that ended in 2005 left two million dead and millions more homeless. One activist described that war as a genocide as long ago as 1992. In the east of Sudan, a low-grade insurgency in the 1990s left still more dead and homeless. It seems to be the fate of Sudan, once Africa's largest country, to produce big statistics, commensurate with the level of violence. In proportion to its population, Sudan produced the largest number of refugees and internally displaced people in the world – six million of them. In Africa, only the Democratic Republic of Congo, perhaps, can rival Sudan's history in terms of continuous death and destruction.

Largely poor and uninhabited, Sudan and South Sudan have also sucked in an extraordinary proportion of the world's political, military and financial resources in attempts to sort them out. Here again, Sudan deals in big numbers. Towards the end of the 2000s, for instance, the UN World Food Programme was running the largest emergency feeding programme in the world in Darfur, and two of the UN's biggest-ever peacekeeping missions were running separately in the same country: one in Darfur (itself taking over from the African Union's first and, to date, biggest peacekeeping operation), peaking with 26,000 soldiers and policemen, and one in south Sudan, with about 10,000 personnel. The UN mission in Darfur alone was costing almost US$1.5 billion a year, the one in the south about $1 billion. Yet not even all this money and manpower has wholly pacified a country that, at independence in 1956, was one of the most promising and sophisticated in Africa. Indeed, in 2011 the country duly split into two. South Sudan declared itself to be the latest nation-state in the world after a referendum overwhelmingly endorsed independence. The first edition of this book took the story of Sudan up to the eve of that referendum in January 2011; this second edition continues the story to August 2016.

The purpose, however, remains the same. I set out to explain how Sudan came to implode so catastrophically, and to suggest what the often well-intentioned foreigners who tried to help the country can learn from their collective failure. No one, perhaps, ever really understood the true extent of Sudan's many dysfunctions, nor the extraordinary depth and variety of this apparently remote country's encounters with the outside world. For in Sudan, all the major forces that shape the contemporary world – religious fundamentalism (both Islamic and Christian), high finance, terrorism, ethnic hatred, oil, nationalism and the rise of Asia – have collided with one another, usually with disastrous consequences. Many of these same forces are at work in much of the rest of the poor and developing world. If the international community's investment of so much time, energy and resources in endeavouring to help the Sudanese people can have had such mixed results, it bodes ill for the rest of Africa and beyond.

One of the reasons for this, I argue, is that outsiders, in particular, have only looked at the areas or particular aspects of Sudan that have reflected their own agendas and interests. They have often failed to consider how their actions (or inactions) in one part of the country might affect another. Too often the big picture has been ignored. Likewise, most accounts of Sudan have focused narrowly on those parts of the country that have attracted attention at any one time: Darfur after 2003, the south in the 1990s, for example. As a corrective, I have tried to look at the country in the round, to explain how all its various conflicts are interlinked.

This is the story of Sudan, then, in as wide a perspective as possible, encompassing, in particular, its relations with the rest of the world. From the very start, the Sudanese government in Khartoum was too weak to exert much control over the vast amount of land that was bequeathed to it by the departing colonialists and so the country was prey to the machinations and territorial ambitions of its neighbours. In addition, more distant and powerful countries became deeply involved in the country's affairs – Britain in the nineteenth century, the USA and China in the twentieth and twenty-first centuries. Sudan's problems, and opportunities, were globalized from the very beginning; the fact that the Sudanese people continue to suffer on such an inhumane scale is a reflection of the nature of globalization today.

Nothing in Sudan has just *happened*; the catalogue of disaster, disease and death has all been man-made. Even the mass killing of Darfur was willed, and allowed to take place, because it suited the interests of certain politicians and nations. Oil-hungry Chinese, meddling Western politicians, over-simplifying activists, spineless African leaders, shamefully silent Muslim countries, land-greedy Arab tribes, myopic Sudanese politicians – all bear some responsibility for the tragedy of

Sudan. There is plenty of blame to go around; certainly more than the American Darfur activists would have us believe.

Sadly, as I argue in Chapter Eight, the 2011 division of Sudan may have finally ended the war between north and south but it has clearly provided no solutions to either country's myriad other problems. South Sudan, in particular, has been a bitter, if all too predictable, disappointment, lapsing into a lethal, ethnically inflected civil war soon after independence, and with no sign that either of the two main antagonists will give up long entrenched hatreds and antagonisms for a peaceful future. Thus the pathologies of Sudanese politics survive and prosper in the south as well as the north. Among other concerns, both countries suffer from a dearth of inspirational, or just incorrupt, leadership.

One way that President Bashir's regime survived the Arab Spring of 2011 and other upheavals has been through restricting access so as to better control the news emanating from Sudan, especially from Darfur and the Nuba mountains. Since 2014 I have been unable to get a visa to return to Khartoum, so the new chapter has been written mostly from secondary sources, as well as interviews with people who have been able to live and work in the country over the past few years.

Despite this, I have tried to tell this history of modern Sudan and the world through the words of the Sudanese themselves, letting them speak as directly as possible to the reader. Inevitably, most of the news in the West about Sudan is filtered through the Western media, of which I am a cheerful and unapologetic representative. During my five years as Africa editor of *The Economist*, I travelled around Sudan on numerous occasions, to as many parts of the country as I could, talking to hundreds of Sudanese about their own experiences and about the people, events and passions that had shaped their lives. Much of what follows draws directly on those interviews, from government ministers through to rebel commanders, from imams to HIV/AIDS activists.

I hope, also, that I manage to convey some sense of the manifold virtues of the Sudanese people. Throughout all the decades of war, famine and political self-immolation, Khartoum has remained the safest and most accepting city in Africa, just as the ordinary Sudanese remain the most hospitable and friendly people on the continent. It is that extraordinary contrast of so much softness, generosity and courtesy amidst so much poverty, grief and hatred that fascinates visitors to Sudan, and draws them back so often. If this book sheds just a little light on this paradox, then it will have gone a long way to succeeding in its task.

THE STRUCTURE OF THE BOOK

The first chapter, 'The one-city state', is an overview of Sudan's physical geography and colonial legacy; it also introduces the reader to the foreign countries that would intervene so fatefully in its post-independence history. The following two chapters are mainly a chronological history of Sudan's post-independence politics and conflicts up to 2001.

Chapter Four charts the way in which Western powers, particularly the USA, became increasingly involved in Sudan on a number of issues in the 1990s and early 2000s. This leads on to Chapter Five, 'Darfur: how the killing was allowed to happen', which looks at the dramatic events of 2003–4 when the conflict in Darfur broke out.

Chapter Six, 'Darfur: the vortex', examines the international and domestic Sudanese responses to the atrocious killings in Darfur, while Chapter Seven is largely an account of how the regime in Khartoum has survived the Darfur war, while the provisional government in South Sudan failed to prepare adequately for independence. The new Chapter Eight gives an account of both South Sudan and Sudan post-2011, up to the present.

CHAPTER ONE

THE ONE-CITY STATE

Khartoum, the capital of Sudan, is situated at the junction of the White Nile and the Blue Nile. Not that there is usually anything very colourful about either river – suffice it to say that in the middle of a desert, this is an obvious place for a city. Traditionally, whoever controlled Khartoum commanded the transport links (and water supply) of much of east and central Africa. By the time the two rivers merge into one, their precious water has already travelled hundreds of miles from what is now Uganda. Beyond Khartoum, the Nile carries on into Egypt and eventually out into the Mediterranean. Given the river's importance, it's natural, perhaps, that the Sudanese capital should take its name from the shape that the Nile describes as it flows through the city. Khartoum literally means 'elephant's trunk' in Arabic, and it's just about possible to imagine the actual meeting point of the two Niles as what one writer has described as 'the delicate cleft in the tip of such a trunk'.[1]

The best place from which to view this, and much else, in contemporary Khartoum is the top floor of one of the city's newest landmarks, located almost exactly at the confluence of the two Niles. This is the Burj Al-Fateh hotel, known to the locals more simply as 'Ghadaffi's Egg' (or even 'Ghadaffi's Grenade'), a not altogether flattering tribute to its quixotic owner and exotic shape. The hotel opened in August 2008, the most spectacular addition to Khartoum's burgeoning skyline. The management, not unnaturally for such a swanky establishment, jib at the comparison with an egg; they prefer to see it as a sail, presumably to conjure up images of opulent Dubai rather than some gigantic chicken. But what is not disputed is the fact that the 'Egg' is indeed Colonel Ghadaffi's project, built for approximately 130 million euros by a Libyan government-owned holding company. It took a long eight years to build, but the result is genuinely impressive, even if Ghadaffi did not live long enough to enjoy it much: he was killed by his own people during the 'Arab Spring' in 2011. The curvaceous glass and steel construction captures the eye from almost any point in the city.

Khartoum has long been the poor relation of Cairo, and the Egg is the most potent symbol of the Sudanese capital's headlong rush to catch up

The Burj Al-Fateh: a sail, egg or grenade

with the neighbours, and even with modernity itself. The view from the top, the eighteenth floor, is the classic one over the meeting point of the two Niles. But a glimpse out of the windows also reveals more, almost equally bombastic office blocks going up on all sides. Behind the hotel is what was once billed as Africa's biggest commercial construction site, Al Mogran. When it was conceived, in the early 2000s, its backers hoped that this huge financial and commercial sprawl would one day be Africa's answer to Dubai, the glittering honeypot of the Gulf.

The ambitious Al Mogran project is symptomatic of a little-appreciated fact about Sudan. On paper, at least, during the early and mid-2000s the country enjoyed an unprecedented economic boom. The country's gross domestic product was US$46 billion in 2007, up about 11 per cent on the previous year. Africa as a whole prided itself on doing well in the mid-2000s, helped by rising commodity prices. Before the global economic downturn, the continent was recording average annual growth rates of about 5 per cent. But Sudan was almost doubling that, growing at an average of about 9 per cent from 2004 onwards. In purely economic terms, it was one of Africa's star performers.

Almost all of this wealth derives from the country's production of oil, sold largely to China. First pumped out from Sudan in 1999, oil now accounts for about 95 per cent of the country's exports and around 50–60 per cent of the government's revenues. It's on the back of these riches that the city government gave Khartoum a makeover, just as the federal government embarked on grandiose plans to turn the capital into a business 'hub', connecting this big Muslim, African capital to the financial centres of the Gulf and the Middle East. Those who lubricate such connections are supposed to stay at places like the Burj Al-Fateh, at the cost of at least $300 a night (rising to $3,500 for the presidential suite, I was told proudly).

This boom, of course, came to an abrupt halt in the summer of 2008 with the world financial crash. Sudan was particularly badly hit as the price of oil plummeted. The Gulf investors who were going to come to Al Mogran put their plans on hold; hard currency became scarce. Nonetheless, the physical results of what was essentially a golden age for

Sudan, at least in economic terms, are still plain to see. Some of the exotic glass temples of Al Mogran, or those farther down the banks of the Blue Nile, survived the crash and now complement Ghadaffi's Egg on the skyline. Appropriately, three of the most lavish of the new buildings belong to Asian oil companies.

For most of Khartoum's modern history there were only two old colonial-era bridges over the Niles. Now there are six – with three more in various stages of completion at the time of writing – all but one of the new ones built in the mid-2000s. There is more evidence of the new wealth throughout Khartoum. Smart, contemporary apartment blocks have gone up all over the city. As well as the Egg, several other high-end international-class hotels have opened. An emerging middle class, confident of Sudan's future as a progressive, open country, sometimes returning home from years overseas, has had a noticeable impact on the character of the city centre and the main residential zones. Though small in numbers, these mainly young and relatively affluent Sudanese accounted for the opening of Khartoum's first shopping mall, as well as new Italian and Chinese restaurants.

Many of these newly rich Khartoumese, together with the perennially well-to-do ex-pats, can be found discussing their good fortune in the comfortable surroundings of the Ozone Café, an open-air coffee house, complete with over-zealous uniformed waiters, just to the north of the city centre. First-timers are sometimes mystified by its location in the middle of one of the city's busiest roundabouts, but that's the fashion in Khartoum, a city with no parks or green spaces. Here you can dip croissants into reassuringly expensive *lattes* and *cappos* and pretend, just for a minute, that you are at least in Cape Town or Cairo, if not quite Paris.

The Khartoumese are already so accustomed to these new signs of prosperity that they barely register, for instance, the extraordinary weight of traffic that has accompanied it. Cars, many of them made in Sudan, now clog up every main street of Khartoum from morning till dusk, in defiance of the newly installed digital traffic lights. Yet to anyone from the West, this impression of the capital clashes incongruously with the images of Sudan that we have become more familiar with over the past thirty years or so: of the burning villages of Darfur, or before that of the emaciated victims of a civil war between the north and south of the country that lasted for the best part of fifty years and killed about two million people, only ending in 2011 when the country was split into two as South Sudan won its independence.

That is only the start of the many paradoxes of modern Sudan. Another is that the economic 'boom' occurred despite the country being subject to comprehensive US sanctions, imposed in the mid-1990s when Sudan was blacklisted as a state sponsor of terrorism. (It still is, according to the US government.) For the visitor, it is absurd that in what has become one of the most expensive cities in Africa it is impossible to use any credit card, or take any local, or other, currency out of an ATM machine, because of the economic embargo. Travellers just have to come armed with large wads of cash. In this respect, it's still old-style Africa.

The Sudanese actually tend to be proud of this, claiming that their recent economic success proves that the country's rupture with the West in the 1990s had little effect, and that there's always a way to get by. To a degree, this is true. Most of the money that has been pouring into Khartoum has been from Asia, the Gulf, North Africa and the Middle East; these are the places that the Sudanese turned to after the USA clamped down. The manager of the Egg, an Englishman, told me that 70 per cent of his clients are business travellers from those regions.

Thus Sudan, Africa's largest country, can present a bewildering, and often contradictory, variety of faces to the world. It is part investment opportunity, part booming oil economy, part economic basket case, part pariah state and part war zone – to name but a few. Take Khartoum itself. The building 'boom' of the mid-2000s was, in fact, confined to only a small part of what the Sudanese refer to as the capital of their country. The farther you venture from Ghadaffi's Egg, the more combustible and fragile the city appears, and with it the whole country. The capital's geography and history embody these paradoxes. It is a mud and brick (and now plate-glass) palimpsest of a traumatic past.

THE 'THREE TOWNS' – PLUS ONE

What most foreigners refer to as Khartoum is, in fact, an entirely artificial construct. For the Sudanese, 'Khartoum' is formally divided into three separate entities, all usually identified as distinct places on Sudanese maps. There is Khartoum itself, on the south bank of the Blue Nile, looking north. There is the city of Omdurman, across the White Nile to the west and north-west of Khartoum. And then there is Khartoum North, traditionally the industrial part of the capital, opposite Khartoum on the north bank of the Blue Nile. The Sudanese often refer to them as 'the Three Towns'. Many in Omdurman rarely venture south – to Khartoum, for instance.

And then there is a fourth Khartoum, the one that does not even appear on Sudanese maps: the so-called black belt. This is the Khartoum that the Khartoumese themselves know little about. In the differences between the Three Towns, and between the towns and the black belt, lies much of the explanation for Sudan's turbulent history.

It is Omdurman, with a population of about 2.4 million, which is regarded by most Sudanese as the real capital of Sudan – the indigenous heart of the country. This is mainly because of its association with the Mahdi. He was the spiritual founder of the country, revered as the man who was responsible for killing the British General Gordon in 1885 and for then setting up the first recognizably Sudanese state, the Mahdiya, which survived from 1885 to 1898. At the centre of Omdurman is the Mahdi's surprisingly modest tomb, still a centre of pilgrimage and worship, with its striking dome. Apart from this landmark, though, which was repaired after being shelled by the British, there is little left of the original Omdurman apart from small stretches of the old mud ramparts built by the Mahdi's army for defence. What the British, on the one hand, call the Battle of Omdurman, in which General Kitchener's army vanquished the Mahdist forces in a bloody confrontation in 1898, ushering in half a century of colonial rule, took place a few miles out of town. The site of what the Sudanese, on the other hand, call the Karari battle is now partly covered by an army base.

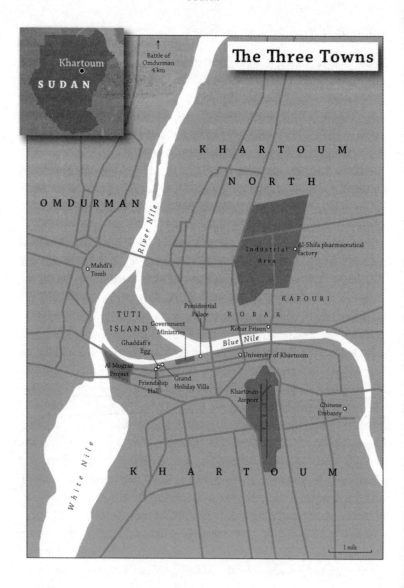

The Three Towns

Battle of
Omdurman
4 km

Khartoum
SUDAN

KHARTOUM

NORTH

OMDURMAN

River Nile

Mahdi's
Tomb

Industrial
Area

Al-Shifa pharmaceutical
factory

KAFOURI

Presidential
Palace

TUTI
ISLAND

Government
Ministries

KOBAR

Kobar Prison

Ghaddafi's
Egg

Blue Nile

Al Mogran
Project

Friendship
Hall

Grand
Holiday Villa

University of Khartoum

Khartoum
Airport

Chinese
Embassy

White Nile

KHARTOUM

1 mile

Originally a humble boat-builder's son, in March 1881, at the age of forty, Muhammad Ahmad ibn Abdallah declared himself to be the *Mahdi*, literally the 'guided one', the man who would lead Muslims to a reform of the Islamic world. Many had expected such a figure to appear and he quickly attracted a huge following from the nomadic tribes of west and north Sudan, known as *ansar* (literally, supporters). He was as much a nationalist leader as a spiritual leader; his declared aim was to kick out the hated Turco-Egyptian administration that at the time misruled Sudan.

The Egyptians, nominally part of the Turkish Empire, had first settled at Khartoum in the 1820s as the first foreign rulers. Their principal interest in the vast empty wastes of this new territory was in procuring slaves, particularly from the African south of the country. The conquered territory became a huge slaving emporium, while the Sudanese were forced to pay taxes to support a foreign administration from which they derived no benefit.

The Mahdi rallied the Arab tribes against Turco-Egyptian rule, and his forces won a series of stunning victories against Egyptian forces. The climax of the Mahdi's revolt came with the siege of General Gordon's troops in Khartoum in 1884–5. With the British by then largely in control of Egypt, Charles Gordon, an icon of British imperialism, fresh from victories in China, had been appointed as governor-general of Sudan to evacuate a territory that Britain considered to be of little strategic or economic importance. But having reached Khartoum, Gordon, wildly exceeding his orders, made the fateful decision to hang on in the capital with just a tiny force of men, thus obliging the main British army to come down from Egypt to rescue him. It was a curious interpretation of evacuation, and embroiled Britain in Sudan on a far larger scale than the politicians back in London had ever anticipated, or desired. However, it didn't help Gordon much. In January 1885 the Mahdi's army stormed the town, skewering Gordon and sticking his severed head on a pike. As it turned out, the relief column from Cairo had set off too late to save him.

In the short term the British decided to cut their losses and complete the evacuation that Gordon should have undertaken in the

The Mahdi

first place.[2] The Mahdi himself died soon after his gory triumph. One of his lieutenants took over, administering the country for the *ansar* for thirteen years. But the British had vowed revenge for the death of Gordon. On the plain of Omdurman, in 1898, Kitchener and his Maxim guns mowed down the massed tribes of the Mahdiya in one of the most one-sided encounters in modern military history. That left the British Empire, then at the zenith of its power, to take control of what had come to be called 'the Sudan', a term used by north-African Arab traders to describe the whole belt below the Sahara across Africa, meaning literally 'land of the blacks'.

The British chose to administer their new conquest from the settlement on the other side of the Nile from Omdurman, in Khartoum. The Egyptians had decided to rule the country from here in the 1820s after they had vanquished the kingdom of the Funj, who had ruled central Sudan from their capital at Sennar, about 150 miles south of Khartoum. After the Battle of Omdurman, General Kitchener set about rebuilding the same governor's palace on the banks of the Blue Nile that had largely been destroyed during the Mahdi's siege fourteen years before. It is still used as the presidential residence to this day, repainted a dazzling white and renamed the Republican Palace. Thus Khartoum was, and remains, the political centre of the country, just as it also came to symbolize, for many, the hated history of foreign occupation.

Indeed, Khartoum, with a population of a little over two million, preserves something of the feel of a colonial city. The British designed the new town largely from scratch, supposedly laying out the street plan based on the Union Jack. With a bit of imagination, the crosses of St George and St Andrew are still vaguely discernible. The sand-coloured, elegant colonial offices of the British administration still cluster around the presidential palace, facing onto the Blue Nile. They continue to be used as government offices. It is thus entirely appropriate that the skyscrapers of Sudan's oil-fuelled golden age are all confined to one tip of Khartoum, around the former centres of colonial power. Much of what reached skywards in Khartoum in the 2000s was paid for, built by and often entirely occupied by yet more foreigners, whether Malaysians, Chinese, Turks, Libyans or Kuwaitis. Sudan's story is still dominated by overseas money and power: the influences that have always shaped the country's destiny.

Khartoum North, by contrast, just over the river, has suffered a very different fate from Khartoum or Omdurman in recent years. This was the working-class district of both British and post-independence Sudan; about 1,725,000 people now live there. The neighbourhood of Khartoum North nearest the river is Kobar, which takes its name from the Arab translation of the name of the British officer who founded the local prison. Heavily protected, standing alone in the middle of a rubbish-strewn wasteland, Kobar prison has changed little since it was built, with rows of cells radiating out from a couple of three-storey buildings in the middle.

Kobar district itself used to house many of the workers for the nearby industrial district. My guide to the area when I visited it was Mudawi Ibrahim Adam, a former lecturer in engineering at the University of Khartoum who moved there in 1995 to set up his own engineering company, Lambda. Employing about twenty-five people, it is a medium-sized company by Sudanese standards. His work includes making spare parts for companies that cannot import new supplies due to US sanctions.

When I visited Mudawi on a weekday in March 2008, his yard was noisy with the grind and whine of machinery. But all around, in the heart of the 'industrial district', everything else was eerily quiet. His yard, he explained, backs onto a former household cutlery factory, as well as a former flour mill and a former textile mill. They all closed, two of them a long time ago; the operative word in Kobar seems to be 'former'. The cutlery factory, Mudawi told me, was one of the under-reported casualties of the war in Sudan's western region, Darfur. The conflict severed the road and rail links between Sudan and west Africa, thus cutting off the export routes to the large markets of Chad, Cameroon, Nigeria and beyond. The area used to be full of biscuit and confectionery factories, also reliant on the west African trade – many of those have now gone too.

Just around the corner from Mudawi's workshop was the Shifa pharmaceutical factory, still pretty much in the same state as it must have been immediately after it was hit by US cruise missiles in 1998. That attack was ordered by President Bill Clinton in retaliation for Sudan's alleged involvement in the bombing of the US embassies in Tanzania and Kenya. The Shifa plant was supposed to be a terrorist bomb-making factory. In fact, it turned out to be no such thing, and the Americans quietly acknowledged their mistake to the owners a few years later.[3]

The Shifa factory may be a pile of rubble, but what is most striking today is how little it differs from the rest of the area. For almost every factory on this vast industrial estate has closed and the remains are crumbling away. Here a single textile factory covered forty acres and employed

15,000 workers; there is almost nothing left of it now. The only signs of life are at the soft-drink bottling plants: Coca-Cola and Pepsi are going strong, produced under licence by Sudanese companies. Apart from that, there is just the odd tobacco factory and medicine production plant. Virtually opposite the bombed-out Shifa factory, Volkswagen has opened a big new sales and repairs centre.

Mudawi told me that with all the jobs lost over the past decade or so, perhaps only 10 per cent of the people in Kobar are still employed. For the Chinese–Sudanese connection that has benefited Khartoum so much has been the death of Kobar and Khartoum North. The textile factories closed as their products were undercut by the flood of cheap Chinese imports, now sold in vast quantities in the souks of Omdurman. In Kobar, with little work and rising prices, there is hardly a family in the area that can afford three meals a day now – breakfast and dinner, maybe, but not lunch. A new meal has been invented, taken at 5 or 6 p.m., combining both lunch and dinner in one.

Another source of local employment that has disappeared in North Khartoum is the Kafouri dairy farm, which used to abut the industrial area. That was levelled some time ago. However, on 'Block Nine' of the redevelopment of the old farm, just about five minutes away from the remains of the Shifa factory, live the country's new elite. This is where President Omar al-Bashir has a compound. He has not strayed far from his roots – his father worked at Kafouri. Indeed, Bashir junior makes much of his humble roots as a 'man of the people'. Other government ministers and officials live in the large, sprawling villas on the banks of Nile facing back to Khartoum – the Kobar prison virtually in their backyards.

Mudawi recalled the riots and protests in the capital in the summer of 2006 against the lack of jobs and the rising costs of food and petrol, especially after the government removed subsidies on many staples. How does the government keep a lid on all the resentment and poverty that Mudawi chronicled for me? After all, twice before in Sudan's post-independence history, as we shall see, military governments have been swept away by popular uprisings. But Mudawi directed me to look closely at Khartoum's brand new Chinese- and Turkish-built bridges. At each end of all them, on both sides of the roads, are police pick-up trucks mounted with machine-guns on the back, ready to shoot. President Bashir, in power since 1989, has learned from the past and is prepared for the worst.

Then there is the last and least-known Khartoum, the black belt, running around the outskirts of Khartoum North, Omdurman and, to a lesser extent, Khartoum itself. The black belt is only an hour's drive from the Ozone Café and its *cappuccini*, yet most Sudanese from the Three Towns will never have visited it. For the black belt betrays the grimmer realities behind the cosmetic face of a prosperous Sudan; its name, for one, is a pejorative reference by the Arab residents of Khartoum to the Africans who largely inhabit it. Those who live and work there call it the 'poverty belt'. Here lives the miserable human detritus of the country's fifty years' worth of post-independence famines, civil wars, ethnic cleansing and economic mismanagement. In a dusty maze of rutted tracks, corrugated iron and mud-brick huts about one-third of the city's nine million or so people cling on to life.

The black belt is, to all intents and purposes, a semi-permanent refugee camp. The vast majority of people here live in dire poverty. Some of the residents have fled from Darfur. Many more escaped, long ago, from the war in the south between the ruling Islamic regimes in Khartoum and the southern African tribes. When the charismatic leader of the southern rebels, John Garang, died in a helicopter crash in 2005, the inhabitants of the black belt, suspecting foul play, rose up in protest, forcing the Khartoumese from the Three Towns to take notice of them for the first time.

Many families that live in these neighbourhoods survive by doing menial jobs in the Three Towns, or in the belt itself. Others rely on humanitarian handouts. With a peace deal signed between the north and the southern rebels in 2005, the UN started a repatriation programme for those who wanted to return to their villages. Standing in one of the UN registration tents, I saw streams of bewildered people giving a few sketchy details of their lives to sympathetic officials. But many had been living in the black belt for so long that they could barely describe where they had come from. And as with everything in Sudan, the numbers were staggering. The UN was planning for 630,000 people to return in the first stage of the programme – at that time, in 2006, the biggest operation of its kind in the world.

THE COLONIAL LEGACY – FOR BETTER AND FOR WORSE

This paradox of Khartoum, of a core of wealth and optimism surrounded by rings of extreme poverty, injustice and political exclusion, is also the paradox of Sudan. For most analysts, this is the key to understanding Sudan's terrible history of instability and civil war. Its post-independence story since the British left in 1956 can seem like nothing more than a long series of armed struggles between the centre of the country and the peripheries – Darfur, the south and the east – as people fight to claim what they feel is theirs from a self-absorbed ruling elite in Khartoum.

Certainly, it is hard to think of anywhere else in Africa where there is such an imbalance between the capital and the rest of the country. It is a phenomenon as immediately noticeable to the African as to the Westerner. When I visited the headquarters of the African Union's peacekeeping mission in Darfur in 2008, I asked some of the troops for their impressions of Sudan. One Nigerian colonel, Augustin Agundu, said that for him Sudan seemed like 'a one-city state'.

It is a good description. In Nigeria, Africa's most populous country, very similar to Sudan in its ethno-religious composition as well as colonial history, several cities compete for stature and influence: Abuja (the capital), Jos, Kano, Port Harcourt, Lagos, Kaduna, Sokoto and Calabar. All these were, to a degree, developed as mega-cities to draw in people from the countryside in order to dilute the traditional ethnic, racial and religious divisions of rural Nigeria. These cities all encompass enormous contrasts between wealth and poverty – but the fact that those contrasts are distributed around the country means that the poverty feels more evenly shared out, as does the wealth. In Sudan, by contrast, Khartoum (the Three Towns) has almost everything, supported by an area 200 miles to its south and north – an expanse that is often called the riverain centre.

Nor is this just happenstance, a random consequence of geography. Modern Sudan, the largest country by land mass in Africa before it was split into two in 2011, was designed this way by the British who ruled from 1899 to 1956. They set a pattern that many foreigners were to follow. Men like Gordon originally arrived in Sudan with the best of intentions: to eradicate the slave trade, then the noblest justification for British imperialism. But in the end the British left behind the most mixed of legacies, of which the most damaging was the extraordinary over-centralization of the country.

After the Battle of Omdurman the British imposed direct rule over Sudan, although beyond Khartoum and the riverain centre the new rulers were fatally uncertain as to exactly what this new country of 'Sudan' should include. Technically, the British ruled in conjunction with Egypt, as one half of what was called the Anglo-Egyptian Condominium. In truth, though, it was the British who filled the senior posts of the administration and decided policy. The British priority, however, was always the control of Egypt; Cairo, after all, commanded the Suez Canal and thus the quickest route to India. The British therefore spent a lot of time and money cultivating Anglo-Egyptian relations. Sudan, the unwanted add-on to Egypt, was, by contrast, to be run on the cheap. Indeed, it had to pay for itself, which was to account for Sudan's particular pattern of colonial economic development.

The Sudanese, particularly those who remember it personally, will acknowledge some benefits of British rule. Uniquely, Sudan was not run out of the Colonial Office, as most of Britain's other possessions were, but rather by a separate cadre of officials reporting directly to the Foreign Office. The Sudan Political Service, as it was called, was thus a cut above the usual colonial administration, socially and intellectually. It had its own selection policy and pay grades. Remarkably, it has been estimated that 91.7 per cent of its recruits came from England's public schools, and of those probably one-third came from the nine most prestigious and exclusive, including Eton, Rugby and Winchester. Every graduate recruit to the service had been to Oxford or Cambridge universities. As the historian of British rule in Sudan notes, almost in awe: 'no graduate of an English provincial university was ever recruited to the service.'[4] At the very least, Sudan got Imperial Britain's most well-bred, if not necessarily the best. Among several remarkable graduates of the service was the explorer Wilfred Thesiger.[5]

Judging by their memoirs, many of the British district commissioners came to care for, even to love, Sudan. Given how little money was available, in some ways they did a good job. Institutionally, for example, by independence in 1956 Sudan was extraordinarily well endowed. The British bequeathed to Sudan an excellent university (of Khartoum), a well-trained civil service and the most professional army in colonial Africa. The capital was one of the most sophisticated intellectual and cultural centres on the continent. There was also an extensive railway network, a good port and some industry.

But what was the main British interest in Sudan? Why did Britain devote even these limited resources to an arid, desert territory with no obvious mineral wealth in the middle of Africa, at a time when the weary titan was already overstretched all round the globe?

The best way to answer that question is to head about a hundred miles south out of Khartoum to Barakat. Here is the main office of the 'Gezira scheme' – in its time the largest irrigated agricultural project on earth and the jewel of colonial development, not only in Sudan but in the whole of Africa. Construction started on the scheme in 1906 and after it started operating in 1925 it was to fix Sudan's role in the Empire, and thus the world, as the principal source of raw cotton for Britain's textile mills.

Almost all investment in colonial Sudan was subjugated to supporting this one enterprise. In its heyday, the Gezira scheme was extremely successful. As late as the 1990s, before the oil began to flow, Gezira was by a good margin still the most important contributor to Sudan's economy. Amid great fanfare, the country's presidents used to come and launch the harvesting season here. Indeed, it is arguable that

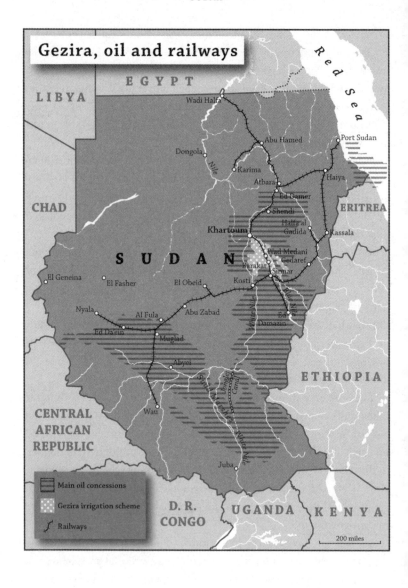

Gezira, oil and railways

Red Sea

EGYPT

LIBYA

Wadi Halfa

Abu Hamed

Port Sudan

Dongola

Karima

Atbara

Haiya

CHAD

Ed Damer

ERITREA

Shendi

Khartoum

Halfa al Gadida

Kassala

S U D A N

Wad Medani
Gedaref

Barakat

Sinnar

El Geneina

El Fasher

El Obeid

Kosti

Nyala

Al Fula

Abu Zabad

Ed Damazin

Ed Da'ein

Muglad

Abyei

ETHIOPIA

Wau

CENTRAL
AFRICAN
REPUBLIC

Juba

Main oil concessions

Gezira irrigation scheme

Railways

D. R.
CONGO

UGANDA

KENYA

200 miles

all Sudan has done over the last decade is swap an over-reliance on one commodity, cotton, for another, oil. At its peak, in the 1950s and 1960s, Gezira would provide up to 6 per cent of the world's cotton and over 70 per cent of Sudan's exports. How all that has changed. Today, oil accounts for over 90 per cent of the value of Sudan's exports and Gezira's farmers and smallholders produce just 5 per cent.

That decline is reflected in the Barakat headquarters today. Everything is a bit shabby and rundown. There is a mild panic when I ask for a copy of a map of the Gezira scheme; we have to drive off to the local market to find a photocopying machine. Hassan Kambal, one of the managers who showed me around, complains that sometimes he will go three or four days without an internet connection.

Nonetheless, past glories still sustain a palpable sense of enthusiasm among the staff at Gezira. They are intensely proud of the scheme and its role in Sudanese and African history, and going out into the fields it's not hard to see why. Having driven for hours through parched desert scrub to get here from Khartoum, suddenly all I can see are orderly fields of green (onions or cotton) interrupted by sandy coloured squares (of wheat). There are long, straight irrigation canals and neat lines of electricity poles fading into the distance. Triangular roofs of metal barns punctuate the horizon. This is a pastoral idyll, an almost unimaginable scene for those used to the barren, polluted wastes of much of the rest of Sudan. It bears more than a passing resemblance to the broad expanses of East Anglia back in England, as, I guess, the British meant it to.

Gezira is the Arabic word for 'island', and the name was all too well chosen. For the irrigation project created an island of green prosperity in the centre of the country, about 2.2 million acres in all, between the Blue Nile and White Nile, with Khartoum at its northern tip. Just to the south-east of Gezira, the British also started large-scale rain-fed agricultural projects near Gedaref. To this day, the whole area is often referred to as 'the Golden Triangle'.

The British created the Gezira scheme where they did for cost reasons. A dam was built at Sennar, on the Blue Nile to the south, and gravity did the rest. The land slopes very gently at an angle of about 4 inches per mile for most of the way north from Sennar to Khartoum, so there was no need for complicated pumps and the like. As Mr Kamal proudly told me, Gezira remains 'the cheapest irrigation system in the world'.

Building Gezira may not have cost a lot, but it still absorbed most of the resources that were available for Sudan as a whole. The rest of the colony was arranged to service the irrigation scheme. The railway, for instance, was built almost entirely to cater to its needs; the trains ran through the Gezira fields and up to a port that was constructed on the Red Sea, now Port Sudan, 750 miles away. Atbara, still one of Sudan's most important towns, started life largely as a railway terminus; in the early 1950s, up to 25,000 people worked on the trains there. At Atbara, the main line from Khartoum split, north on to Egypt or north-east up to Port Sudan. From there the cotton was exported to Britain and elsewhere.

From the town of Kosti, a transport hub on the south-west tip of the Gezira scheme, the railway was extended in the later 1950s to Nyala in south Darfur. That was the sole connection to the rest of west and southern Africa. To this day, this is largely how the main arteries of the country's infrastructure remain. Rusty, ghostly old trains still half-heartedly ply the same few routes, usually at intervals of four or five days apart.

For labour, Gezira sucked in thousands of people not only from Sudan but from west Africa as well. The cotton harvesting season lasted from about December to May. Many Hausa and Fulani people came from northern Nigeria, for instance, on their way to do the *hajj*, the pilgrimage to Mecca in Saudi Arabia that every Muslim has to complete once in his or her life. Many Nigerians stayed; their descendants still live in villages on the White Nile, near to Gezira, or in eastern Sudan near Kassala. It is estimated that nearly one-quarter of the Muslim population of contemporary Sudan is regarded as 'Nigerian', a term that refers to other west African migrants too.[6] Migrant workers arrived also from the lands that now constitute Chad, Niger, Mali and Libya.

Indeed, to regulate the flow of workers to Gezira, the British introduced the Closed District Ordinance Act. This restricted travel around the country unless people were employed on the scheme, purportedly to prevent a potentially dangerous build-up of idle labour there. More to the point, though, this legislation also closed off anyone from the south of the country from working on the Gezira scheme. The British effectively created a two-tier nation, composed of those who could work on its most remunerative economic project, mainly from the Muslim north and the west, and those who could not, from the south. This fitted into a more general policy of keeping the non-Muslim south, then being colonized mainly by churchman and missionaries, separate from the north.

The hyper-development of Khartoum and the riverain centre of Sudan at the expense of the regions had begun. Gezira was overseen with clockwork precision by the punctilious British administrators. As one Sudanese who remembered Gezira from the colonial days told me, it was all run like 'a military camp'. I got a good flavour of this when I visited the archive centre of the Gezira scheme. Like the rest of head office, it is well on the way to decrepitude. Nevertheless, the very welcoming Sudanese archivist likes to put on a good show.

The photographic portraits of the British directors of the scheme are still propped up on a shelf, all looking as though they might never have set foot in Sudan. Here is D.P. Macillvray, in a tweed cap and jacket, doing his best impression of a man out on a Scottish grouse shoot. Another former director leans intently on the tiller of his yacht, presumably, to judge by his clothes, somewhere in the Solent. And in six or seven rooms are preserved what must be the entire run of files of the British Gezira administration. No detail of expenditure was, apparently, overlooked to ensure the smooth running of the scheme. Here is a stentorian letter from a C.V. Waite, of the Gezira Board, to his Chief Mechanical Officer:

On leaving Rest House No. 1 after lunch yesterday my Morris Oxford car BN 3261 became bogged down in the mud in the drive. Every endeavour was made to manhandle the car out of the mud with the aid of gardeners but without success. Mr Eshof in the Meringen Workshop Landrover then arrived and his offer of a push out of the mud was very gratefully accepted. Immediately the fenders of the two cars touched, however, the rear side bumper of my car snapped off the fender and this in turn broke the glass of the near side rear lamp. Inspection of the bumper revealed that welding of the bumper to the fender was very thin indeed with no strength; this obviously accounted for the mishap.

I should be very glad if a new glass cover for the lamp could be fitted and the bumper re-welded onto the fender.

This was written on 23 July 1956, after the scheme had been formally handed over to the Sudanese after independence was declared on 1 January of that year. Mr Waite must have been one of the last of the British to leave the scheme. The next piece of correspondence in his file relates to his application for a new job in England at one of London's smarter gentleman's clubs.

After the Sudanese took over, Gezira still grew in size and importance. It became the country's largest employer, with about 13,000 staff as well as the 130,000 or so farmers and their families, as well as seasonal workers, who produced the cotton. Moreover, Gezira drew in Sudan's only other large-scale employers to the same area. On its fringes, attracted by the bounteous supplies of irrigated water and good transport links, the Sudanese, with the help of some foreign investors, set up sugar-processing factories.

One of these was the vast Kenana mill, started as a showcase project by the Sudanese president General Numeiri together with one of Britain's most buccaneering entrepreneurs, Roland 'Tiny' Rowland. The plant has since been upgraded as a joint venture between the Sudanese government and Kuwaiti and Saudi Arabian investors. The Sudanese Sugar Company, a wholly government-owned corporation, now has four factories in the area; the White Nile Sugar Company was digging the foundations for a vast new factory just up the road from

Kenana when I visited it in 2008. Like the produce of the Gezira scheme, the bagged, processed sugar is then put on the train for the long, slow journey up to Port Sudan and overseas markets.

The siting of the sugar factories around Gezira in the 1970s and 1980s merely perpetuated the over-concentration of wealth and economic activity in the riverain centre that the British had begun. In comparison, the regions continued to be starved out. One prominent Sudanese economist, Ali Abdalla Ali, now an adviser to the Khartoum Stock Exchange, told me: 'We have been imprisoned by the past.' If it was the fault of the British colonial administrators that all development and employment was concentrated only in the centre of the country in the first place, then it was also the fault of successive Sudanese post-independence governments to continue relentlessly with the same pattern.

To have done things differently would have involved some sacrifices by the elites of Khartoum, and a little imagination. As it was, capital merely went on following the path of least resistance. In 1994 the vast industrial complex of GIAD, now probably Sudan's largest single employer, was set up just 25 miles south of the capital. This is the heart of Sudan's military-industrial complex. As well as churning out saloon cars, GIAD produces arms, tanks and ammunitions for the army's seemingly endless wars.

LUCKY IF YOU LIVE IN THE CENTRE

The oil boom of the 2000s, unfortunately, merely accentuated the existing imbalances of development. The main oil refinery, a joint China–Sudan venture, is a handy two hours north of the capital. The major oil wells might be clustered in the middle belt of the country, in regions like Abyei, where the savannah of the north meets the wetlands of the south, but all the pipelines and investment head north, to the refinery and then on to Port Sudan.

As a consequence, the African Dinka tribespeople of Abyei have seen almost no benefit from the oil that has been extracted from under their land. Contrast their territory, though, with the heartland of the

Arab tribal elites north of Khartoum, all the way up to Dongola and Hamid. There is no oil here, or other natural resources – apart from the waters of the Nile. Yet there is an awful lot of development. It is easy to appreciate just how far the centre has raced ahead compared to the rest of the country by just driving around it.

For example, immediately below the fourth cataract of the Nile, about 220 miles due north of the capital, is the Merowe dam, the country's largest construction project. In all, the project may have cost up to $2 billion. It is partly funded and built by the Chinese, but has also sucked in a good part of the Sudanese government's entire national budget for development. The dam is meant to benefit the whole country – yet for the moment it will only benefit the desert region north of the capital, much as Gezira did for the land due south of Khartoum. Driving as close as possible to see it, in the autumn of 2008, we could glimpse the enormous dam wall from a mile off before we were stopped from going any farther by Sudanese security guards. Like most other such projects in Sudan, the dam has been highly controversial. Thousands of people were, allegedly, forcefully evacuated from local villages to make way for the building works.

The Merowe project also includes a new airport and a Chinese-built bridge over the Nile, opened, with appropriate pomp, circumstance, singing and dancing, by President Bashir. The bridge connects Merowe on the north bank of the Nile with Karima, one of Sudan's few tourist destinations, with its ruined temple and ancient Kushite pyramids. But as Darfuris point out, the whole Merowe enterprise will help just one million people in the surrounding area, as well as the population of Khartoum. Darfuris may see some electricity from it, one day in the distant future. But Darfur, with over six million people, has still never had anything even approaching the size and scope of the Merowe project.

Along with the dam have come thousands of miles of high-quality all-weather bitumen roads criss-crossing remote parts of the desert to connect up the towns of the north: Atbara to Merowe, Karima to Dongola, Kosti to Khartoum and so on. This is the territory of the Arabized tribes who have traditionally run the centre, and thus

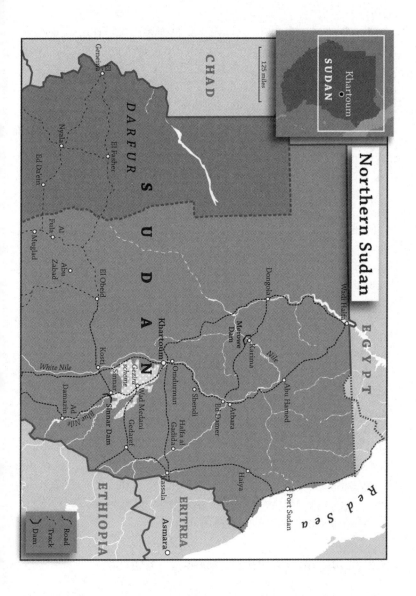

Northern Sudan

Sudan. Tribes such as the Shaygiyya, Danaqla and Jaaliyyin became sedentary and urbanized along the Nile long ago. Others of the Arab tribes remained nomadic, such as the Misseriyya. They pushed out west and south to the areas of Kordofan and Bahr al-Ghazel.

Driving through the region north of Khartoum in October 2008, apart from the bridge at Merowe we always crossed the Nile on alarmingly ancient-looking ferries, apparently dating back to colonial times. When we were on the river, however, in the background usually loomed an enormous Chinese-sponsored bridge in various stages of near completion. When all the bridges are open the riverain centre will want for nothing in terms of fast transportation links – even if almost nobody uses the roads. Most Sudanese are too poor to own a car; we drove for hours without passing a single other vehicle. All the same, it is now possible to do the 300-mile journey to Khartoum from Dongola, the capital of the north and the birthplace of many of Sudan's leaders, in about five hours. The same trip used to take at least two days.

By way of contrast, as far as I could ascertain the south of Sudan still had only about 30 miles of tarmac road in the entire region by the end of 2009, and about half of that total was to be found in the centre of the capital, Juba. Several projects were mooted, all to be paid for by Western donors, but nothing had yet happened. Thus the main commercial artery from the border town of Nimule, linking Sudan with Uganda, to Juba, a distance of about 100 miles, took me a bone-shaking five hours in a good Toyota Landcruiser on a road that was little more than caked mud. And that was during the dry season. In the rainy season, for six months of the year, many of these 'roads' become anything but; the lucky few, UN officials and aid workers, fly. Such are the glaring disparities of modern Sudan.

SURVIVING, OR NOT, ON THE MARGINS: DARFUR

So wealth, and thus power, has continued to accumulate in the capital and its immediate surroundings. About half the nation's income and assets are in the Three Towns that compose 'Khartoum', according to one expert on Sudan, Alex de Waal, as well as about a quarter of the country's people. Another telling statistic is that three-quarters of the country's health professionals live in Khartoum.[7] All the nation's major institutions are in the city, as are the only decent universities apart from the University of Juba – and even some departments of that are in the capital.

All this points to another profound truth about Sudan. Just as 'Khartoum' is, to a great degree, an artificial construct, so is 'Sudan' itself. The British were, essentially, only interested in the riverain centre. The two other parts of what they handed on as 'Sudan' in 1956 were only late additions. Darfur, as big as France, home to the non-Arabized, Muslim tribes such as the Zaghawa and Fur, was only vaguely joined to the lands ruled from Khartoum when the British conquered it in 1916. South Sudan, formerly known as Equatoria, entirely different in every conceivable way, geographically, religiously and ethnically, was administered as an almost completely separate country by the British and only grafted onto 'Sudan' a few years before the end of colonial rule.

The northern Sudanese Arabs were thus trained to think almost exclusively about themselves. Their most important relationship was with Egypt, the real centre of British rule in the region, from where much of their country had always been administered. They regarded themselves as Arab, linked to the Arab world to the north and east by religion, race, politics and commerce. They very rarely looked south, and hardly ever west. These attitudes persist to this day, with deadly consequences.

Just in terms of basic geography, it is easy to see how the inhabitants of the Three Towns might overlook the rest of Sudan. Khartoum is, after all, a very long way away from the country's other main urban centres. El Fasher, the capital of Darfur, is about 750 miles to the west; El Geneina, the capital of West Darfur and the country's last town before reaching Chad, is a few more hundred miles beyond that. The most important town of south Sudan, Juba, is 870 miles south of Khartoum.

But geography only explains so much. Take, for instance, the deep-seated grievances of Darfuris against the centre. These were explained to me in more detail by Ahmed Diraige, the last Darfuri governor (in the early 1980s) of a unified Darfur. He now lives in a modest flat in London's Swiss Cottage district. His father was a tribal chief of the Fur, the biggest local tribe (Darfur is Arabic for 'the home of the Fur'). As Ahmed told me, it was not, in fact, poverty that concerned Darfuris the most; in fact, the Darfuris were relatively well off in the context of sub-Saharan Africa. Rather, it was a sense that they contributed a lot of money in taxes out of their wealth to the central government in Khartoum but got almost none of it back in the form of development or investment. It was this, more than anything, that provoked a feeling of resentment and then rebelliousness.

As Ahmed explained to me: 'Darfur is one of the richer parts of Sudan . . . in cattle, animal husbandry, gum arabic, groundnuts . . . all produced in Darfur and Kordofan.' A tax was levied on the plentiful animals owned by the people. It was called *diynia*, meaning 'beard', because the tax was charged when the owner became an adult. Horses incurred the most *diynia*, followed by camels, cows, donkeys, sheep and goats. These taxes were levied by the British and were then continued after 1956 by the post-independence governments. Yet the Darfuris seemed to get nothing in return.

The trigger for the British invasion and annexation of Darfur in 1916 was the decision by the last independent sultan of the Fur to back his fellow Muslims in Turkey, Germany's ally, on the outbreak of the First World War. As a consequence of this, Ahmed Diraige remembers, the British 'always treated Darfur as a security situation'. The British thus purposefully underdeveloped Darfur to keep it under control. They were afraid, for example, that a little bit of education for Darfuris would provoke dissent from a 'discontented class of semi-literate trouble-makers', as one official put it.[8] This set a pattern that, again, the post-independence governments seemed unable to break.

By 1935, almost two decades after colonial rule started, Darfur still had only one elementary school and two sub-grade 'literary schools' for a school-age population of 500,000. As the best historian of modern Sudan, Robert Collins, characterizes it: 'When the British departed from Sudan at independence in 1956 they left behind in Darfur a record of conspicuous lack of interest and studied indifference.' But the same situation continued after 1956 too. Diraige started a movement called the Darfur Development Front to give political expression to this sense of neglect and marginalization as early as 1964; it was the forerunner of the organized, armed resistance to Khartoum's rule in the 1990s and 2000s.

Ethnic differences would provide the other major fault lines in the country. Darfur might have been incorporated into Sudan, but the Arab tribal groups of Khartoum and the riverain centre nonetheless looked down on the African tribes of Darfur, such as the Fur or Zaghawa, even though they were fellow Muslims. Tribes like the Fur had migrated to the fertile parts of the Darfur region, around the Jebel Marra, from deeper in Africa, from the south and south-west of the continent. They therefore had little in common, apart from religion, with the Arab tribes of the north. There was a good deal of racism in the attitudes of the Arabic centre towards the African tribes, as we shall see throughout the book. Those in Khartoum who wanted to bring the Fur to heel for political purposes in 2003 knew that they could easily manipulate the racism of some of the nomadic Arabic tribes towards the Fur farmers. Here lie, in part, the roots of the *janjaweed* killers, the Arab militias that have terrorized the Fur villages in Darfur.

So what has it been like to live, largely out of sight and mind of the rulers of your own country, in a 'periphery', as Sudan's remoter regions have often been called? To find out, I had dinner with Mohammed Sadiq at his house in El Fasher, the capital of Darfur. A charming, alert, wiry father of four young children, he is now the country director of a British NGO called Practical Action. He was born in the village of Akoma, 50 miles to the east of El Fasher, in 1961. He is from the Zayadiya tribe, and went to school in one of El Fasher's two secondary schools; there were only four schools then in the whole of north Darfur, an area roughly the size of England. Being bright, he was obviously university material. But there was no university in Darfur, so he was sent off to the University of Khartoum.

Just getting to Khartoum was an adventure in its own right. The few flights were far too expensive and booked out weeks in advance. The only option for most people was to go by truck. In the dry season, the journey of about 750 miles took Mohammed at least seven days; in the rainy season far more. Trucks would regularly get trapped in the sand. He recalls one such journey of twenty-seven days, getting stuck on one occasion for four nights in the same place. Yet this was a journey that people like Mohammed would have to do several times a year. One of the first things that astonished him in Khartoum was how easy – and how cheap – it was to travel from Khartoum to other places in the centre of the country.

Given the small number of schools in Darfur, it was perhaps little surprise that there were so few Darfuris at the University of Khartoum when Mohammed got there, despite the fact they made up about a third of the population of the country. There were just forty-seven in his year; he remembers the exact number because there was an informal society of Darfuri students. In all, there were just 450 Darfuris out of a total of about 9,000 students at the university. Being such a rare creature, however, conferred a rare status on Mohammed back home. 'It meant you were very famous in Fasher, earned very high respect.'

Mohammed was excited and surprised by the little things that marked his step up in the world from Darfur to Khartoum. In the university he had a cupboard, a table for reading and more than five courses for the evening meal. 'I could not believe it,' he exclaims. He was treated differently as a Darfuri, but he was never made to feel racially inferior. He did, however, get an early taste of the capital's wilful ignorance of Darfur's affairs during the dreadful famine of 1984–5, an important staging post along the way to the region's full-blown conflict twenty years later.

The famine was a catastrophic event for his region: 20,000 cattle belonging to his relatively small tribe died, most near the sources of water, thereby contaminating them. People were driven from their villages by the stink of rotting carcasses. Yet, as a student in Khartoum at the time, Mohammed recalls, 'The government hid it all . . . they did not even want to talk about the crisis, until people arrived in Kordofan or from Darfur, begging on the streets.' Letters could take more than twenty days either way between Khartoum and Darfur, so no one could find out much. 'But after two months people arrived in Khartoum, and then we knew. At the university, we would donate one meal a day to the beggars. Then the government announced the crisis . . . thousands of people from the north migrated to Khartoum or to the south.'

Mohammed returned to Darfur in 1987, to support his family. One of the crucial events in the build-up to the widespread rebellion which broke out against the government in Darfur in 2003 was the publication of what its authors called the 'Black Book' the previous year. This was compiled and written by certain members of Darfur's intelligentsia in Khartoum who would go on to form one of the main rebel groups, the Justice and Equality Movement (JEM). The book had a very restricted circulation, perhaps just over a thousand or so copies. But it outlined in detail the accumulated grievances of the Darfuris against the governments of Khartoum over many years, how Darfur had received so little of the development money that had been spent in Sudan. Instead, the book asserted, almost all the money had gone to a small cabal of Muslim Arab tribes in the centre.

It was largely the same story in the east of the country. Like Darfur, the vast, flat desert area giving onto the Red Sea contained some of Sudan's most valuable commodities – not cattle, but the huge facilities at Port Sudan and the large, rain-irrigated farms of Gedaref state. Yet almost all the revenues from these enterprises, as we shall see in more detail, went straight to Khartoum, leaving the local Beja tribespeople, for instance, even poorer than the Fur in western Sudan. The Beja, consisting of four sub-groups, are a mainly nomadic people, infamously dubbed the 'fuzzy-wuzzy' by the colonial British in tribute to their distinctive hair. Only two years after independence the Beja started to agitate for a fairer distribution of the wealth coming out of their own region by founding the Beja Congress. Eventually, their accumulated grievances were to lead to armed conflict with the riverain Arabs in Khartoum in the 1990s. This insurrection was less visible than the ones

35

in the south and Darfur but still inflicted a great deal of destruction on the region.

Often, the rest of the country seems to be as much psychologically as geographically out of reach for those who work and live in the Three Towns and Gezira. For example, despite all the headlines and moral outrage that the fighting in Darfur has attracted in the West, many Khartoumese have only the haziest notion of the conflict and show little interest in finding out more. I have come across this split reality between Khartoum and the rest of this vast country many times, and will give only one example here. I was interviewing a forty-year-old Sudanese economist who had been seconded from the ministry of finance to work in the local offices of the International Monetary Fund. He was from Kosti, on the edge of the Gezira scheme. We were idly chatting about Sudan's enormous public debt (as one does with IMF economists), when we strayed onto the issue of Darfur.

This sort of conflict, he said, could 'happen anywhere, the result of competition between farmers and pastoralists'. Fair enough – many argue just that. But then he started to warm to his main theme. The whole Darfur conflict 'had been invented by the Western media', he claimed. All of Sudan was underdeveloped, he argued, not just Darfur; thus he could not understand why the Darfuri rebels got so much attention. 'They are just bandits', he said.

But, I replied, what about all the killings? 'I have no idea about that,' he snapped, leaning back in his leather office chair. I gave him my litany of facts and figures on the war in Darfur; maybe as many as 200,000 dead up to that time, certainly over 2.5 million displaced peoples in refugee camps. In answer, he simply laughed. 'It's unbelievable,' he repeated several times, unsure of himself. 'Darfur is a Muslim society. I can't believe it . . . they are fellow Muslims. They can't kill and rape each other. I don't want to believe it because they all Muslims . . . It must be exaggerated, must be a hidden agenda.' He told me that most of the people in the refugee camps were merely 'enjoying the free food, watching television, chatting on their cell phones . . . relaxing and enjoying themselves, with nice clothes'.

His was just an extreme version of a very common point of view, typical of the highly educated professional classes in Khartoum who simply don't want to know. The visiting African peacekeeping soldiers I spoke to in 2008 noticed this as well. A Nigerian major was amazed, after spending a few days in the capital, at how little anyone knew about Darfur. 'In Nigeria, everybody knows what is happening everywhere else,' he said. 'There is a much greater awareness of what's happening in the rest of the country.' He himself had travelled to all thirty-six of Nigeria's states. Yet in Sudan, it is unusual to find people who have explored their own towns, let alone visited other parts of the country.

FATAL DIVISIONS, NORTH VERSUS SOUTH

We have seen how the Darfuri and Beja found themselves ignored, isolated and passed over by the riverain ruling class of Sudan. Yet at least they had Islam to bind them to the north. The people of southern Sudan, however, mainly the distinctively tall Dinka and Nuer, did not share that tie. The southerners would be cut off from the centre not only by underdevelopment and neglect but by ethnicity, religion and culture as well.

Indeed, so enormous were the differences between 'south Sudan' and the rest of the colony that for a long time the British themselves dithered over whether the Muslim north and Christian and animist south should really be grouped together as one country at all. This dilemma reflected the realities of two different lands. As distinct from a 'north' of deserts and plains, the 'south' was an area of jungles and marshes. Indeed, the great *sudd*, that expanse of marsh and swamp that dominates much of the area of southern Sudan before giving way to the scrub and savannah of the north, is well named – in Arabic, it literally means 'barrier'.

The British only penetrated into the *sudd* in a systematic way after 1904, and it took them about another thirty years to conquer the whole of the south. However, the colonialists not only found huge differences

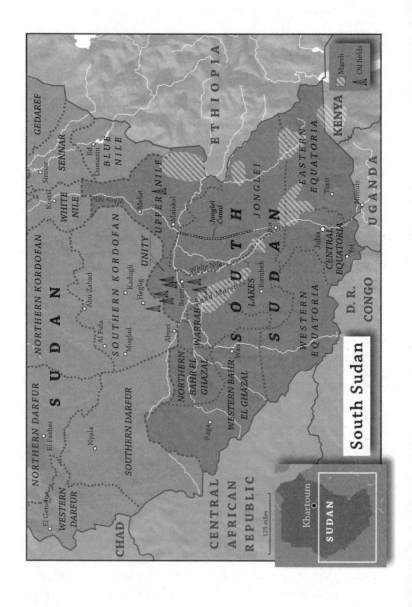

between the Equatorial region and the northern deserts, they also consciously sharpened those differences for their own purposes. Their main concern was to shape the south as a sort of religious and cultural bulwark against the spread of Islam, in order to protect the colonized Christian territories to the south (Uganda and Kenya today). Thus, for instance, the British encouraged Christian missionaries to convert the indigenous animists. As Mohamed Omer Beshir, probably the greatest of Sudan's modern historians, writes: 'While education in the north was geared to employment, this was not the case in the south where it was geared to the spread of Christianity and the prevention of the southward spread of Islam.'[19]

From the end of the First World War, the British therefore initiated a comprehensive, if largely surreptitious, policy of creating a southern Sudan separate from the north. English rather than Arabic was made the official language of instruction in schools. The use of Arabic anywhere was actively discouraged and Arab clothing was banned. A separate southern army, the Equatoria Corps, was established in December 1910, when the last of the northern Sudanese troops left the region. In the 1920s most of the Arab merchants, the *gallaba*, who traded in the main towns of the south such as Juba and Rumbek, were repatriated to the north. The Closed Districts Order of 1922 declared the whole of the south to be off-limits to northerners unless they had the express permission of the governor. This, together with the expulsion of the *gallaba* Arabs, effectively severed the south from the commercial and economic life of the rest of Sudan – or anywhere else. Greek, Syrian and Jewish traders were, however, allowed to continue commerce in the south.

The British were intent anyway on strangling any chance of development in the south. Arguing against people being given more money for their meagre crops of cotton at auction, the British governor of Upper Nile Province wrote with cold-blooded clarity in 1928: 'To provide means for the present generation to acquire sufficient wealth to enable them to obtain all the various luxuries civilization brings and to make it possible for such comparative wealth to be easily gained

would, in my opinion, be a mistake.' Britain's general lack of enthusiasm for the south was reflected in their choice of administrators to
run the place. As distinct from the Oxbridge district commissioners
swanning around in the north, the British who ran the mosquito-
infested south were mostly non-pensionable military officers, derisively known as the 'bog barons'. The nickname says it all about the
British disdain for the south in contrast to what they regarded as the
sophisticated and romantic Muslim culture of the north.

The cumulative effects of these twin colonial policies, of purposeful
underdevelopment and the elimination of all Arabic influences, would
have dire consequences for the whole region. As Mohamed Beshir
concludes:

> The rigid control of traders and marketing, justified by the need to
> protect the primitive southern communities against the exploita-
> tion of northern merchants, did not encourage the development of
> an exchange economy or trade. 'State control' prevented the free
> interplay of the forces of the market and the development of
> economic incentives. The reason for . . . economic backwardness
> was not the lack of financial resources only, it was also an outcome
> of the extreme application of the policy of indirect rule and its
> philosophy of protecting the primitive societies against outside
> influences.

The Christian mission schools, in particular, were co-opted into the
government's plan, and received increasing amounts of government
money. Specific missions were asked to open schools in areas where the
government sought, in the words of one British official, to 'counteract
the spread of Arabic and Islam'. The preponderance of church schools
in the south was to have important consequences after independence.
The churches remained strong despite the imposition of Islamic *sharia*
law in the 1980s from the north, and were to be a vital component of
the southern fightback against the Islamist regime in Khartoum in the
1990s.

However, having followed a policy that might have led to a coherent and acceptable separation of the north and south in the interwar years, in 1946 the British eventually decided that the south's destiny lay with the north in a single country after all, ruled from Khartoum. Why? Partly because of objections from the northern Muslims, who were demanding ever more stridently that the south be incorporated back into Sudan as a whole. Also, after Britain had been bankrupted by the war, the other equally cash-strapped east African colonial territories did not want to assume financial responsibility for the administration, let alone development, of the vast, apparently valueless swamp of southern Sudan. In other words, there was nowhere else for the south to go.

By now, however, it was far too late to forge a single national identity, particularly so in the rush towards independence. The differences were too great, as indeed had been intended. Even more so than in the western region of Darfur, southerners felt utterly cut off from Khartoum, the nominal capital of the country. Darfuris, at least, could take a dirt road to Khartoum, however long it took. Southerners did not even have that luxury. There were no roads, as remains the case to this day. So it was either a journey by boat, up the Nile, which could take a month, or by plane, which was far too expensive for the southerners, who even then were among the poorest people in the world.

Indeed, travelling through the south in the years after 2005, I would meet many younger or middle-aged southerners who had still never been to Khartoum, or anywhere else in the north. This was partly the result of the years of civil war, but also the natural consequence of the original lack of sympathy between the 'rulers' in Khartoum and the 'ruled' in the south. Not surprisingly, as one thirty-year-old doctor from Nimule on the Ugandan border told me, his generation therefore had 'no empathy with the north at all'.

The British might have been responsible for erecting the barriers between north and south Sudan in the first place and for treating southerners as second-class citizens. But here, as in other respects, the Muslim politicians who succeeded the British in Khartoum merely took their cue from their former colonial masters. Perhaps even more so, for the Muslims of the north, themselves on the fringes of the Arab world, had their own reasons to be dismissive of southern claims to equal rights and economic opportunities. As one of the most authoritative Sudanese writers, Francis Deng, puts it: 'The northern Sudanese tendency to exaggerate Arabism and Islam and to look down on the Negroid races as slaves could well be the result of a deep-seated inferiority complex, or, to put it in reverse, a superiority complex as a compensational device for their obvious marginality as Arabs.[10]

As a result of northern indifference, most southern Sudanese simply looked farther south for education and jobs, to Uganda and Kenya, countries with which they had more in common than north Sudan. Those southerners who did travel to Khartoum usually did so only out of necessity. They would go there as refugees, fleeing the war in their own territory, and once in the capital they disappeared into the black belt, where they were constantly reminded of how much better off the northerners were than themselves.

David Nyma, a doctor working at the Nimule hospital, explained to me how he saw the north though southern eyes. He is from the Madi tribe, which straddles the Sudan–Uganda border. David was forced to go to Khartoum in the mid-1980s for his education, first at secondary school and then at the University of Juba, which was relocated to the capital during the civil war. Training as a doctor, he discovered that not only were there prestigious government-run federal hospitals in Khartoum, but also hospitals in the northern provincial capitals and even in the rural areas, where there were also plenty of dispensaries: 'So the service reached almost everybody,' he told me. In the provincial hospitals there were even specialists: a paediatrician, a surgeon and a gynaecologist. In strictly professional terms, David thought it was 'pretty good'.

Rather than making David feel proud of Sudan, however, this merely rubbed in how little his own people had. When he left the south in the mid-1980s, healthcare provision for the Madi was composed of one small clinic in Nimule and a dispensary in Loa, covering an area of hundreds of square miles. For anything serious, he told me, people had to go to the southern capital of Juba: 'But this was usually impossible, as there was no transport. Friends had to wait three or four days to get a ride to Juba.' Even when they arrived, there was only one hospital in the city, 'and that had very few doctors'.

People like David were from the 'deep south' of Sudan. But it was the same story much nearer to Khartoum. Take the Nuba Mountains for example, an area relatively close to the capital, just south of El Obeid, the capital of Kordofan. El Obeid is the last big Arab city before the Nuba Mountains; it is the centre, among other things, for Sudan's very profitable production of gum arabic, essential for the production of sweet fizzy drinks. A good road runs from El Obeid east to Kosti, and then up to Khartoum. The distance is about 370 miles, but it can be done easily in a day. South of El Obeid, however, the infrastructure deteriorates drastically; it's a much longer and bumpier ride to get down to Kadugli, the capital of the Nuba Mountains. Here again, despite their proximity to the north, Nubans have always been painfully aware of how little they have compared to the Khartoumese.

Take the experiences of Ali Abdulrahman Abbas, for instance, who was born in the Nuba town of Delami in 1973 and is now head of an NGO called Nuba Relief, Rehabilitation and Development Organization, based in Nairobi, where I met him. He was forced to flee the Nuba Mountains after his village was burned to the ground in the civil war in the mid-1990s. But he had also spent time in Khartoum before that, as his father had been an officer in the Sudanese army. His memories were overshadowed by the glaring inequalities between Khartoum and the area where his family lived.

In the whole of the Nuba Mountains there were only two clinics, in Dilling and Delami. 'If a child was sick, you would have to be carried on your father's back to Dilling for two or three days.' There were no roads at all. Schools had no classrooms and few teachers; you started primary school 'under a tree'. 'When I saw the infrastructure, the development in Khartoum,' Ali told me, 'I thought, why can't this be done in Nuba? There must be something wrong. I am not a part of this country.' Even to this day, he says: 'Nuba is so close to Khartoum, but still feels very remote.'

Thus, from the very beginning of independence, African southerners, whether Dinka or Nuban, were never made to feel that they were an integral part of the new nation. Just as everything that the southerners had experienced of 'rule' from Khartoum for the 150-odd years before independence had taught them to be resistant to, or at the very least sceptical of, government from the north, so this continued after independence. In practice, it seemed to matter little to southerners whether foreigners or 'Sudanese' lorded it over them from Khartoum. Turco-Egyptian rule had brought only slave raids, and in southern folklore the Mahdist liberating heroes of the northern imagination had behaved little better. Indeed, the two eras were grouped together by the Dinka as the time when 'the world was spoiled'. During their own time in Sudan, the self-regarding British were always referred to as *Turuk* in the south – the Sudanese word for the Turks.[11]

To the southerners, the customary northern ignorance and indifference towards them continued up to self-rule in 1956. The Sudanese elite, very much focused on organizing themselves for independence from Britain, were barely concerned with the sensitivities of the south. As Sudan rushed towards independence, the main issue at stake for the northern Arabs was whether to win their freedom together with Egypt, as part of a new Condominium, or alone. They just *assumed* that they would rule over the south, and thus saw no need to address the yawning political and religious differences between them and the southerners, which might have been accommodated in some sort of federal arrangement.

Thus not a single southerner was invited to attend the talks in Cairo in 1953 that set the terms for independence with the British and Egyptians. In 1954, the Sudanization Committee preparing for independent rule, almost entirely staffed by Muslim northerners, replaced 800 British and Egyptian posts with Sudanese, but only six southerners were appointed to posts in the entire country. All the main government jobs in the south went to northerners. This created outrage in the south, where it looked very much like they had simply swapped one lot of colonial rulers for another. As one of the southern politicians complained:

'Each boat and aircraft . . . brought northerners for appointment to the administration, police or the army, and the flow at times looked like an invasion.'[12] Many southerners blamed the British for not fighting their corner hard enough.

Small wonder, therefore, that even before the British left southern Sudanese suspicion and resentment at their high-handed treatment by the northern Muslims had boiled over into armed resistance. In August 1955 the first act of a southern rebellion took place when the Equatoria Corps rioted, killing all northerners at its base in Torit. The southern soldiers of the corps were resisting a Khartoum edict to transfer them north; the mutinous soldiers feared that this would leave the south with no army to protect it from northern oppression. After independence in January 1956 the rebellion only worsened, led by a southern guerrilla movement called the Anya-Nya (a term for snake venom).

To southerners, fears of aggressive northern intentions towards them were quickly realized. Southern requests to reopen the question of federal arrangements to allow for a limited measure of southern self-rule were snuffed out. Indeed, calls for a federal system were effectively 'rendered criminal'.[13] Instead, the new administrators seemed intent on creating a new Sudan simply by imposing Arab, Islamist rule on the entire country.

Thus Friday instead of Sunday was declared a holiday. Particularly devastating for southerners was the closure of all the Christian mission schools in the region by the first military government in Khartoum in 1964. Instead, Islamic schools were introduced and southern children were given Muslim names; learning the Koran became a compulsory subject. Yet still northern politicians could not grasp southern grievances. Mohamed Beshir was chair of a round-table conference in Khartoum in 1965, when the parties sat down for a rare chance to listen to each others' points of view. Beshir, himself a northerner, later wrote: 'Many northerners were shocked when they realized that the southerners looked upon them as nothing more than descendants of Arab slave traders and colonizers. Very few of them had, until then, realized the extent of mistrust and bitterness among the educated Southerners.'

But that conference, like many others, did little to help. As Francis Deng (a southerner) has written, for the south: 'The true struggle for self-liberation had just begun with independence.' The draining north–south war was to continue on and off (with a break from 1972 to 1983) until 2005, costing, in the end, over two million lives. The newly independent Sudan was born in blood and has yet to learn another way to live.

THE WORLD BEYOND: THE NEIGHBOURS INTRUDE

The remoteness of the regions and their underdevelopment, as well as their misrule from Khartoum, had another grave consequence for Sudan. It made the regions prey to the malevolent ambitions of Sudan's neighbours, something that might have been avoided if Khartoum had taken a greater interest in developing and thus strengthening them in the first place. For the involvement of the neighbouring countries is one of the factors that has made pacifying Sudan's rebellious regions so hard; the neighbours usually held as much, if not more, sway over Sudan's west, south and east than Khartoum did. Ironically, for all of the capital's wealth and power, Sudan's long civil wars have been symptomatic of the failure of the centre to exert sufficient military or political control over the peripheries.

Thus Darfur, so far from Khartoum, was an easy picking for Colonel Ghadaffi, the self-styled revolutionary socialist who came to power in Libya in 1969. He conceived of a new Arab Maghreb, uniting Sudan, and particularly Darfur, with Libya. Sharing hundreds of miles of unprotected border, the African tribes of Darfur were helpless as the Libyan-sponsored Arab tribes of the self-proclaimed 'Islamic Pan-African Legion' started invading the territory in the 1970s. Soon Darfur was awash with guns, and the destructive dynamic of Arab nomadic tribes versus Fur settled farmers became dangerously exacerbated. This was to become a pattern in Sudan. Existing ethnic and religious tensions over access to the best grazing land or water had previously been contained by local mediation as tribal chiefs sorted things out between themselves. But those ethnic and religious differences were to be cleaved open for political gain by outsiders, as well as by competing Sudanese political factions.

Like Libya, Chad probably had a greater bearing on the politics of Darfur than Khartoum. For the Zaghawa people, in particular, the long colonial boundary between Darfur and Chad was meaningless; all the inter-tribal conflicts would reverberate in both countries. Idriss Déby, a Zaghawa, launched the coup that brought him to power in Chad in 1990 from Darfur, just as the attempted counter-coups against him in 2004, 2006 and 2008 would be launched from Darfur. One of the main Darfuri rebel groups after 2003, the JEM, is composed mainly of Zaghawa, and operates quite freely either side of the border. The JEM fighters owe a loyalty to Déby, who (among others) armed them. They repaid the inept and corrupt dictator handsomely when they formed his last line of defence, literally at the palace gates, when Chadian rebels came perilously close to overthrowing him in 2008.

Likewise, in eastern Sudan local politics and allegiances have often been dictated more by Eritrea and Ethiopia than by Khartoum. So porous are the borders between the three countries, so erratic Khartoum's interest in and control over its eastern states, that the various civil wars within Ethiopia and Eritrea since the 1960s always spilled over into Gedaref and Kassala states in east Sudan. Similarly, it was easy for the Sudanese armed groups opposed to Khartoum to use bases in Eritrea and Ethiopia, aided and abetted by those governments. This was particularly so in the 1990s after the Islamist regime in Khartoum virtually declared war on their largely Christian neighbours; indeed, much of the opposition to the Islamic government in Khartoum was organized from the Eritrean capital of Asmara. It was here, for instance, that the armed and civilian Sudanese resistance to Khartoum's rule came together in the mid-1990s as the National Democratic Alliance, dedicated to overthrowing President Omar al-Bashir.

The self-proclaimed Eastern Front – the armed insurgency against Khartoum's rule in east Sudan – owed what little military success it had almost entirely to Eritrean arms and tactics. Sudan's rulers tacitly acknowledged Eritrea's enormous influence over east Sudan when it asked Eritrea to broker the peace deal between it and its eastern rebels at the beginning of 2006. Eritrea did the job remarkably quickly, getting the East Sudan Peace Agreement signed in October of the same year. That this happened so fast was a reflection of the fact that Sudan's eastern rebels had to accept what Eritrea wanted, so dominant was that country's role within the Eastern Front.[14]

It was not only the immediate neighbours who got involved, however. From the very start of independence, there were plenty of countries that viewed the south, for instance, in the same terms as the British had, as a bulwark against the expansionist ambitions of north African Islamism.

Bishop Elias Taban has as good a memory as anyone of the whole course of the southern wars with the north. Born in Yei in 1955, tall, fit and energetic, he is now the much-respected and very respectable-looking head of the Evangelical Presbyterian Church in the south. But the bishop was once a child soldier, recruited by the Anya-Nya guerrillas in 1964 when he was just nine years old. The people who trained him in the bush camps around Yei as he grew up were the Israelis. He recalls how Israeli officers drilled the young boys and taught them the basics of guerrilla warfare.

The children were told 'that they were fighting for freedom from Islam'. With the forced closing of the Christian mission schools, young boys like Elias had been obliged to go to the new Islamic schools where they were forced to adopt Muslim names. He remembers his own very well: Mohamed Ali Monsur. So the message of 'freedom from Islam' certainly resonated with these boys. They nicknamed the fighters from the north *mudukur*, meaning 'praying on your knees'.

Once recruited, Elias's main contribution to the cause was to spy on government army convoys along the main roads. To do this, he and his friends had to climb the tall trees bordering the roadsides and count the numbers of trucks that rumbled past. Each truck or car could only carry a certain number of troops in it, so from the boys' tally the guerrillas could calculate the number of troops ranged against them fairly accurately. They would then plan their ambushes and attacks accordingly.

But it became increasingly dangerous work, as the northern soldiers got wind of the little spies and grew gradually more adept at picking them off in the branches. Elias's friends began to die in alarming numbers. After a year of this, Elias's father, himself an Anya-Nya fighter, complained that too many children were being killed this way 'for the good of the future of the country', and so Elias's commander officially reassigned him to other duties.

The Israelis trained not only the boy soldiers but many of the Anya-Nya commanders as well, sometimes in Israel itself. The Israelis brought in guns and ammunition and advised on tactics, although they did not do any frontline fighting themselves. Discreet as they were, the Israelis nonetheless remained the principal backers of the southern rebels throughout the 1960s up to the first peace agreement with the north in 1972. The Israelis were close allies with Uganda, and so they could ship arms and men in over the southern border on the main road leading from Kampala. For the Israelis, backing the southern rebels was part of a wider strategy of containing anti-Israeli, Islamic forces throughout the Horn of Africa and the Red Sea region.

Elias Taban, who went on to train as a Presbyterian pastor in Uganda, explained to me how other east African countries saw the southern cause in similar terms. Nigeria in the west and Sudan in the east were the two countries where Islamism could penetrate into the rest of the continent from north Africa. In these terms Sudan, so the thinking went, was the major prize: through Sudan, Islam could penetrate into Congo, Kenya, Uganda, the Central African Republic and elsewhere, if it were allowed to. 'Sudan was the gateway to central Africa', as Elias told me.

Thus Christian southern Sudan had to be supported to prevent this. The two major Christian neighbours, Kenya and Uganda, were therefore faithful allies of the cause. Kenya, in particular, was to become a major conduit for arms and supplies to the Sudan People's Liberation Movement, the successor to the Anya-Nya.

The USA first became heavily involved in Sudan in the 1970s as a function of Cold War politics. It became the main foreign backer of

President Numeiri in the mid-1970s. But, as we shall see, its involvement deepened even further in the early 1990s, mostly in defending the southern Sudanese Christian churches from the *jihad* declared against them by the northern Muslim government. Christian activists proved remarkably adept at mobilizing domestic US public opinion around this cause, and also around the issue of slavery. In the 1990s and 2000s, the USA's relationship with the country would become Sudan's most important external concern as many other issues crowded onto their bilateral agenda, not least terrorism and al-Qaeda. On Sudan, the USA would be taught a salutary lesson about the limits of its global influence.

Thus in southern Sudan the causes of religious freedom, human rights, the defence against Islam and national self-determination all became inextricably linked – and fighters would rally to the southerners' side for any one of these causes. During Sudan's second civil war in the 1990s, for example, Eritrea played much the same role as Israel had in the first war. Eritrea was already heavily involved in protecting its own frontier by backing Sudan's eastern rebels against Khartoum's Islamist regime. Helping the southern rebels put further pressure on Khartoum. Ironically, many of the Eritreans who were sent by their government to fight for the south against Khartoum's army were Muslims themselves, but they saw their own long, bloody battle for freedom against what they saw as bullying Ethiopia reflected in southern Sudan's struggle against the north. As Elias Taban remembers: 'They were motivated by a sympathy with a small nation of people, battling against oppression by a more dominant country.'

The Eritreans might have been few in number, like the Israelis, but they proved to be extremely effective fighters. They had been combat trained over years of harsh guerrilla warfare in the mountains of Tigray against the Ethiopian army. Particularly impressive were the fearless women tank drivers – the men were mainly on the artillery. To this day, there are many Eritrean men and women in Juba and Yei who stayed on after the end of the war in 2005. Some of the men are now taxi drivers, skilfully plying the awful roads in battered old Landcruisers and minivans.

EGYPT AND CHINA CAST THE LONGEST SHADOWS

As well as these near neighbours and a more distant superpower, the newly independent Sudan was also subject to the ambitions and internal politics of two other countries: Egypt and China. Indeed, together with the USA after the 1970s, these two countries were to wield the most external influence over Sudan after 1956.

Egypt, together with Britain, was the old colonial power. Unlike the British, however, the Egyptians could not just pack up and go home – the very survival of the Egyptian state rested on a pliant, pacific Sudan, in two ways.

First, Egypt's economic well-being relies heavily on the waters of the Nile, and the river runs through Sudan for most of the journey from its source to the Mediterranean. And secondly, as post-independence Egypt was founded as a pan-Arabist, socialist state after General Nasser's revolution, the priority for its leaders was to keep at bay the spread of political Islam and Islamic fundamentalism. From the 1960s onwards, the nearest source of contagion, as they saw it, was Sudan. The organized expression of political Islam, the Muslim Brotherhood, was founded in Egypt in 1928, as we shall see in the next chapter. But there it was banned and its leaders imprisoned or executed. The Sudanese branch of the Brotherhood, however, flourished in Khartoum, where it broke off from its Egyptian parent and grew into a distinct, home-grown version of the same.

The primary interest of Egypt's leaders, therefore, was to prop up those Sudanese politicians who would be a bulwark against the spread of Islamism. Thus, for example, the (initially) socialist Jafar Numeiri was Egypt's favourite Sudanese president, and the Egyptians provided plenty of military support for his vain attempts to suppress the Islamist parties in Sudan. Egypt was also to be the main regional enemy of Sudan's 1989 Islamist revolution. Egypt's president, Hosni Mubarak, contributed greatly to the ousting of its leader, Dr Hassan al-Turabi.

But most important of all for the northern Sudanese governments, whatever their religious creed or political complexion, were the Chinese.

Many in the West presume that the Chinese connection, harshly exposed over Darfur since 2004, is a comparatively recent affair, consummated by the large-scale Sino-Sudanese exploitation of oil in the country in the 2000s. But in fact the Chinese were in Sudan from the very beginnings of independence, and from the start they identified themselves with the interests of the northern Muslims in Khartoum. In the Israeli-run guerrilla camps in the bush in the mid-1960s, Elias Taban remembers how all the child soldiers enthusiastically chanted songs boasting of how they would 'knock Chinese bombers out of the sky'.

If religion, cotton and human rights (in the guise of anti-slaving) drew the British into Sudan, the Chinese were drawn to the country by a search for like-minded allies in a largely hostile world. There is an emotional, historical tinge to the beginnings of this affair. Unlikely as it seems, Britain's General Gordon played a part. In the early days of Chinese visits to Khartoum it became something of a ritual for new arrivals to pay their respects at the tomb of the Mahdi, the slayer of Gordon. Why? Because the British general was already well known to the new arrivals from Asia. He had been 'Chinese Gordon' before he ever became 'Gordon of Khartoum'.

Before he embarked on his first mission to Sudan in 1877, Gordon had led the imperial Western armies in the Opium Wars against the indigenous rebel Taiping army in Shanghai. The Chinese paid homage to the Mahdi as the man who vanquished their own imperial oppressor. Thus the Chinese and the Sudanese saw themselves as fellow victims of Western imperialism. Sudan was the first sub-Saharan African country to recognize the new Communist China, in 1959. Sudan also acknowledged 'one China' from the beginning.

The man to talk to about the China connection in Sudan is Ali Abdalla Ali, once a professor of economics at the Sudan University of Science and Technology and now the main adviser to the Khartoum Stock Exchange, which he helped to set up in 1992. Like the rest of the elder generation of Khartoum's ruling class, he is highly educated, with degrees from Sudan, New Delhi and Hertford College, Oxford University, which he attended in the early 1970s. In his airless office on the fifth floor of the concrete warren that is the stock exchange, he nostalgically reflects that he might have stayed at Oxford and become a don were it not for the summer pollen that set off his asthma.

He first wrote about the Chinese in Sudan in 1976. Even then, the pattern of Chinese aid and investment to the country was firmly established; China extended interest-free loans to be repaid in goods years after the completion of specific projects. From the 1960s to the 1970s, in the midst of the Cold War, China pointedly challenged the superpower hegemony of the USA and Soviet Union by building close ties to post-colonial, non-aligned African countries. The construction of the Tazara (Tanzania–Zambia) railway, opened in 1975, by 25,000 Chinese technicians and up to 100,000 African labourers was but the most extreme example of the aid programme that developed out of this political and diplomatic imperative.

The more modest Sudanese equivalent of the railway was the Friendship Hall, a multi-purpose conference centre in central Khartoum, minutes away from the banks of the Blue Nile; it was completed in 1976. A functional, modernist block, very much in the style of the era, it has weathered well, although it is now rather overshadowed by Ghadaffi's Egg.

In his essay of the same year, Ali could not have been more generous in his praise of the Chinese and their role in the construction of Friendship Hall. For Ali it was a model of what made the Chinese so popular with the Sudanese. Two hundred Chinese technicians worked 'in real partnership with the Sudanese labourers and engineers'. The hall was completed on time, in three years. 'When the hot summer months came the technicians worked in the interior of the Hall and when the cooler weather approached they shifted to work on the exterior of the building, thus saving energy and time.' And there was grudging praise for the Chinese workers' application: 'All those who collaborate with the Chinese admit their invincible but (sometimes) irritating discipline which they nevertheless agree to accept.'

Then there were the cultural and political affinities as well. 'Non-interference' in the affairs of Sudan, or in any other developing country, was already official Chinese policy, as it was to remain into the 2000s. This was welcomed by African leaders, in contrast to the lectures they had to endure on how to run their countries from self-righteous Westerners. Whereas the West has always blown hot and cold on Sudan, with aid money coming and going according to the vagaries of domestic politics and economic fashion in London, Brussels or Washington, the Chinese have been consistent partners right from the start. As if to emphasize the point, the Chinese returned to the scene of their first triumph at Friendship Hall to add an extension onto it in 2003.

It was only later that the Chinese–Sudan relationship came to revolve so much around oil. Ironically given later events, in 1970, when the Chinese were first approached by President Numeiri to prospect for oil, they admitted that they did not have the technology to do the job. Instead, they recommended Chevron, the US major, thus precipitating the original US involvement in the country's nascent petroleum industry. Chevron subsequently struck oil in 1979, only for its operations to be violently curtailed after 1983 when the north–south civil war resumed. It was only when Chevron pulled out of the country completely, and at the same time the Chinese demand for hydrocarbons became urgent, that China was lured in.

By the mid-1990s China was entering its new phase of quasi-capitalist industrial expansion and was scouring the globe for natural resources, especially in places where the West had not tied up everything already. Sudan was the perfect destination. Oil had already been discovered, courtesy of Chevron, and it was relatively easy to extract.

The first oil deals between China and Sudan were signed during a high-profile visit by President Bashir to Beijing in 1995. The first joint-venture oil consortium, the Greater Nile Petroleum Operating Company (GNPOC), was set up two years later and began pumping out crude from Sudan in 1999. By about 2003, only four years later, the Sudanese government was boasting that its oil industry was producing 500,000 or so barrels of oil every day. Even if the real figure was rather lower than this, as many analysts reckoned, maybe 300,000, that still proved enough to fuel the economic boom in Khartoum.

GNPOC, however, is just as much an Asian as a Chinese venture. The China National Petroleum Corporation (CNPC) owns 40 per cent of GNPOC, but Malaysia's Petronas is not far behind with 30 per cent. Petronas was a joint partner in starting the company in 1995, and also helped to set up Sudapet, the Sudanese government's state-owned oil company which has a 5 per cent share in GNPOC. Also, the Indian national oil company, ONGC Videsh, bought a quarter share of the business in 2003, after a Canadian company, Talisman, was forced to withdraw from GNPOC after it was targeted by activists in a disinvestment campaign.

MORE TERRIBLE THAN BEAUTIFUL

These, then, were the colonial and foreign influences that were to shape the ungainly and artificial state of Sudan that gained independence on 1 January 1956. From the very beginning the new country could barely live with itself. Much of the blame for that should be attributed to the colonial powers; Britain, and to a lesser extent, Egypt. The historian of the Anglo-Egyptian Condominium, M.W. Daly, concludes that the colonial government left 'an economy seriously skewed, dangerously dependent on one crop, virtually without modern industry, with a tiny educated elite enjoying expensive social services, and vast areas and millions of people left further and further behind'.[15]

But despite the newly independent Sudan's obvious problems, how did the country's own politicians, now finally in command of their own country, fail so miserably to do any better?

CHAPTER TWO

POPULISTS AND CIVIL WAR, 1956–89

Contrary to what an outsider might conclude from the two decades of one-party authoritarian rule in Sudan since 1989, in fact there has always been an impressive plurality of religious and political visions in the country. Indeed, if anything there has probably been a surfeit of political competition. For, as we shall see, the democratic system inherited from the British quickly collapsed under the dead weight of Sudanese politicking. This failure to govern effectively *by consent* has been Sudan's principal weakness since independence.

Throughout, though, there has been only a handful of political groupings or parties that have mattered in Sudan, competing for power in Khartoum. A couple of these were the original parties that jostled to inherit power from the British; the rest grew up largely in opposition to them after the 1950s. However, although the leaders of these parties might have regarded the disagreements between themselves to be so profound as to be almost unbridgeable, to many Sudanese on the peripheries of the country these same Khartoum-based parties all seemed to be much of a muchness in their illiberalism and venality. Despite the differences in rhetoric, in the end they all acted in roughly the same way, trapped, apparently, in the strait-jacket of the Sudanese state's peculiar economic and political make-up bequeathed to them by the British. Indeed, for all their superficial differences, Sudan's leaders were (and remain) products of exactly the same political class and were often educated at the same school; as we shall see, they even married into each others' families. It is little wonder that the southern Sudanese, the perennial victims of Khartoum's politicians, scarcely bothered to distinguish between them. Only one northern leader showed any genuine interest in forging a new, peaceful country, and even then for only a few years before he too was consumed by the vortex of Sudan's dysfunctional politics.

AN ABUNDANCE OF POLITICS AND THE FAILURE OF DEMOCRACY

The most important political thread running through Sudanese history (or at least, that of the country now called Sudan) remains the Umma party. It owes its existence to the enduring legend of the Mahdi who, in his opposition to British and Egyptian rule in the 1880s, created the first independent Sudan. The British did their best to obliterate the lineage of the Mahdi, executing two of his sons and dumping their bodies in the Nile after the battle of Omdurman. But one posthumous son did survive, Sayyid Abd al-Rahman al-Mahdi. He founded the modern Mahdist movement, out of which grew the Umma party. A descendant, Mubarak al-Mahdi, told me the Umma version of Sudanese political history in the opulent surroundings of his Khartoum townhouse.

Retreating to the historic home of the Mahdi, Aba Island, on the White Nile close to Kosti, from the First World War onwards Sayyid Mahdi rebuilt the fortunes of the family after the disaster of Omdurman by turning his attention from warfare to commerce. In particular, he specialized in the less glorious but more lucrative activity of irrigated agricultural schemes. He invested in oil-seed crushing and won contracts from the British colonial government for wood, fuel and meat. Thus he revived the fortunes of the Ansar sect, the original followers of the Mahdi.

Vitally, he abandoned the Ansars' original hostility to the British and instead decided to co-operate with the colonial rulers. In the First World War he supported the British cause, and was duly rewarded. As we have seen, the Sultan of Darfur, by contrast, supported the Turks and the Germans, and his land was invaded and annexed. In 1945, with the prospect of independence in the offing and elections coming, Sayyid Mahdi founded the Umma party as the political expression of the Ansars.

The Umma party has always commanded more support among ordinary Sudanese than any other political movement. Sadiq al-Mahdi has been the leader of the Umma since the 1960s. He enjoyed the gilded upbringing of the rest of Sudan's elite, including a degree in politics from Oxford University, and by the mid-2000s was probably still the only politician who could truly say that he commanded mass support across the whole of the country, or at least in the Muslim north. Mubarak argues that just as only the Mahdi was able to unite the Sudanese tribes together to fight for an independent Sudan, so only the Umma party has been able to unite the Sudanese since.

Judging by election results, Mubarak certainly has a case. In the west of Sudan, in Darfur and Kordofan, from where many of the original Mahdi's fighters came, the Umma party has always been strong. In the last free national elections in Sudan, in 1986, the Umma party won thirty-four out of thirty-nine seats in Darfur, whereas the rival political arm of the Muslim Brotherhood, the National Islamic Front (NIF), won only three seats, despite spending lavishly on trying to win more. In the country as a whole, the Umma secured 38.2 per cent of the vote, the highest percentage, and won the biggest block of seats in parliament, 99 out of a total 273.

The other strongest party at independence in 1956, and very similar in character to the Umma, was the National Unionist Party (NUP), now called the Democratic Unionist Party (DUP). Just as the Umma was founded on the Ansar sect, so the Unionist party was founded on the Khatmiyyah sect. The DUP has traditionally been the party of the urban centres, largely led by and paid for by businessmen, but it has been supported in the rural areas by peasants who believe in al-Khatim, another name for the prophet Mohammad.

The founder of the Khatmiyyah sect was Mohammed Osman al-Mirghani. He brought his strain of Sufi Islam from Arabia, in the early nineteenth century, to east Sudan, a region that remains the power base of both the sect and the political party. The centre of pilgrimage for the Khatmiyyah is the beautiful mosque in Kassala, at the base of the spectacular massif of the Taka hills with their distinctive dome-shaped peaks. Beyond are the rugged highlands of Eritrea. In the mosque are supposed to be the remains of Mohammed's son, Seyyid Hassan al-Mirghani, who died in 1869. The mosque was partly destroyed by the Ansar during the Mahdiya, a reminder of the often bloody rivalry between the two sects.

In the arguments over independence in the early 1950s, the Khatmiyyah favoured Sudan becoming independent from Britain in

The mosque and massif at Kassala

union with Egypt, hence the Unionist name, while the Ansar favoured Sudanese independence from Britain and Egypt all at the same time. The NUP won a majority of seats in the first parliamentary elections held under British rule in 1954, but, even so, an anti-unionist majority in the parliament ensured that there would never be any union with Egypt.

Both the Umma party and the DUP remain traditional, dynastic parties, led by either a direct descendant of the Mahdi or a member of the Mirghani family. If these two parties dictated the immediate course of post-independence politics, two more parties arose as self-proclaimed 'modernizing' projects, to liberate Sudan, supposedly, from the bondage of hierarchical, dynastic politics. These were the Communist Party and the Muslim Brotherhood, which were largely to dominate politics from the late 1960s onwards.

But such spirited political competition came at a price – the self-destruction of democracy. One party could never dominate at the polls, which meant that governments were usually made up of three or four parties, often following each other in and out of coalitions in rapid succession. This paralysed decision- and policy-making. Mubarak el-Mahdi, looking back, described the country's governance as 'being like Italy'. He also points to another factor in Sudan's failure of democracy: the meddling of the neighbours, mainly authoritarian Egypt and Libya. Both countries were unenthusiastic about their own citizens having a successful model of democracy so close at hand.

From the very beginning, therefore, Sudan lapsed into a familiar cycle: unstable, democratically elected coalition governments would become weak, chaotic and unworkable, only to be swept away by military-led coups in league with one of the main political factions, acting in the name of law and order. The new military ruler was accepted at first, but in his turn became overbearing, dictatorial and unpopular. He would then be overthrown by a popular uprising that returned the country to democracy again. But the newly elected government would be unable to command any authority in parliament and be overthrown by the military in league with one or other of the parties – and so it went on. No parliament in independent Sudan has ever served its full term, except the first (which anyway started before independence). Meanwhile, the ability of both democratic and military governments to govern from Khartoum was constantly undermined by the draining civil war with the south.

Thus from 1954 to 1958, first the DUP and then the Umma party dominated democratically elected governments before the army launched its first coup. General Aboub ruled until 1964, when he was swept from power in a popular uprising, the so-called 'October Revolution'. From 1965 until 1969 the DUP and Umma party again shared a number of uneasy coalitions, which 'rose and fell with increasing rapidity' before General Numeiri became president in a coup in 1969.[1] He was ousted from power in 1985 and another Umma/DUP coalition government took power in 1986 after national elections. But that government proved to be no stronger than its predecessors, and was swept aside in its turn by Bashir's coup in 1989.

THE TRIUMPH OF NUMEIRI

Jafar Numeiri was the only leader who succeeded in stitching together the disparate parts of Sudan for any length of time, so his record deserves to be studied in some detail. He came to power largely with the help of the communists, who since the 1940s had been the avowedly modernizing force in Sudanese politics, hostile to what they perceived to be the anachronistic feudalism of the Umma and Khatmiyya. Communism gained a following throughout Africa because it offered a compelling critique of the injustices of imperialism. But it became unusually strong in Sudan because, exceptionally, the country had very strong trade unions, on the Gezira schemes, in agriculture generally and on the railways. The epicentre of communist organization in Sudan, therefore, was the railway-junction city of Atbara.

Sudan's Communist Party was one of the best organized political bodies in Africa. Like in other countries, the Communist Party was extremely popular among the young and the educated – the intelligentsia.

It was the strongest party in the universities throughout the 1950s and 1960s. Many communists were inspired by the example of Egypt. The socialist revolution of General Nasser was then in full swing, and the cause was given a big fillip by Nasser's victory over the British and French during the Suez Crisis of 1956. Nasser's remarkable success against the former colonial powers came only a few months after Sudan's own independence from Britain. General Numeiri's seizure of power, allied to the communists and with the support of Egypt, represented the peak of communist and left-wing influence in Sudan. And in obeisance to the party, in his first years in power Numeiri did at least try to follow a broadly socialist programme.

General Numeiri was only thirty-nine when he launched his coup. Hailing from Dongola in the north, he had been an athlete and a good footballer in his youth, although he grew up to be physically small and unimposing, even in his full-dress uniform. Judith Miller, a reporter for the *New York Times*, was certainly unimpressed. She lived in Khartoum on and off during the 1970s and 1980s and met him several times. She wrote of him thus: 'Flabby, black-skinned, and tainted in the eyes of many of his racist northern countrymen by his facial scars – inflicted by tribal healers to protect children against the Nile's innumerable eye diseases – he was a poor orator.'

Nonetheless, he was also energetic, clever and ruthless. And despite his despotic instincts, he remains the only Sudanese leader to have even attempted to govern the country in the name of all Sudanese, and to have presided over a period, however short-lived, of peace. He charted a highly erratic course through the domestic and international politics of his era, yet his rule can still be divided, roughly, into three distinct phases: a socialist phase (1969–71), followed by a Western-orientated phase (until the late 1970s) and finally an Islamist phase, until his fall in 1985.

Numeiri's coup on 25 May 1969 was swift and bloodless, and modelled closely on Nasser's achievements. Numeiri had become enamoured of Nasser and his pan-Arabic socialist movement as a young man, and had enrolled into the Free Officers' Movement. When he came to power, Numeiri ruled through a Revolutionary Command Council, again following Nasser's example.

Numeiri quickly and lethally moved against his political opponents, particularly the despised Umma party. In 1970, responding to an Ansar demonstration against him in Khartoum, Numeiri attacked their spiritual base (and the original home of the Mahdi) on Aba Island. Egyptian fighter-bombers supported the attack, allegedly directed by a youngish air force chief-of-staff called Hosni Mubarak.

This assault left about 12,000 Ansar dead, including the imam of the sect, the uncle of a young Sadiq al-Mahdi, who escaped into what would be the first of several exiles. The extensive holdings and property of the Mahdi family were sequestered by the state. Today, a visitor to Aba Island can still catch a glimpse of how grand the Mahdis must once have been. Their palace, probably the biggest and most ornate residence in Sudan apart from the presidential palace in Khartoum, still survives. It is now the rather shabby law faculty of the local university. Numeiri's Egyptian-led destruction of Aba Island to destroy the descendants of the Mahdi was a terrible echo of earlier Egyptian aggression against the island. In 1881, the Egyptian governor of the Sudan had torched its buildings, farms and orchards in pursuit of the original Mahdi at the beginning of his uprising.

Then, in 1971, Numeiri took advantage of an attempted coup by the Communist Party against him to turn on his erstwhile allies and destroy them as a political force. The leaders were executed and the organization shattered, especially among the working-class trade unions. Nobody and nothing were spared. The railways, for instance, were deliberately run down in order to break one of the party's main power bases. Little remains today of the old communist movement, once such a powerful force in Sudan.

The subsequent years saw the profound reorientation of Sudan's foreign policy, away from the East and towards the West. The attempted communist coup made Numeiri wary of the Eastern bloc and in 1972 he resumed diplomatic relations with the USA. It was the height of the Cold War, and the USA was happy to cultivate the Sudanese president as a regional counterweight to terrorist-supporting, socialist Libya, and the grim Marxist regime of the dictator Haile Mariam Mengistu in Ethiopia following the 1974 overthrow of Emperor Haile Selassie. In addition, Numeiri could always count on the Chinese, who first started investing heavily in Sudan during the years of his regime.

The mid-1970s were his best years. Indeed many people look back to the mid- to late-1970s as the best years in Sudan's history, especially given what was to come. It is true that Numeiri had demonstrated a merciless streak in dealing with his rivals. He was certainly no democrat. But he also made peace with the south in 1972 and presided over a period of relative prosperity. By contrast with his blood-soaked regional peers, Idi Amin in Uganda, Haile Mariam Mengistu and Mobutu in Zaire, he seemed to be a model of reasonableness and liberalism. For a moment, it looked as if a unified Sudan, encompassing all religions and races, with some power devolved to the regions, might actually work.

Brothers in arms, at first: Nasser, Numeiri, and Ghadaffi

The peace deal of 1972 with the southern rebels, concluded at negotiations in Addis Ababa, brought Numeiri great acclaim in Africa and beyond. Khartoum allowed a regional assembly in the south, and the two sides' armed forces were to be integrated. A southerner was made vice-president and several southern politicians served in the government. Certainly, Numeiri's cultivation of the south was laced with a certain degree of political self-interest; after turning on the communists he urgently needed new sources of political support. But the Addis Ababa agreement also appeared to be a logical, quasi-federal solution to the country's most besetting problem since independence.

For a while, everything went well. For the first time a northern government seemed genuinely interested in the south, without imposing an Islamist agenda on the region. The government presided over several lasting contributions to the development of the south: the University of Juba was opened; radio and television stations were set up; some roads were built; and scholarships were provided for young southerners to study at universities in Egypt.

As the man who had brought peace and relative prosperity to the south, Numeiri, the northerner from Dongola, was, as some remember, 'loved' in the south during the 1970s. His visits to southern towns are still vividly remembered. They turned into triumphal processions. The Reverend Elias Taban, the boy soldier who fought for the south against the north in the first civil war, told me of the euphoria when Numeiri visited Yei, Taban's hometown. Everyone turned out in a display of genuine affection, with the children chanting in Arabic: 'Who is your father? Numeiri. Who is your brother? Numeiri.' People lined the streets to acclaim the president. Taban says that he was 'the strongest secular leader of Sudan'. A Dinka I spoke to remembered the president's visit to Abyei in 1972:

> The whole population came to the streets, gave him a big welcome. There was dancing from morning to the evening. We slaughtered bulls for him, we did traditional dancing, we marched around Abyei, all nine Dinka tribes. It was a graduation day, with

all the Dinka youth in their traditional clothes standing in the main square waiting for Numeiri.

The president's most ambitious plan was – finally – to link the south to the north via a waterway and road. This was the famous Jonglei canal, the mother of all development projects. Just as Gezira had been, in its time, the biggest irrigated agricultural project in the world, so the Jonglei was planned to be the longest navigable canal in the world, with a road running along beside it. The canal would connect Bor, in the heart of the south, with Malakal, over 200 miles to the north-east and the navigable gateway to north Sudan.

The idea was to prevent the waters of the White Nile, after they left Uganda's Lake Victoria, from disappearing into the boggy marsh of the *sudd*. A contemporary pamphlet, printed to encourage foreign investors, explained that no less than half of the mighty river flowed uselessly into the *sudd*, about 530 billion cubic feet a year. If this water could be saved and channelled, so the argument went, it would go a long way towards overcoming the water shortages that plagued both Sudan and Egypt. Contracts were signed in 1974 with a French company, and the world's largest mechanical digger, called 'Bucketwheel', began work a few years later. Standing five storeys high, consuming 900 tons of fuel a day, this behemoth shifted over a million cubic feet of earth per day. The project would cost US$75 million.

Some Western environmentalists were alarmed, but most others were happy. Patrick Orr, an Englishman running his own public-relations business out of Nairobi, was hired by one of the few southerners in the new national government, Bona Malwal, the Minister of Culture and Information, to spread the good news about the new Sudan and all the investment that was coming in. Orr accompanied Numeiri on several visits to the south. On one particular visit to Juba in 1977 he was mobbed by adoring crowds alongside the president. Orr recalls that Numeiri 'used to take pride in his popularity in the south'.

This was also the era when the Arabs first envisaged Sudan, with its cheap labour, plentiful land and Nile waters, as the 'breadbasket' of the

Middle East. Money poured in from the Gulf to expand the irrigated agricultural schemes around Gezira.

DR TURABI AND THE RISE OF THE MUSLIM BROTHERHOOD

Despite Numeiri's apparent successes, however, all the while his political base was being eroded by the remorseless rise of the other self-consciously modernizing force in Sudanese politics, the Muslim Brotherhood. The Brotherhood developed in direct opposition to the secular communists, but also in flattering imitation of them.

The dominant figure in the Brotherhood was Dr Hassan al-Turabi, often regarded as one of the most renowned thinkers and activists in the whole of the Arab world since the Second World War. In this respect, he is usually compared to Sayyid Qutb, the Egyptian leader of the Muslim Brotherhood in the 1940s and 1950s. As one scholar has written: 'Rarely in the modern world can radical political philosophers such as Sayyid Qutb and Hassan Turabi have been so influential in shaping the thoughts and actions of generations of activists.'[2]

Like Sayyid Qutb, whose followers included Dr Ayman al-Zawahiri, the founder of al-Qaeda, Turabi grew up in a country under foreign colonial occupation. Like Qutb, Turabi's intellectual development was thus shaped by the imposition of British and Western values. Both, however, were also beneficiaries of that same Western rule. As precociously talented young men, obviously destined to be members of their respective countries' ruling classes, both were granted the privilege of being able to travel extensively in the West. Just as the course of another contemporary revolutionary's life, Che Guevara's, was to be changed by his own youthful travels in the Americas, so too were Qutb's and Turabi's – but in significantly different ways.

Take Qutb. Stern and ascetic, he travelled to the USA in 1948 on a generous Egyptian government scholarship. Like many of his class and generation he was steeped in Western literature and culture, particularly French and English. He had expected that the USA would help the

Arabs overcome the oppression of colonial rule by the old European powers and so, like every other Arab, was bitterly disappointed when the USA recognized the new state of Israel in 1948. He felt that the Arabs had exchanged one exercise in oppression for another, and his disenchantment with the USA and his deepening hatred of Western values only increased as he travelled across the continent to Greeley, Colorado, where he stayed for six months. I have never been to Greeley, but imagine it to be as inoffensive and unremarkable a place as most towns in Colorado. Qutb, on the other hand, was outraged, particularly by what he experienced as the aggressive, overt sexuality of the women. Famously, he wrote: 'A girl looks at you, appearing as if she were an enchanting nymph or an escaped mermaid, but as she approaches, you sense only the screaming instinct inside her, and you can smell her burning body, not the scent of perfume but flesh, only flesh. Tasty flesh, truly, but flesh nonetheless.'

He was equally scandalized by the relaxed, informal manners, the poor food and even bad haircuts. It was in the USA, he wrote, that he had found a 'primitiveness that reminds us of the ages of jungles and caves'. With his darker skin, Qutb also experienced some of the racism of US society. All in all, he returned to Egypt in 1950 convinced that modern Western values, such as tolerance, sexual equality and democracy, represented a direct threat to Islam. The rest of his life was dedicated, as Lawrence Wright, a historian of al-Qaeda, has written, to picking apart 'the entire political and philosophical structure of modernity and return[ing] Islam to its unpolluted origins'.

It is easy to see how this world view would lead ineluctably to the terrorism of al-Qaeda. It also put the Muslim Brotherhood of Egypt, which Qutb came to lead, at perpetual odds with the Egyptian state, led as it was by the secular-minded Nasser and his successor Anwar Sadat. The leaders of the Muslim Brotherhood were often arrested for opposing Egyptian governments, just as the Brotherhood used increasingly violent means to try to destabilize and overthrow those governments. In 1981 they assassinated President Sadat after he had signed the Camp David peace agreement with the Israelis three years earlier. Qutb himself was executed, albeit on the flimsiest of evidence, after being implicated in an earlier plot in 1966 to topple Nasser's government.

Turabi followed Qutb to the West. However, the lessons that he drew from his experiences, at least as he likes to tell it, were significantly different. Turabi was born in the eastern town of Kassala. His father was a *sharia* law judge, so Turabi grew up in a family where legal and constitutional debates about Islam were natural; these same debates would engage him for the rest of his life. Also, importantly, the Turabi family moved all over the country, living in Kordofan, Blue Nile state and elsewhere. Unlike most Sudanese, this wandering gave Turabi what he calls a 'pan-Sudanese' outlook. Certainly, what distinguished the later Islamist movement in Sudan would be a pan-Sudanese mission; Islam was promoted (bizarrely) as a creed to unite Africa's largest and most religiously diverse country.

As a privileged son of a judge, Turabi was sent to the 'Eton' of Sudan, Hantoub School in the town of Wad Madani, just south of Khartoum. Fond of replicating their own institutions in the most unlikely places, the British did just this for their public schools in Sudan: 'Harrow', in contrast to Eton, was at Wadi Saydna, just outside Omdurman. The headmasters and most of the staff were British. The indigenous elite of post-independence Sudan were groomed at these schools, just as Eton had traditionally provided the governing class of the British Empire – and of colonial Sudan too.

Ahmed Diraige was also a pupil at Hantoub and remembers the experience well. Turabi was three years above him, 'very intelligent, always at the top of his class'. Whereas 'we all played football, basketball and athletics . . . he [Turabi] did nothing of that'. Diraige, on the other hand, was captain of athletics for three years, and of the cadet force. Another 'hearty', to use the British parlance, was Jafar Numeiri, in the year above Turabi. Numeiri did athletics with Diraige.

Also in Numeiri's year was the future head of the Sudanese Communist Party, Muhammad Ibrahim Nugd; he played a vital role in helping his classmate seize power in 1969. Diraige remembers him as an 'intellectual' like Turabi, and already 'busy recruiting new students to Marxism'. A few years behind Numeiri was Osman Mudawi, one of the earliest adherents of the Muslim Brotherhood and a stalwart of the ruling National Congress Party in the 1990s and 2000s.

Turabi was thus at school with many of the key figures in Sudan's modern history. He also married the sister of Sadiq al-Mahdi; she was a student of Turabi's at the University of Khartoum. This closeness of north Sudan's politicians to each other sometimes surprises outsiders. Despite the venomous insults that they hurl at each other, they are often bound by ties of marriage, which are much more important in Sudanese culture than political differences. Thus Ali Osman Taha, a leading member of President Bashir's regime, married a cousin of Sadiq's; another Bashir insider, Ghazi Atabani, married a full sister of Mubarak al-Mahdi. A leading light of the DUP, Hassan Hilal, was the son of a woman from a leading Umma family. And so on. Indeed, northern Sudanese politics can sometimes seem like little more than a big family squabble as a small number of inter-married politicians incessantly cut deals with each other to share the spoils of power, rotating in and out of governments and coalitions with bewildering rapidity. This explains some of the ritual courtesies that Sudanese politicians extend to each other personally, even at the same time as they might be incarcerating or exiling one another.

On completing his university studies in Sudan in 1956, the year of the country's independence, Turabi went abroad to gain further degrees. He studied for a year at the Institute of Legal Studies in London, and then went to the Sorbonne in Paris to study for a doctorate in law. In 1960 he also obtained a scholarship, like Qutb, to travel around the USA, where he stayed with American families. In his own words, he 'saw everything', and returned to Sudan only in 1964.

In contrast to Qutb, Turabi was excited and stimulated, he told me, inspired even, by most of what he found in the West. Sure, when he first arrived in London he recalls that as a Muslim he was tempted by the novelties of women and drink. He saw other fellow Muslims capitulate, although he says that he 'resisted'. This sort of exposure to Western temptations was a familiar rite of passage for the wealthy students of the post-independent Middle East. Sudan's famous novelist, Tayeb Salih, wrote his best and most renowned novel about the encounter between young Islamic students and Europe – or as one character calls it in the book, 'the land of hanky-panky'. *Season of Migration to the North*, first published in 1966, is a bleak and mysterious novel; the Sudanese traveller to England seduces and possibly kills several women and is then imprisoned. He is lauded by his fellow Sudanese as being so clever because he got to England, but he is undone and overpowered by what he finds there.

However, as Turabi recalled for me, rather than seeing all Western customs and recreations 'as the devil', as 'traditional [Muslim] scholars did', he became more interested in trying to integrate the best features of Western modernity into a new, contemporary version of Islam. Rather than attempting to purify Islam of modern life, as Qutb would do, Turabi, in his own words, would try to 'integrate all life into religion'. This became, rhetorically at least, his life project. While never wavering in his conviction that Sudan should be an Islamic state, in his writings Turabi could appear remarkably democratic and progressive on how this might be achieved. In 1983, for instance, he wrote:

> Religion is based on sincere conviction and voluntary compliance . . . In circumstances where Islam is allowed free expression, social change takes place peacefully and gradually, and the Islamic movement develops programs of Islamization before it takes over the destiny of the state because Islamic thought – like all thought – only flourishes in a social environment of freedom and public consultation.[3]

This sort of thinking was extremely attractive to the first generation of ambitious, post-independence Sudanese, especially students. They flocked to Turabi when he returned from the West and became leader of the political wing of the Muslim Brotherhood in Sudan in 1964. One of these eager acolytes was al Tayib Zein al-Abdin, for much of his career a lecturer in political science at the University of Khartoum. Himself a graduate of London's School of Oriental and African Studies and the holder of a doctorate from the University of Cambridge, he estimates that '90 per cent of the leaders of the Muslim Brotherhood were educated in the West', mostly in Britain or the USA. From the very beginning the Islamist movement led by Turabi was principally an elite project, a product of the universities and the intelligentsia, and in particular the student body of the University of Khartoum, where Turabi became acting dean of the faculty of law in 1965. Could Sudan be modern, they asked, and at the same time true to its Islamic roots?

Sayid el-Khatib, now the director of Khartoum's Centre for Strategic Studies, the government's main think-tank, joined the Muslim Brotherhood at high school in 1969 and was one of many, he says, 'enamoured of Turabi's education in the Sorbonne and in Britain'. Turabi, for him, quickly became a 'mentor' at the university. Many of Turabi's other disciples from this time went on, like el-Khatib, to run the Sudanese government in the 1990s and 2000s. Several were to become familiar figures to Western governments in negotiations over Darfur and southern Sudan. Ali Osman Taha graduated from the University of Khartoum in 1970 and was later foreign minister; he was always the liberal face of President Bashir's government. Ghazi Atabani studied at the Khartoum medical school before going to the University of Surrey in England where he finished his training as a physician; he led the government's peace negotiations over southern Sudan in 2002–3. Mustafa Osman Ismael also trained in Britain, as a dentist, and became President Bashir's foreign minister. Both Sulaf al Din Salih Tahir, formerly head of the Humanitarian Affairs Commission, and Yassin al haj Abdin, another veteran Islamist, completed PhDs at Reading University in England – and so on.

El-Khatib attributes the Muslim Brotherhood's success in attracting so many high-calibre disciples directly to 'Turabi's leadership and organization'. The Brotherhood started recruiting in high schools and the universities and then spread outwards to create, eventually, 'the most successful Islamic movement in the Sunni world'. It also grew in strength independent of the original Muslim Brotherhood in Egypt, whose agents had done much to lay the roots of the Islamic movement in Sudan in the 1940s and 1950s. This would allow the National Islamic Front (NIF), the party of Turabi's political Islam, to burnish its Sudanese nationalist credentials, untainted by any connection with the former imperial oppressor Egypt.

Al Tayib al-Abdin, who also joined the Brotherhood in 1969, argues that it was also principally a reaction 'against the dominance of the communists'. As the two parties were both opposed to what they regarded as the sect-based politics of the Umma and the DUP, they had much in common – but were also in direct competition. The Muslim Brotherhood in the 1960s was much smaller than the Communist Party. But, rather than being overawed by the communists, Turabi set out to learn from them. Thus he carefully expropriated the tactics and organizational prowess of the communists to expand his own movement. Abdin argues that the Muslims therefore embarked on the 'politicization of everything'; they set up cells and 'cadres' in those sections of society that Islamists would not traditionally engage with, such as trade unions, women's groups, middle-class professional bodies and trade associations. The army was also targeted. In Marxist-Leninist parlance, the Muslim Brotherhood would become the 'vanguard' of consciousness-raising, at the apex – theoretically – of a much wider mass movement. So what began in the frothy, intellectual hothouse of the University of Khartoum spread, to a certain degree, outwards to become a grassroots political force. Indeed, it is no coincidence that the Islamic revolution of Sudan (or even that of Iran) reads much like the history of the Bolshevik revolution in Russia – the one was largely modelled on the other, complete with the Red Terror, show trials and secret police.

There was one other vital element to Turabi's success. He positioned the Muslim Brotherhood as a nationalist movement just as much as an Islamic one. So, in el-Khatib's words, Turabi 'tied national aspirations to Islamic aspirations'. This appealed enormously to those who had participated in the anti-colonial struggle and still resented the trappings of colonial rule in post-independence Sudan. The Sudanese Communist Party, on the other hand, could be portrayed as just another instrument of foreign control in the Cold War. To Abdin, the

Brotherhood's Islamic nationalism gave him and his generation a 'strong sense of dignity . . . to face the colonialists'. The Brotherhood was thus influenced by Western values and controlled by men who were at ease with those values. Yet it was also a movement in reaction against those values. This created a fundamental tension at the heart of the Islamist movement that is still to be adequately resolved.

Abdin, sitting in his bare office in the original buildings of what had been the British-built Gordon College, now the University of Khartoum (as it was renamed after independence), offered me his own early life story by way of explanation. He went to Britain as a young student in 1969 'thinking that Britain was the best country in the world'. Britain, as a leader of the anti-communist bloc in the Cold War, should, in his own mind, have been on the side of the Muslim Brotherhood against the Communist Party. But his experiences in the former colonial power left him disillusioned. He discovered that Britain was 'anti-Muslim, anti-Arab and anti-Africa'. It was the 1960s and Britain seemed to be on the side of the apartheid regimes in Africa (in South Africa and what was then white-run Southern Rhodesia).

He also found the British to be 'discriminating'. I pressed him on this – had he suffered any racist abuse personally, or been discriminated against in any way? All Abdin could tell me was that 'all white women refused to sit beside me in the bus . . . they would stand'. Wasn't this being just a bit oversensitive? He admitted that he had not suffered 'personally', nor had he been directly called any names or suffered any insults. But, he argued, 'The more educated you are, the more you feel the humiliation of the Western powers. Those who are educated are most sensitive to colonial slights.'

Thus the ideology of the Muslim Brotherhood was, broadly, the anti-colonialism of the educated classes. Yet Abdin argues that its positive values were just as important. He told me that he himself had always been a democrat and had believed passionately in the rest of Turabi's modernizing programme. Abdin admired the way that Turabi actually implemented his ideas too, against often hostile opposition. He claims that Turabi cleverly altered the rules of election to the council of the Muslim Brotherhood, for instance, to get women onto the council as well as representatives of the students and trade unions. Turabi's brand of Islam offered a compelling, modern alternative for those who could not support what they regarded as the fossilized feudalism of the other Islamic parties in Sudan.

THE RISE OF ISLAM AND THE FALL OF NUMEIRI

The rising strength of political Islam in Sudan was first demonstrated in 1976, when all the Islamist parties, the Brotherhood as well as the sect-based parties, backed by Libya and the Soviet Union, combined forces to try to topple Numeiri in a coup. For the Ansars, this was an attempt to exact revenge for the massacre on Aba Island in 1970. For the young acolytes of the Muslim Brotherhood like Sayid el-Khatib, appalled by the secular socialism of Numeiri's first phase in power, it was an opportunity to reorientate the course of Sudanese politics along more Islamist lines. Khatib and many others were sent to Libyan military training camps in the Sahara desert to train for the coup. He remembers it as a time when Colonel Ghadaffi was 'funding every liberation movement on the continent . . . and was flirting with Arab unity'. A united Sudanese Islamic front, of the Umma party, the DUP and the Muslim Brotherhood, suited the Libyan dictator's interests at this time; he dreamt of carving off Darfur and incorporating it into a Libyan Arab Sudanic empire. The Soviets wanted their own revenge for Numeiri's decapitation of the communists in 1971.

In the event, the coup failed, but it was a near-run thing. Numeiri and his supporters were besieged in Khartoum for three days before the plotters were pushed back. The event had a lasting, even traumatic, effect on the president. The near success of the coup revealed his weakness in the face of this new alliance of Islamist parties. So Numeiri was forced to change tack. Rather than ruling as a secularist satrap of Egyptian socialism, in 1977 he decided to invite the Islamist parties into a government of 'National Reconciliation'. Thus Turabi and his brother-in-law Sadiq al-Mahdi (albeit temporarily) both joined the government. Turabi became attorney-general in 1979, from which position he could begin to formulate his plans for introducing *sharia* law; later he became presidential adviser on international affairs between 1983 and 1985. It was a decisive moment in Sudanese history. Numeiri had ditched his leftist allies and turned to the Islamic parties for support instead. The whisky-drinking, cigar-smoking president now became correspondingly more pious himself. Some said that he saw divine inspiration in having survived the two coup attempts of 1971 and 1976.

As a result, the nature of his regime became increasingly contradictory. At home Numeiri was moving in a nationalist and Islamic direction, while for foreign consumption Numeiri tried to keep up, and even deepen, his key alliance with the USA. Sudan received hundreds of millions of dollars worth of US aid in the later 1970s and early 1980s. Sudan also bought weapons from the USA, and US troops were allowed to carry out joint manoeuvres with the Sudanese army on Sudanese soil.

What probably endeared Numeiri most to the USA, however, was his sustained support for the evacuation of the Falasha Jews out of Ethiopia in the early 1980s. Faced by increasing discrimination at the hands of Mengistu's Derg regime, the Falasha Jews began to escape over the north-western border of Ethiopia into eastern Sudan from where, with the government's full co-operation, they were taken by US transporters to Israel. The operation culminated in a celebrated last airlift with a CIA C-130 airplane in 1984. The USA attached great importance to the operation; Vice-President George Bush was intimately involved. Numeiri's help earned the Sudanese president and his government a special place in the affections of President Ronald Reagan. Several Sudanese ministers were invited to meet Reagan, including, probably, Attorney-General Turabi, the future mentor of Osama bin Laden.

But however helpful he was to Israel and the USA, Numeiri's 'Western phase' did him little good at home. Indeed, his enthusiasm for Ronald Reagan was a positive liability. The US embassy in Khartoum, the biggest in Africa by this time, reported back to Washington on the widespread criticism that Numeiri received from ordinary Sudanese for lending such public help to the 'Zionists' and their Christian ally. Gayle Smith, a US journalist, lived in Khartoum during the 1980s and watched from close up the slow-motion crash that became the end of Numeiri's regime. It was an experience that informed her thinking later in the 1990s when she served on Bill Clinton's National Security Council (NSC) as a Sudan expert. Looking back in 2008, she recalled that although the Sudanese enjoyed some aspects of their president's Western tilt, such as jeans and Coca-Cola, she was also very aware of a backlash against 'consumerism' and the accompanying Westernization. What Gayle called Numeiri's 'suck-up' to the USA was, she observed: 'humiliating for a generation of young men . . . and Numeiri had once been a proud socialist. So there was a real desire to reassert their identity through Islam.' The main beneficiaries of this feeling were those who combined their Islamism with Sudanese nationalism, such as Turabi. → bin Laden

Indeed, it was an attempt by a desperate president to appease this rising tide of Islamist discontent, especially after the success of the Islamist revolution in Iran in 1979, that accounted for the last, most controversial, phase of his rule. Numeiri himself became more devout. He swapped his trademark safari suits for Arab clothes and in 1980 he published a book advocating a more Islamic lifestyle for his ministers and countrymen. He had seen the fate of his brother-in-arms Anwar Sadat, the president of Egypt, who had been killed by the Muslim Brothers in 1981 for making peace with Israel. He did not want to go the same way.

Numeiri's embrace of political Islam culminated, fatally, in the dramatic and unexpected introduction of *sharia* law throughout the country, north and south, in the 'September Laws' of 1983. They were drawn up hastily and badly, and were damned as such even by those who had been slowly working to introduce *sharia* themselves, such as Turabi. It may have been bad law, but politically it sent out a clear message about the new direction of the country.

Just as importantly, Numeiri also abrogated crucial clauses in the Addis Ababa peace agreement with the south, suspending its semi-autonomous status. The Christian south, to no one's surprise, unable to tolerate the imposition of a Muslim legal system and the suspension of its putative autonomy, went back to war with the north almost instantaneously. To this day, southerners are at a loss to explain why their former hero turned so vehemently against them. A common phrase that I still hear in the south is that Numeiri was 'bewitched' by the Islamists. For other southerners, these developments proved that Numeiri had never been sincere about his vision of a new Sudan.[4]

The president merely became increasingly autocratic and unpredictable as his troubles closed in on him. In the name of *sharia* law he introduced the whole panoply of courts of 'decisive justice' presided over by the Muslim Brotherhood, together with the *hudud* punishments. Public amputations and executions started; those who were unable to get to them in person could watch them on television. Turabi fainted while watching his first amputation, but defended the punishments all the same to Judith Miller. Despite plenty of evidence to the contrary, he reassured Miller that the Sudanese would not be shocked by these events. 'In Zaire and elsewhere in Africa,' he said coolly, 'thieves are often crucified or beaten to death. So Africans are used to amputations and flogging.' Numeiri subjected all banks in Sudan to Islamic law; profits, known as *morabaha*, were still allowed, but not interest.

Numeiri also marked his embrace of political Islam by presiding over a more farcical event, a mass throwing of alcohol into the Nile. Hundreds watched in varying degrees of cynical stupefaction as Numeiri himself, standing on the bank of the Nile in front of the presidential palace, smashed bottles of beer and whisky on the embankment wall before hurling them into the river. He was followed by hundreds of his delirious supporters. The joke on the day afterwards was that nothing had changed except that the fishermen had caught a lot of drunken fish. Since everyone knew that Numeiri and his circle were heavy drinkers, few took these gestures very seriously.

Turabi might not have had a hand in the actual drafting of the September Laws, but he almost certainly played a role in the final, barbarous act of Numeiri's Islamist phase. Right at the end, Numeiri turned on the Islamists. He had courted their support, but they were also his most savage critics. And the most articulate of them was Mahmoud Mohammed Taha, leader of a small but influential Sufi-inspired sect called the Republican Brothers. Taha, an ideological critic of political Islam and the approach of the Muslim Brotherhood, had warned against the dangers of Islamic fundamentalism, especially after the Iranian revolution of 1979 seemed, for the first time, to ignite such passions in Sudan. Taha specifically opposed the introduction of *sharia* law. Not only, he argued, would *sharia* set back the advance of women in Islam, one of his great causes, but it would also reignite the war with the south. He was proved right on both counts. Nonetheless, in December 1984 he was arrested, together with four other Brothers, for sedition. An appeal court added the far more damaging charge of apostasy (*ridda*) and he was sentenced to death.

The accusation of apostasy came from a collapsing regime desperate to strike back against its critics, and to prove that it was serious about *sharia*. More to the point, the execution was probably also partly the work of Turabi, exploiting his position in the government to take the opportunity to remove his most important rival as a source of Islamic guidance. Taha's was the first show trial of the Soviet-style era of Islamic government.

On 15 January 1985, Taha was hanged in public in the courtyard of Kobar prison in Khartoum North. Judith Miller, wrapped in a white cloak and head scarf, hoping that no one would notice her, went along and has left this account of what she witnessed:

> The scaffolding was at the far end of the courtyard, elevated but still lower than the prison's sandstone walls. The scene at Kobar was gay, nothing like the grim photographs I had seen of prisons where Americans are executed, with friends and relatives of the condemned huddling outside the walls amid protestors holding candles in the [early morning dark].
>
> I seemed to be the only woman in the yard. Many of the several hundred men appeared to know one another. They greeted each other in the traditional Islamic welcome: '*Assalam Aleykum*', peace

be with you. '*Aleykum Salam*,' and unto you, came the reply again and again. The tall dark-skinned men in their foot-high turbans and flowing white robes laughed and chatted about the weather, prospects for this year's crops, and the unending civil war in southern Sudan. Gradually, everyone sat down in the sand to wait under the sun that seemed to grow harsher by the minute. The execution was scheduled for ten o'clock.

Shortly before the appointed time, Mahmoud Mohammed Taha was led into the courtyard. The condemned man, his hands tied behind him, was smaller than I had expected him to be, and from where I sat, as his guards hustled him along, he looked younger than his seventy-six years. When they first saw him, many in the crowd leaped to their feet, jeering and shaking their fists at him. A few waved their Korans in the air.

I managed to catch only a glimpse of Taha's face before the executioner placed an oatmeal-coloured sack over his head and body, but I shall never forget his expression. His eyes were defiant; his mouth firm. He showed no hint of fear.

The crowd began cheering as two Sudanese guards in sand-coloured uniforms tightened a noose around the sack where Mahmoud Taha's neck must have been. Though the bubble of the crowd drowned out their words, they seemed to be screaming at him. Suddenly, the guards stood back, the platform snapped open, the rope became taut, and the sack that covered Taha wriggled in the air. A few seconds later, the sack merely swayed a bit at the end of the rope. Idiotically, I thought of potatoes.

A roar erupted in the courtyard: '*Allahu Akbar!*' the crowd screamed – God is great! The din intensified as the men began chanting in unison: '*Allahu Akbar! Allahu Akbar! Islam huwa al-hall!*' (Islam is the solution).

The exuberant men hugged and kissed one another. Justice has been done, a man next to me shrieked, falling to his knees, touching his forehead to the sand, uttering a Muslim prayer. Stunned and sickened by the jubilation around me ... [we began to leave].

When we reached the exit I craned my neck to catch one last look
at the scaffolding. The sack, Taha's body, was still dangling from the
rope. I wondered whether they would cut it down.

A small number of Islamists might have been satisfied, but most
Sudanese, including many in the Muslim Brotherhood, were appalled,
as were Numeiri's increasingly bewildered allies in the West and in the
Arab world.

As we have seen, the declaration of *sharia* law reignited war with the
south. The newly formed Sudan People's Liberation Army (SPLA),
the successor to Anya-Nya, started fighting against the north again in
the summer of 1983, initially with about 2,500 guerrillas. Finding the
money to fight the renewed civil war with the south compounded
the woes of a Sudanese economy that was dipping into a steep decline.
The national debt ballooned to over $7 billion in 1983, and the country
regularly defaulted on its repayments. A decline in the prices of wheat
and cotton meant that there was less money coming in from these
export staples. The value of the currency plummeted, leading to inflation and steep rises in bread and gas prices. This hit the middle classes
particularly hard as judges, doctors, engineers and teachers witnessed
the erosion of their pay differentials. It was therefore the professionals'
associations and unions that came to organize most of the opposition to
Numeiri's decaying regime.

Then in 1983–5 came the final blow to Numeiri's hold on power, the
first of the great droughts, leading to famine in Darfur. By now living
in a tightly sealed fantasy world, the president refused to heed any of
the warnings about the looming crisis. Ahmed Diraige, the respected
governor of Darfur, appointed by Numeiri himself, tried to warn the
president of what was happening. At the end of 1983, he recalls, he
begged Numeiri 'to declare an emergency, to declare there was a
famine', but he refused to listen. In the end, desperate, Diraige travelled to Khartoum to see the president in person, but was refused an
interview for a full month. Eventually, Numeiri had to see him. In
front of the council of ministers, the governor said his piece, but

Numeiri just exploded and shouted back: 'This is my revolution. You don't tell me what to do. Go and do your job!' He then stalked out of the chamber.

Diraige left the country in despair soon afterwards. By 1985, probably 95,000 Darfuris had died of starvation. Hundreds of thousands of desperately hungry people descended on Khartoum, bringing the reality of starvation onto the streets of the capital. It was a grim time. By 1985 there were more and more strikes and protests on the streets of Khartoum and Numeiri's only response was to deploy the police and security forces in an attempt to intimidate the growing numbers of demonstrators.

Appropriately, the end came as Numeiri flew off to attend a meeting in Washington DC with Ronald Reagan in the first week of April 1985. By then the economic situation had deteriorated further as the subsidies on sugar, bread and oil had been lifted to try to cut government spending. Prices had soared and for days crowds of people protested on the streets of the capital, led by the Bar Association, the Sudanese Medical Association, the Banking Officials' Trade Union, the Sudanese Engineers' Association and the University of Khartoum Lecturers' Union. A lawyer called Omer Abdel Ati unexpectedly found himself cast in the role of de facto leader of the revolt by virtue of the fact that he just happened to be president of the Bar Association at the time. The lawyers had become particularly hostile to Numeiri on account of the government's extrajudicial murder of Taha.

One organizer on the streets was Hafiz Mohamed, now an activist for Justice Africa, an NGO in London. He remembers it all vividly. He worked in a bank, and was a union leader as well. He and his union convenors 'managed to close all the banks, and they all demonstrated against Numeiri'. On 2 April the first great demonstration started in the centre of Khartoum in front of the faculty of medicine of the university. The whole city seemed to be on strike. There were more demonstrations on the following days.

Despite the crisis, Numeiri still insisted on seeing Reagan. The deputy US ambassador, David Shinn, accompanied the USA's loyal ally to the airport to see him off. Shinn still retains a clear image of plumes of black smoke rising from the streets of the capital behind the plane on the runway, as vehicles and buildings burned. 'What was he thinking? Why did he leave?' Shinn recalls asking himself as Numeiri's plane took off. Presumably, Numeiri believed that his security forces could contain the situation. In fact, as Omer Ati observed, by that stage the riot police were less aggressive than usual, 'almost as if they were sympathetic to the demonstrators'.

By 6 April it was all over. With Numeiri out of the country, a group of generals who had kept in touch with the demonstrators announced the formation of a new interim government. The news came just as Numeiri's private jet landed at Cairo on the way back from his meeting with Reagan. As it turned out, the deposed Sudanese president had to wait almost another fifteen years before being allowed to complete the return leg to his homeland. He died, largely forgotten, in Khartoum in 2009.

As for the Jonglei canal, the great symbol of hope for Numeiri's vision of a new, united Sudan, the giant 'Bucketwheel' got about three-quarters of the way from Malakal to Bor before the war restarted and workers on the project had to be evacuated. The giant machine was bombed by the SPLA on the resumption of hostilities; some militants argued that all along the whole project had been nothing more than a clever northern ruse to steal the south's water for the benefit of Egypt and the riverain elite.

The marsh and jungle of the *sudd* has reclaimed much of the canal now. But the great wheel is still visible, I am told, stuck in the mud where it was sabotaged. An American friend, a wildlife conservationist, has to criss-cross the territory regularly to track animal movements and has inspected the 'Bucketwheel' close-up. He tells me that it is now home to, among many other flora and fauna, a giant colony of African killer bees.

THE DESCENT INTO ETHNIC CONFLICT – THE FAILURE OF SADIQ AL-MAHDI

So ended Sudan's last prospects for country-wide peace. At the final count, Numeiri's regime ended in profound disappointment. But his rule showed that a multi-racial, multi-ethnic country tolerating religious differences was possible – if only for a while, and at a price.

Political scientist al Tayib Zein al-Abdin, looking back with me on these events from his office in the University of Khartoum in 2008, argued that the main beneficiary of Numeiri's rule turned out to be Hassan al-Turabi. He benefited the most from the complicated tangle of alliances that Numeiri constructed and then destroyed in order to keep himself in power. Turabi's political rivals were fatally damaged, or even eliminated, as was Taha. Moreover, with Turabi in office, the Muslim Brotherhood was able to 'organize within the government', infiltrating the army and the civil service, and setting up the secret cells that would be activated in the coup of 1989. In Marxist–Leninist terms, it was classic 'entryism'; working from within a system in order to destroy it.

A privatization programme, forced on a bankrupt Sudan by the IMF and West, also allowed the Muslim brothers to prosper financially. They bought up a lot of the privatized assets with the proceeds from their own Islamic businesses and the new 'Islamic banks' floated on a sea of money from supporters in Saudi Arabia and elsewhere. All the time, the aim was to build clear Islamic alternatives to Western-dominated institutions and initiatives. Thus, for example, a movement was set up called Dawa, to promote the cause of Islam in Africa; an offshoot of this was the Islamic African Relief Agency, which was supposed to rival Western humanitarian NGOs. A missionary arm was also set up, the Association of Muslims in Southern Sudan.

However, even after the fall of Numeiri Sudan still had a chance to save itself before being pitched into Turabi's Islamic revolution. The military regime that replaced Numeiri relinquished power quickly and restored democracy. In the general election of 1986, the Umma party won the most seats in the parliament (ninety-nine) and so Sadiq al-Mahdi became the prime minister, ruling in coalition with the DUP and an assortment of other smaller parties.

Yet, as it turned out, his government was the most disappointing of all Sudan's post-war administrations. A decent and charming man, Sadiq had a broad idea of what was needed to reverse the excesses of

Numeiri's rule, but failed dismally to do anything about it. Crucially, Sadiq failed to overturn Numeiri's most controversial legacy, the September Laws. Sadiq had made their repeal a major plank of his election platform as it was obvious that the civil war would only be stopped if *sharia* law was abandoned, at least in the south. But Sadiq never managed to carry out his promise. Robert Collins writes that Sadiq's 'vacillation and indecision over the September Laws exasperated the Islamic fundamentalists, alienated the secular Sudanese, and convinced the southerners he was not to be trusted'. In the end, for Collins, Sadiq 'ironically resembled Numeiri in his obsession to remain in power at any price, which led to deals with the DUP, the NIF and the army; but he lacked the skills of the "master manipulator" '.

I met up with Sadiq on the fringes of a conference in England in 2008; still courteous and youthful-looking, a striking figure in his white *jellabiya*, he was anxious to defend himself against his critics. He argued that, in fact, his hands were tied on repealing *sharia* because the DUP, his coalition partner, wanted to keep it. And without the DUP, his government would have collapsed – so the repeal of the September Laws was another casualty of Sudan's coalition politics. The Umma position was that the September Laws were 'a mutilation' of Islam, not a fulfilment of it; but without an outright majority in parliament, there was little they could do about it. Instead, Sadiq's government did the next best thing. It 'suspended' the September Laws while ministers embarked on an ultimately fruitless search for legislative alternatives. During his government, Sadiq claimed to me that, 'no hands were chopped, [there was] no flogging'.

Be that as it may, the September Laws remained in place, making any lasting peace with the south impossible. But there was worse. It was at this point, fatally for the later history of Sudan, that the northern governments began to arm and organize the first Arab militias. In this, as in much else, Sadiq's government proved to be a precursor of the violence to come. Arming the Baqqara (and their sub-tribes the Misseriyya and Rizeigat) to fight alongside the regular Sudanese army against the so-called 'African' rebels in the south was not only a dreadful escalation of the civil war, it also foreshadowed the tactics that were to be employed in Darfur after 2003.

The strategy of arming the Arab nomads and pastoralists originated principally as a counter-insurgency tactic, against what was said to be the penetration of the SPLA into the Nuba Mountains. The move began with the transitional government of Major-General Siwar al-Dhabab which took over after the fall of Numeiri. A sympathizer of the Muslim Brotherood, Dhabab ruled from 1985 to 1986 while the elections of May 1986 were organized.

Adam Madibu, another of Sadiq's relations and a minister in his government, blames the arming of the Baqqara and Misseriyya Arab tribes in the Kordofan region specifically on Major-General Burma Fadlallah Nasir, who, as minister of defence, was in charge of security in the transitional government. Like other northern Muslim politicians, Madibu, when I discussed this with him in 2008, explained it to me as an act of self-defence: 'What he [Burma] did was to give the Arab tribes arms to protect themselves from the SPLA. It happened, and the Arabs thought that they were protecting their land.'

The academic who has studied this most closely, Jago Salmon, argues that Burma Fadlallah's involvement began when one specific Misseriyya village, al-Garud, in Kordofan, was attacked in July 1985, and sixty people were killed. The attackers were armed Dinka, and the Baqqara immediately retaliated. The government in Khartoum sent a delegation down to the village to arrange for security, headed by Burma. Confronted by angry villagers, and unable to redeploy the overstretched and feeble Sudanese army from its other duties fighting the civil war in the south, the delegation unilaterally took the decision to arm the Misseriyya and Rizeigat. In the words of Salmon: 'Truckloads of ammunitions and light weapons, mostly AK-47s and G3 rifles, were distributed directly to members of allied tribes, specifically the Rizeigat and the Misseriyya Humr, through native administrative structures and leaders.'[5]

The victims of these paramilitaries would call them *murahileen*, named after the traditional Misseriyya migratory routes, the *murhals*. They were the forerunners of Darfur's *janjaweed*. By 1986, Salmon writes, 'Well-armed raiding parties of 500–1,000 men had begun systematically to strip the assets of the Ngok, Abiem, Malual and Tuic Dinka populations . . . and forced their displacement into pro-government territories.'

Even if it was the transitional government of 1985–6 that was responsible for arming the nomadic tribes first, Sadiq al-Mahdi's government of 1986–9 was certainly implicated in the decision as well. Furthermore, Sadiq's government inherited the strategy and intensified it. The Misseriyya, in particular, were closely connected to the Umma party; western Sudan was, after all, the Umma's heartland. One of the paramount chiefs of the Misseriyya, Babo Nimir, married into the Mahdi family. Sadiq's government would have been in close contact with the Misseriyya tribal leaders, and Burna Fadlallah was a leading Ansar himself.

According to Madibu, attempting to play down their role in the formation of the militias, he and Sadiq, the prime minister, 'thought that it was nothing unusual, just part of the campaign against the SPLA'. Sometimes the Arab tribes went 'too far', he told me, but if there were 'certain atrocities, they were not planned'. Eventually, Madibu told me, when the scale of those atrocities became obvious, Sadiq's government did order an internal enquiry into what had taken place.

However, from the point of the view of the African southerners such as the Dinka, who bore the brunt of these new militia attacks, this latest phase of conflict seemed to be anything but usual. The new strategy marked not just a turning point in the war with the south, but in the whole way that the Arab tribes did business with their African brethren. The traditional architecture of inter-ethnic and inter-tribal dialogue was now purposefully shattered to turn the young Arab nomads into armed militias, supposedly to support the military's counter-insurgency war.

The young men from the Baqqara, made up of the Rizeigat, Misseriyya and Humr (a sub-section of the Misseriyya) tribes, made willing recruits. After all, many of them had lost much, including their cattle – their birthright and most precious asset – in the drought and famine of 1983–5. This was the important context of the time.

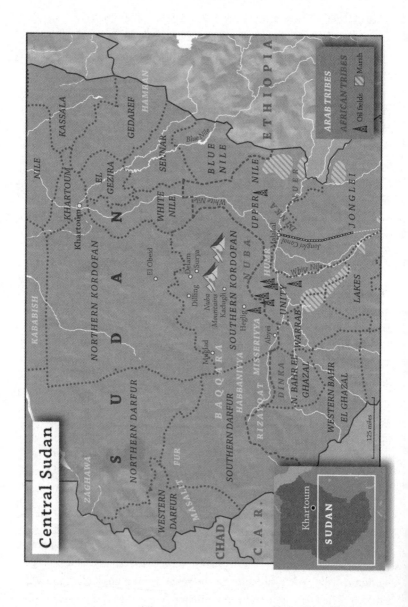

Central Sudan

125 miles

ARAB TRIBES
AFRICAN TRIBES
Oil fields
Marsh

ETHIOPIA

C.A.R.

CHAD

ZAGHAWA

WESTERN DARFUR

MASALIT

NORTHERN DARFUR

SOUTHERN DARFUR

FUR

S U D A N

KABABISH

NORTHERN KORDOFAN

Khartoum

KHARTOUM

NILE

EL GEZIRA

KASSALA

GEDAREF

HAMRAN

SENNAR

Blue Nile

BLUE NILE

WHITE NILE

White Nile

El Obed

Delam
Surya

Dilling

Nuba Mountains

Kadugli

SOUTHERN KORDOFAN

NUBA

UPPER NILE

JONGLEI

Jonglei Canal

Malakal

White Nile

HUMR

Heglig

Abyei

UNITY

WARRAB

LAKES

Muglad

BAQQARA

HABBANIYA

RIZAYGAT

MISSERIYA

DINKA

N. BAHR EL GHAZAL

WESTERN BAHR EL GHAZAL

SUDAN

Khartoum

88

Throughout Sudan, the nomadic tribes were devastated by the environmental cataclysm of the mid-1980s; it was a phenomenon that changed forever the old ways of life throughout much of the country. We have already noted the impact of the droughts in Darfur. Take another region, such as the east. Here, the Beja pastoralists are estimated to have lost 80 per cent of their animals in the mid-1980s. As a consequence, one sub-group, the Amar'ar, shifted completely from camel rearing to breeding smaller animals. Others abandoned the nomadic life completely to look for jobs in Port Sudan.

Impoverished and desperate, the Baqqara of Kordofan regarded themselves as victims just as much as anybody else. They were thus easily persuaded that they could revive their fortunes by attacking the Dinka. They had always coveted the more fertile, wet lands of the south where the Nuba and Dinka lived. Relations between the Misseriyya and the Ngok Dinka in the Abyei region in particular had anyway been deteriorating over the issue of grazing rights since the 1960s. Now the young Misseriyya men were told that they could loot and take whatever they wanted; their village leaders and elders no longer had the authority to restrain them. For these Misseriyya, the idea that they were part of a 'coordinated counter-insurgency' strategy with the army mattered rather less than the prospect of seizing their rivals' land and cattle.[6]

The onslaught was particularly harsh in the Nuba Mountains. This was a very mixed area of Arab tribes and African Nuba; it was, and remains, Sudan's fault line, running between the two worlds and cultures. Ali Abdulrahman of the Nuba Relief, Rehabilitation and Development Organisation, an NGO based in Nairobi, gave me a graphic account of what happened on the ground. His story is fairly representative of several others that I was told.

Born in the Nuba Mountains in 1973, Ali was raised in a culture where the central dynamic was what he called 'the old conflict between the Nuba farmers and the Baqqara cattle-farmers'. But these conflicts were usually sorted out in customary ways, which Ali described to me:

When the dry season came, traditionally the Baqqara elders would send a team [south] to the Nuba Mountains from El Obeid to different parts of the Nuba to find out whether the Nuba had harvested, and whether it was free for them to move in. They would chat with the Nuba elders and negotiate the passage into the Nuba . . . If the fields were not cleared, maybe they would be given a dateline for them to come.

This all changed, however, after 1985. All along, Ali was aware that although the differences between the Nuba and the Baqqara had always been negotiated, fundamentally 'The Baqqara never believed that the Nuba had equal rights with them.' So in 1985: 'When the northern government asked [the Baqqara], they did not need much encouragement [to raze the Nuba villages]. They did not regard it as a crime. After they were armed, they no longer negotiated, they just came.'

As a schoolboy, Ali witnessed the increasingly tense relations between the Nuba and Baqqara break down altogether after 1985. His twelve- or thirteen-year-old Baqqara classmates suddenly began to tell Ali: 'We will kill you, we will kill you. You will only be drinking the milk of your pigs, you will not have cows.' Baqqara children brought empty cartridges to school to taunt Ali: 'If you argue with us, next time it will be a live cartridge.'

In 1986, Ali remembers that he got into a fight with one of the Baqqara who was insulting him, but the headmaster blamed Ali for the fight and punished him instead. Later, the headmaster, a Nuban, invited Ali to his house and told him: 'I blame you not because you are on the wrong side. But the Baqqara have been armed to fight against our Nuba people. If I don't blame you, the case may become major. You are not wrong; they are not supposed to bring cartridges to school. But for your own safety, I blamed you. Matters are not in our own hands anymore.' To Ali, his Baqqara classmates 'regarded themselves as Arabs and first-class citizens. And they didn't think the Nuba had the right to be in the same classroom as the Baqqara.'

Ali stayed on at the school in this extremely intimidating atmosphere simply because there was nowhere else where he could finish his studies. He left eventually in 1988. Clearly, some of the teachers, many of them Arab, must have been implicated in the organized violence and aggression against the Dinka or Nuba children; a few probably would have been members of the Muslim Brotherhood. Teachers were among their favourite recruits. One Dinka I met, now a vet in Abyei, came across one of his Misseriyya classroom tormentors years later and asked him why he had attacked him twenty years before: 'We were pushed by Arab teachers,' he replied.

As soon as Ali had finished his studies, because of the violence sweeping through the region he decided to get out of the Nuba Mountains completely and escape abroad. After a two-month trek across south Sudan he reached Ethiopia and safety. By that time Ali had little option but to leave. The Baqqara, including some of Ali's classmates, were well into their campaign of burning many of the Nuba villages to the ground. In fact, Ali's own village, Surya, just south of Delami, barely escaped the same fate.

One evening, Ali's uncle, the chief of the village, received a letter; being illiterate, he took it to Ali to read. The letter gave warning of an impending Baqqara attack at five the next morning. Ali was sent round the village to wake everyone up to decide what to do, whether to fight or flee. After a brief discussion, it was decided to evacuate the village that night with all the livestock and gather behind a nearby hill. When the attackers arrived, disappointed at finding nothing in the village, they turned instead on another village, burning it to the ground and killing many people. The Baqqara attacks on the Nuban villages followed the same pattern. Young men, if not killed, would be press-ganged into the army; all the precious cattle and other livestock would be stolen; young children would be taken off to Islamic schools for Arabization and young women would often be taken as slaves. The remainder would be put in camps, concentration camps effectively, to restrict their freedom of movement.

Thus the Nuba people would be ethnically cleansed from their own land. Ali says, 'It was genocide in Nuba, exactly what happens in today's Darfur.' In 1980 there were about 2.5 million Nuba; between 1984 and 2005 Ali claims that about 200,000 to 250,000 were killed and about 1.2 million or so displaced. 'The attacks did destroy the Nuba way of life', says Ali, 'and today, most people do not want to go back still because of the insecurity.'

The ferocity and intensity of the militia attacks were undoubtedly fuelled by the racist attitudes of the Baqqara towards the Nuba and Dinka. In inciting the Baqqara to attack the African tribes, the Khartoum governments must have known that they were playing with fire; 'atrocities', at least, should have been expected. It was not only the Dinka and Nuba who could testify to the racism that turned a counter-insurgency exercise into widespread massacres. Foreign observers who spend any time with the Misseriyya experience it too, to this day.

Probably no outsider has spent more time recently with the Misseriyya than Sarah Pantuliano, an Italian-born academic based at the Overseas Development Institute in London who spent months with the nomads in the late 2000s. She told me that the Misseriyya, particularly the older ones, still referred to the Dinka mainly as *genghei*, which translates as 'slave'. This attitude seemed to absolve them of any moral responsibility for what the *murahaleen* did in the 1980s and 1990s. 'The Misseriyya are in denial about this,' Sarah told me. 'They don't feel that they did anything wrong. They say that they did it as the Dinka were a threat. The emphasis is always on "service" for the government against the SPLA.' The word slave in this context was not used merely as a figure of speech. During the 1990s slaving itself became part of the *murahaleen*'s mix of assault tactics on the Dinka. As we shall see, it was the issue of slaving that alerted the outside world to what was really going on in Sudan's north–south civil war.[7]

It was thus a combustible mix of victimhood, poverty and racism that drove the militias to be so murderous and destructive. Looking back on the 1980s now, Ali Abdulrahman concedes the Baqqara their sense of victimhood, the feeling that they had lost nearly everything in the droughts of 1983–5. But he argues, rightly, that this was no excuse for unleashing such extreme violence on the Nuba people. After all, he says, they had had problems like this before, yet 'the Baqqara had never been denied access to the fields and water' to the south.

Rather than the northern politicians taking on the difficult task of addressing the losses and impoverishment of the Baqqara after the droughts, they took the easier course of exploiting and sharpening those grievances for their own ends. Rather than working out a long-term solution to common problems, the message from Khartoum's politicians to the Arab tribes was that they had impunity to pillage and loot their neighbours to compensate themselves for what they had lost in the droughts. The result was carnage.

Islam, too, was part of the mix. Like the issue of race, it was exploited to the same end. The Nuba people are diverse in terms of religion; before the 1980s it had never been a determining factor of anything very much in the region. Take Ali's family for example. His grandmother was a Protestant, his uncle a Catholic, his father and mother were Muslims. Ali himself was brought up as a Muslim, but, influenced by his granny, he went to church, and eventually ended up as a Catholic. This diversity and religious tolerance was natural in the Nuba Mountains. 'All houses in Nuba had this type of mix,' Ali told me, 'and all lived peacefully. Never had a problem. You couldn't tell who was who when Christmas came, or Eid.' But, again, this balance was purposefully upset for political ends. Ali, who later spoke to several Baqqara about this, says that they were told that the Islam of the Nuba was 'not a real Islam, not an authentic Islam'. From this came the impetus for a *jihad* not only against non-Muslims, but against 'fake Muslims' as well.

Thus the northern governments, particularly after Turabi's Islamic revolution of 1989, 'politicized the situation and split up Muslims vs Christians'. It was easy, eventually, to transform the *murahileen* of the mid-1980s into the Popular Defence Forces (PDF) of the 1990s. This was the explicitly Islamist militia of Turabi's rule, modelled on Iran's Revolutionary Guards. In fact, it was Sadiq al-Mahdi's government, in the spring of 1989, just before it was overthrown, that first suggested the formation of a national paramilitary force, the forerunner of the dreaded PDF. All along the north–south fault line the same thing was happening from the mid-1980s onwards; the old ways of reconciling race and religion were breaking down. A Dinka, Monyluak Kol, told me about what was happening in the Abyei region, right in the centre of the country. An accountant by training, Kol was, at the time of our meeting in 2008, the acting administrator of the Abyei region.

Kol explained the local history to me. Here too, in Abyei, the Misseriyya and Dinka Ngok, the local Dinka sub-tribe, had once contentedly negotiated the nomadic migrations of the Misseriyya and their cattle south into the wetlands of the Dinka territory during the dry seasons. The negotiations would take place under a tree, or in Abyei, between the elders. Consequently, the Misseriyya 'were always given permission' to go south, even if they were often confined to certain areas. But once the Misseriyya began to get arms from Khartoum, 'Those negotiations broke down because the Misseriyya thought that they would always be supported by the government, so there was no need to honour any agreement or negotiate properly.'

Kol could date the first time this happened very precisely, to the end of February 1965. In the migration of that year, he told me, the Misseriyya 'looted cattle, and cut the right arm off a Dinka man. There was fighting, and the government intervened to help the Misseriyya.' Could he be sure it was the end of February 1965? I asked (Kol himself could scarcely have been born then). Yes, it was definitely so, chorused the fifteen or so Dinka seated around the table with us. 'Everybody here knows the date,' Kol told me. 'The first direct conflict between the Dinka Nor and Misseriyya.' Who won? I asked. The Dinka, they said. In those days, both sides used spears; but the Misseriyya had just one in their hands, and the Dinka seven or more. It was an easy victory.

But the terms of fighting began to change in the 1970s. In Numeiri's time, the Misseriyya began to get rifles, and then in the mid-1980s they began to be armed more heavily by Sadiq al-Mahdi's government. Kol knew of the allegations that the Misseriyya were armed to defend themselves against the SPLA attacks, 'but that is not true, there were no SPLA around here', Kol told me. Soon, the whole Abyei area 'was devastated'. The Misseriyya 'looted cattle, burned houses, abducted children and raped women. It was a surprise. The attacks were so devastating.' Repeating the pattern of destruction in the Nuba Mountains, a short way to the north-east, the regular Sudanese army would often attack first, followed by the Misseriyya militias. It is impossible to prove, but Kol claims that 700 or so villages were destroyed. It is a sad indictment of the incompetence and wretchedness of Sudan's last democratic government that it parlayed the anguish and loss from the terrible natural disasters of the mid-1980s into Sudan's most feared means of warfare and ethnic violence.

The intensity of the attacks in the Abyei region, indeed along the whole middle belt of Sudan, can also be explained by oil. This is where the biggest fields are, where Sudan's best and most profitable crude can be found. In the 1990s, clearing the Dinka villages was also a way of clearing the lands for exploration and then exploitation. The Heglig oilfields, to the east of Abyei, became completely closed off to the Dinka by the Sudanese army. This was the ruthless exploitation of natural resources for commercial gain. The Chinese, who run the Heglig fields, connived in this process simply by asking no questions about how the way was cleared for the pumps and derricks. Indeed, locals told me that the Chinese seemed to be completely indifferent to their fate. Oil extraction also led to large-scale deforestation and the contamination of the water supplies on which the farmers and nomads depended. The process of oil production itself thus also contributed to the degradation of the Dinka way of life.

CHAPTER THREE

THE NATIONAL ISLAMIC FRONT AND TURABI IN POWER, 1989–2000

'A mixture of religion and organized crime'

Osama bin Laden

While Sudan's last democratic government was tottering to its shameful end, at some point in 1988 or early 1989 Hassan al-Turabi, the avowed democrat, decided on a *coup d'état* to get into power. For some of his followers, Turabi's complicity in the execution of Taha in 1985 and his apparent enthusiasm for amputations had already shaken their faith in his decency. Now Turabi disappointed them yet more by turning against the very democratic values that he had previously championed.

Why? Because by now it was clear that the ballot box was not going to give him the power he craved. The elections of 1986 were a disaster for Turabi's party, the National Islamic Front (NIF). As we have seen, the NIF won fifty-three seats in parliament, a respectable number against the Democratic Unionist Party's (DUP) sixty-three and the Umma's ninety-nine. But of those fifty-three, twenty-three were special 'graduate seats', only open to university students. This confirmed the fact that the Muslim Brotherhood, for all its organizational skills, money and experience, remained largely a party for the educated few.

Particularly shocking was the result in Darfur. The Mahdists cleaned up, winning thirty-four of the thirty-nine available seats in their traditional heartland, while the NIF won only two, whose incumbents later defected to another party anyway. Less surprisingly, the NIF did no better in the south. Humiliatingly, Turabi himself did not even win his own seat in Khartoum. Observing Turabi from close quarters, Sayid el-Khatib believes that: 'Up to this time he was a strong believer in democracy, but now he changed.' In particular, according to el-Khatib, Turabi thought it was 'unfair' that all the other parties had ganged up against him to deprive him of a seat.

Al Tayib al-Abdin was on the NIF committee of about twenty members that, in Turabi's paradoxical way, 'voted' on the proposed coup after a long discussion at a private house in Khartoum in May 1989. The arguments that Turabi advanced for such a drastic course of action were threefold. For a start, at least two other groups, he said, were already plotting their own coups – so if the NIF did not seize power, they risked letting in somebody else. Secondly, the war against the south was going extremely badly again, with the Sudan People's Liberation Army (SPLA) now in control of about 80 per cent of the region; there was even a fear that the guerrilla army might exploit its good fortune and invade the north. A new NIF government, Turabi asserted, would provide a more resolute defence against the SPLA. Finally, he argued that the West would never allow an Islamic group to take power democratically, citing the example of Turkey. Thus, he claimed, there was no option but to force the issue and grab power by military means.

He may have been prescient. Turabi was taking his decision in 1989, three years before the 1992 elections in Algeria. On that occasion an Islamist party was on the verge of winning an election democratically, but was denied power by the Western-backed military government, triggering an extremely bloody decade-long civil war. Would the West have allowed the NIF to come to power if it had won a majority at the polls? We will never know, as the NIF never had sufficient popular support to do so. Was the West using the SPLA to spearhead an invasion of north Sudan? Many countries, including Israel, Ethiopia and

Uganda, had supported the southern rebels in the first and second civil wars. The USA gave the SPLA a lot of non-lethal help from the mid-1990s onwards. But none of these countries ever contemplated a wholesale invasion of north Sudan.

More to the point, Turabi's decision to risk a coup was an acknowledgement of the failure of his overall strategy to vanquish the sect-based Islamic parties with an appeal to a broad-based populist Islam. From now on it would be political Islam by coercion, from the top down.

At least one person in the Muslim Brotherhood argued against a coup. Al Tayib al-Abdin told me that he warned his colleagues at the time how damaging such a course of action would be for the Islamist movement. He argued that the supposedly Islamic values of equality and justice that the Brotherhood had burnished over the previous decades would be undermined by the very act of overthrowing a democratically elected government. It would be terrible for 'the image of Islam', as much as for those who participated in it. Turabi, on the other hand, promised that once in power, even via a coup, the purpose of the new regime would be to work towards the apparently laudable goals of 'federalizing the country and then gradually democratizing it'.

This has become, post-2001, a depressingly familiar argument: espousing the use of force to impose liberal, democratic values on a country. It was deployed by the USA in Iraq in the early 2000s, for example. In 1989, in Khartoum however, al-Abdin found himself in a minority of one, and the coup date was set for 30 June.

Meticulous planning ensured that there was almost no bloodshed on the day of the coup itself. The NIF had at its disposal several hundred people who had been trained in the Libyan terrorist training camps during the 1970s. They had only just failed to oust Numeiri; now they proved more than equal to the task of toppling Sadiq al-Mahdi's fragile government. On 30 June these Libyan-trained cadres donned military uniforms to arrest senior ministers and army commanders hostile to the NIF, including the commander-in-chief of the army.

After years of work by the Muslim Brotherhood on infiltrating the army, a sufficient numbers of officers, led by Colonel Omar al-Bashir, were now willing to give the coup the vital military support it needed. Army officers were in a receptive frame of mind at the time as many of them blamed the squabbling politicians in Khartoum for the failure to defeat the SPLA rebels in the south. The politicians, in their turn, blamed the army; there was little mutual respect left between the two sides. In this context, the exact date of the coup was extremely significant. Exhausted by war, unable to find a strategy to win it, Sadiq al-Mahdi's government had reluctantly agreed to a peace conference with the southern rebels. This had taken months to organize and was due to begin the very next day. As much as anything, the coup was therefore a pre-emptive strike by the Islamist hardliners and the army against what they saw as surrender to the south.

So much for the plotters. What was it like to be on the receiving end of a coup? A young Mubarak al-Mahdi was the interior minister at the time in his cousin's government. He had been fully aware of the strained relations between the government and the army in the previous years. Khartoum does not keep secrets well, and Bashir's name had cropped up in intelligence reports as a likely plotter. Mubarak had launched an investigation, but his intelligence officers couldn't prove anything. Everyone knew, though, about the scheming Turabi.

Mubarak was also aware that the NIF had a number of well-placed supporters, members of the Muslim Brotherhood, in military intelligence, and that they might be a problem. Indeed, their contribution proved crucial on the night. They relayed false messages to local army officers that it was the commander-in-chief himself who was launching the coup. Meanwhile, of course, these very same military intelligence officers were arresting the said commander-in-chief.

June 30 was a Thursday, and Mubarak was at a late session of parliament as legislators were trying to pass the budget. Getting away at 12.30 a.m., he drove straight to a friend's daughter's wedding that the host had insisted he attend despite the late hour. Mubarak was given dinner and stayed on while his wife and his nephew left for home at 2.30 a.m. When the two got back, they found the house surrounded by soldiers, who claimed that they were there only to protect them. Inside, however, the omens were not good – the telephone lines had been cut. In fact, the soldiers were not there to stop anyone getting in, but to stop anyone getting out.

Realizing that they had been tricked, the two escaped via a secret door leading out of the back of the house. Mubarak's wife hastened back to the wedding and got there at about 4 a.m. to warn her husband what was happening. Mubarak immediately phoned the head of police, only to learn that the commissioner was himself a key member of the plot. Sensing that the game was up, he 'went into hiding' in Khartoum, moving from house to house to evade capture for several weeks before slipping out of the country via the Libyan desert and then on to London. He was not to return to Sudan until 2000.

He was lucky. Mubarak was the only member of the government not to be arrested. Prime Minister Sadiq al-Mahdi evaded capture for a week before he was caught. He was imprisoned for months, and then spent years under house arrest in Omdurman. He finally escaped from Sudan via Eritrea in 1996. Other members of the government spent six months to a year in jail, being constantly harassed, arrested and rearrested. Hassan al-Turabi and the Muslim Brotherhood, in the guise of the NIF, were now in control of the country.

But not too obviously so. The politically astute Turabi was aware that a full-blooded Islamist revolution in north Africa would provoke an immediate and possibly fatal response from Sudan's neighbours, particularly secular Egypt. The master plotter thus went through an elaborate charade of sending himself to prison as well, so he could pose as merely another hapless victim of a normal, comparatively unthreatening, military coup.

Thus, as Mubarak al-Mahdi was vanishing into the darkness of the streets of Khartoum, Turabi was packing a suitcase for his show stay in Kobar prison. There, bizarrely, he shared the cells with the most prominent of the coup's victims: his brother-in-law Sadiq al-Mahdi, and his old classmate Muhammad Ibrahim Nugd of the Sudanese Communist Party. According to the historian Robert Collins, Turabi spent his months of confinement attempting to lecture his unsympathetic fellow prisoners 'on how a new chapter in Sudanese history was about to be written. *Sharia* would remain the law of the land, and an Islamic state would be created despite the protestations of southern Sudanese and Muslim heretics, the Kafirin.'[1]

DESTROYING THE OPPOSITION, AND THE COUNTRY

Turabi was true to his boasts. As soon as he released himself from prison in December 1989, the true nature of the regime was revealed. Omar Bashir, the leader of the rebellious army officers, was the new president of the country and the public face of the new government. But Bashir and the military leaders of the coup, who were grouped together in what they called the Revolutionary Command Council, all swore an oath of allegiance to Turabi. Bashir, the Muslim Brother, seemed quite willing to follow Turabi's instructions. Indeed, even before Turabi's self-release from Kobar, the new government had self-consciously described itself as 'Islamist', to distinguish it from other governments in the Arab world led by Muslims, let alone secular communists, or even Baathists in Iraq.

A new 'Council of Defenders of the Revolution', chaired by Turabi's acolyte Ali Osman Taha, quickly began to impose the new Islamic programme on a country in which political Islam was still relatively unpopular. Their work was to be helped along by the creation of a new Internal Security Bureau, every bit as sinister as it sounds. What this amounted to in practice was a reign of terror to wipe out all centres of resistance to the new regime in the name of Islam. Most of the victims of this terror were, of course, themselves Muslims. *They* saw Turabi's 'political Islam' as nothing much more than an ideological pretext to exercise absolute power.

The first people that the new regime targeted were those whom Bashir and Turabi considered to be their most dangerous opponents – the very same people who had risen up against the previous non-democratic government, Numeiri's, in 1985. 'Which is why,' according

Hassan al-Turabi in 2009

to Hafiz Mohamed, one of the protestors on the streets in 1985, 'when the NIF came to power they deliberately set out to destroy the middle classes.' It had been the doctors, engineers, lawyers, journalists, academics, bankers and teachers who had led the overthrow of Numeiri, and who now therefore bore the brunt of the NIF's repression.

Hafiz, for instance, who had trained as an accountant, was working in his by now Islamized bank; he was targeted as a trade-union convenor. He remembers when his moment came. He was called into his manager's office in December 1989, and told that 'presidential decree 973', all two lines of it, ordered his immediate dismissal. Decree 973 gave no legal justification for the sacking; the manager simply told Hafiz that if he did not enforce it he himself would also be out of a job. Hafiz recalls that six of his close colleagues were sacked, and fifty-seven altogether from the banks in Khartoum – all leaders of the unions. Unable to get any further employment, Hafiz set up on his own as a business consultant in Omdurman before leaving the country altogether three years later.

This is why, Hafiz concludes: 'Sudan today has no middle class.' What the new regime achieved was nothing less than the complete destruction of the intellectual and professional capacity of the entire country, leaving Sudan fatally enfeebled.

Particularly galling to the educated middle classes was the demand that everyone be indoctrinated into the ruling ideology of political Islam by serving in the new Islamist militia, the Popular Defence Forces (PDF). This was formed as a legal entity in November 1989. Recruits were to be drilled at new training camps, initially set up around Khartoum. In the words of the historian of the PDF, the force was conceived of by the NIF leaders as a sort of praetorian guard of the new regime, 'an authentic Islamic model of military organization – a citizen's army of volunteer *mujahidin* prepared for frontline battle'. In fact, when volunteers proved lacking, all male citizens over the age of sixteen were obliged to attend PDF training.[2] Tens of thousands of young PDF men would fight – and die – alongside the regular army in the war against the SPLA in the 1990s.

Just avoiding service in the PDF cost many skilled Sudanese their jobs. Abduljabbar Abdellah Fadul, a Muslim Fur, remains one of Darfur's most respected experts on livestock production and environmental management. Now at the University of El Fasher in Darfur, he graduated from the University of Khartoum in 1975 and witnessed the new regime from close up, as one of those whom the NIF now targeted.

He remembers what happened at Gezira University, just south of Khartoum, when the orders went out that all staff had to retrain for three months in the PDF, whatever their age or job. If they refused, they faced the sack. Thirteen professors resigned on the same day that they got the order. All of them went overseas. One of them, the most prominent, got a job in Saudi Arabia for US$4,000 a month, whereas in Khartoum he had been earning $750 a month. Abduljabbar himself was sacked in February 1991; he watched as five desperately needed doctors were thrown out of the medical faculty of the hospital in

El Fasher for refusing to join up. Some stayed in private practice in Darfur, others joined a gathering exodus to Europe, the USA, the Gulf and elsewhere.

These were all, Abduljabbar, laments, 'educated, skilled people lost to Sudan'. He was lucky, getting a better-paid job almost immediately with the United Nations Development Programme. Foreigners, and foreign aid, were also unwelcome in the new Islamic republic. With the rains again faltering in Darfur in 1990, one of Abduljabbar's last acts in government employment (working for an innovative famine early-warning unit) in November of that year was to do a 'needs assessment' of Darfur. He was alarmed to find that the region was threatened by a complete harvest failure and that, yet again, famine was imminent. He recommended the swift delivery of food aid from outside the country to avert a disaster. This did not please his immediate superiors in Khartoum. He was told: 'You want to bring foreigners, why do you want to do that? We don't want USAID food; we are capable of feeding our own people.'

This was a patent untruth, but it didn't matter; he was not telling the new regime what it wanted to hear. His famine early-warning unit was closed down and he lost his job, with, as we shall see, awful consequences for Darfur. Reflecting on all this in 2008, still angry, Abduljabbar said that the government spent the early 1990s 'sacking qualified, skilled professionals and replacing them with their own unskilled, loyal cadres . . . so now there is no longer any knowledge . . . no one who can do anything'.

The old universities, which since independence had been among the greatest centres of learning in sub-Saharan Africa, were savaged. After all, the University of Khartoum had provided the most militant and well-organized resistance to previous regimes, as Turabi and the NIF leadership, almost all graduates of the university, were only too aware. Furthermore, the university had been opposed to Turabi's own coup. So the independent-minded student unions were banned. Free meals and accommodation for students were discontinued after 1989, making it almost impossible for the children of less well-off parents to go to university.

It is true that the intellectual Turabi founded twenty or so new universities after the 1989 coup, including the first one in Darfur, in El Fasher. But al Tayib al-Abdin, the former Muslim Brother and colleague of Turabi's, remembers the ulterior motive here: 'The idea was to reduce the status of the University of Khartoum.' Its lecturers were redistributed around the country, to dilute their influence, and the university was starved of money. In 1964 al-Abdin was teaching political science there to classes of forty or so students. When I spoke to him in 2008 he had classes of 400; this allowed for little meaningful education. In his own words, the NIF assault on the universities was all about 'knocking out another power point of resistance'.

Anyone who had the opportunity to compare the Sudanese universities of the pre-revolutionary era with what followed was shocked. One such was Dr Mukesh Kapila, an Anglo-Indian who was to play an important role in exposing the crimes of Darfur to the world when he spent a year in Sudan for the UN in 2003–4. Over twenty years before, however, in 1979, he had come to the University of Khartoum Medical School from Oxford University to complete his degree in medicine. He was sent to Khartoum because of its international excellence, especially in tropical medicine: 'The curriculum was the most advanced you could think of . . . it was well on a par with anything at Oxford.' The Sudanese professor who taught him was 'very good' and he had to work extremely hard just to keep up with his Sudanese peers.

In 2003 he returned to his alma mater for a nostalgic pilgrimage. But things had changed. He was 'shocked by how much it had declined . . . there was almost nothing left'. It was like a 'kindergarten, so low had the standards sunk'. All the old professors and doctors had left. His own local hospital at Peterborough in England, by contrast, was full of highly qualified and skilful Sudanese doctors who had left their own country in the 1990s to work for the National Health Service.

The quality of education in the whole system, from primary school through to the universities, went into wholesale decline. Islamization of the curriculum was accompanied by Arabization, which meant that all instruction was now to be in Arabic rather than English. This may have satisfied some legitimate nationalist aspirations, but it also cut off subsequent generations of young boys and girls from important areas of study. Even at the University of Khartoum Medical School, Dr Kapila noted, all instruction was in Arabic, yet it is impossible to learn medicine without at least a rudimentary knowledge of English, as so much of the medical literature is in that language.

Instead, a lot of time was now devoted to learning the Koran, while other subjects were compressed into educationally useless 'combined studies' courses. It didn't escape the notice of many Sudanese that this educational vandalism was, in Abduljabbar's words, 'forced on the country by the ruling ideologues who had benefited from a fantastic education'. When I brought this up with the multi-lingual, multi-degreed Turabi in 2008, he merely replied, 'Arabic is richer than English.'

So bad did the public universities become that by the mid-2000s, many businessmen and others who I spoke to lamented that the Sudanese graduates from these institutions were 'unemployable', without even basic skills in literacy or numeracy. Meanwhile, stories abounded of regime members escaping the destructive consequences of their own policies by sending their children to British and US universities instead. Certainly, by the mid-2000s a new generation of fee-paying, private universities had started to flourish in the Three Towns to cater for the sons and daughters of the government and the new moneyed, ruling class. There one can learn English, other foreign languages and a range of subjects, almost like any Western university. Yet such is the poverty in Sudan that only very few have access to them.

Then there was *sharia* law, first introduced by Numeiri's government. Under Turabi, naturally, *sharia* became an important pillar of political Islam in practice, to be enforced by a new Popular Police Force. An Islamic Penal Code was introduced in 1991 which sanctioned amputations, floggings and other punishments. Any last outposts of judicial independence were eliminated; the Sudanese Bar Association was discontinued, and a member of the NIF was appointed chief justice to ensure that *sharia* operated throughout the judicial system.

THE *JIHAD* FOUNDERS ON THE ROCK OF JOHN GARANG

If the coup itself seemed to contradict everything that Turabi had taught his followers about democracy, the new regime also proved to be uninterested in implementing any sort of constitutional federalism. Turabi, and many others, had often touted federalism as the long-term solution to Sudan's problem of ethnic and religious diversity. But once the NIF was in control of the country the reality was very different. Rather than federalism, there was a great deal more Arabization, especially in the west of the country, and a lot more confrontation, especially in the south.

In Darfur, the new government continued the same policy of ethnic aggression against the local African tribes that Libya's President Ghadaffi had started in the 1970s as part of his dream of a greater Libya–Sudan Arab integration in the Maghreb. Ghadaffi's chosen instrument to fulfil his ambitions, the Islamic Pan-Arab Legion, was fully supported by the new regime in Khartoum. In 1990 Sudan, acknowledging Libyan influence in the region, signed a Libya–Sudan integration charter. In 1991 a new governor of Darfur was appointed, the NIF extremist Colonel al-Tayib Ibrahim Muhammad Khair, known as *al-sjikka* (the Iron Bar), a tribute to his not-so-gentle methods of suppressing anti-Islamic street demonstrations in Khartoum. He began an offensive against the non-Arab Fur, Zaghawa and later the Masalit tribes, forcibly disarming them and driving many from their homes, often across the border into Chad.

This was not only ethnic warfare, but also a function of domestic politics. The NIF had been chastened by the victory of the Umma party in the 1986 elections in Darfur – so, once in power the NIF sought systematically to destroy the Umma's grip on the region by attacking its power base among the Fur and other tribes. To this end, under the guise of 'modernizing' local administration, as Numeiri had done previously, Khartoum split Darfur into three new administrative districts, or 'states', in 1994. This made the Fur, the main enemies of Arabization, easier to deal with; rather than having their own unified lands, they would become marginalized minorities in the new administrative districts.

New officials from Khartoum came in, riding roughshod over local customs, including, fatally, the traditional mechanisms of conflict resolution. Most worryingly, as Abduljabar Fadul quickly found out, they were also unconcerned by droughts and famine. All the main dynamics for the conflict after 2003 were firmly set in motion in these years.

In the south, instead of 'federalism' the war against the SPLA was stepped up and intensified. Indeed, the war against the southern rebels was formally declared to be a *jihad* (holy war) in 1992. This encouraged the recruitment of young men into the PDF to fight the war, but at the same time removed any room for negotiation with the SPLA. The PDF was used in large numbers; there may have been as many as 40,000–50,000 of them in Kordofan alone by the early 1990s. By 1994, the demands for manpower had become so heavy that press gangs roamed the streets of Khartoum to seize people for the PDF. Many of the recruits that fought against the SPLA were, in fact, from Darfur, a region that had traditionally provided most troops for the army. Young Darfuri men were indoctrinated into the Islamist revolution, and the *jihad*, in training camps in the north. The poor and ignorant teenagers were soft targets for their PDF Islamist teachers. They could be easily manipulated, and readily believed all the lies that were fed to them.

The boy soldier-turned-priest Elias Taban, then fighting with the SPLA, learned all about this at close quarters when 400 or so of the self-styled *mujahideen* fighters were captured after the SPLA took the town of Yei, south-west of Juba, from government forces. The evangelical priest volunteered to take twenty of the prisoners into his own house and feed them before they were to be handed over to the International Red Cross. Every evening, Taban and his 'prisoners' would sit around and eat together. 'They were very friendly, very social,' Taban recalled for me. They explained to him how they had all been forcefully recruited and indoctrinated at special camps. They had been told that 'Christians were the Number One enemy and that if they were captured they would be killed.' According to Taban, they were instructed that 'if a Muslim kills a non-Muslim in the cause of bringing the person to Allah, then his blood is not on your hands'.

To Taban, they seemed more like naïve youngsters than fanatical ideologues. When they were eventually released in 1998, many of these captured *mujahideen* refused to return to the north, fearful that they might be press-ganged back into the PDF. Some of them remain to this day in Yei as small traders and shopkeepers.

Travelling throughout the south in the late 2000s, I heard many similar stories. Take Ring Kuol, the Ngok-Dinka vet from the Abyei region in the centre of the country. As Abyei is a mixed African and Arab area, Ring shared most of his upbringing with the local Misseriyya and other Arab tribes, but had to flee to Khartoum in the early 1990s after his village was burned down by those very same Arabs. Nonetheless, he retained several close Arab friends from his schooldays, even after they had left to join the *jihad* against the south. One of these, from north Kordofan, invited Ring to eat with him after he had himself returned from three months of fighting the *jihad* in the south. Ring was surprised to be asked, but went along anyway.

Ring remembers: 'I thought he would be changed, but he was quite normal.' His friend told him that the message he had received from his own government was that the southerners were just one among many peoples 'who are against Islam, so Muslims have to protect Islam from people who want to destroy it'. So he had left home for his *jihad*, expecting to find people waiting to kill him for his faith. Instead, however, as Ring told me, his friend 'had not seen anything abnormal. Southerners seemed ordinary people, not aggressive against Islam. He was surprised. He had just believed what he had been told. It was political lies.' On his return he invited the Christian Ring to eat as a sign of peace.

Yet despite the mass mobilization of the PDF by Turabi and Bashir, throughout the 1990s the Khartoum government never achieved a decisive military defeat of the SPLA. Indeed, for most of this time the government's forces were often confined just to holding on to their 'garrison towns' in the south, such as Juba, while the SPLA controlled most of the countryside. For all the manufactured ferocity of the PDF and the heavy weaponry that Khartoum was able to deploy in the field, these were more than matched on the southern rebel side by the iron discipline and rigorous training of the SPLA, as well as the strategic acumen of its charismatic commander, John Garang. He was perhaps the only Sudanese politician in the post-independence era who had a real vision of the how the country might be united and function properly. From 1983, when he assumed command of the SPLA, until his death in a helicopter crash in 2005, he was Khartoum's most formidable opponent.

One of the brightest of the southern leaders, he had gained a PhD in agricultural economics at Iowa State University and had also completed the US Army Infantry Officer's Advanced Course at Fort Benning, Georgia, in 1974. He then served in the Sudanese army after the Addis Ababa agreement brought peace to the south in 1972. When hostilities resumed in 1983 he was serving as head of the Staff College in Omdurman, but he quickly decided to desert the Sudanese army and join the southern rebellion. Given his background and training he was an obvious choice to lead the SPLA.

Garang ran the guerrilla army in a dictatorial and often ruthless manner; dissent was never tolerated and those suspected of plotting against him were liable to be executed. In this sense, he was a divisive figure. The SPLA was run very much as a top-down military organization, with little regard for the niceties of building a broad-based, more political mass movement of resistance. Nonetheless, Garang's high-handed ways, resented by many, were usually vindicated on the battlefield.

His cause was greatly helped from 1983 to 1991 by the backing of the Marxist regime of Haile Mariam Mengistu in neighbouring Ethiopia. Mengistu not only provided weapons for the SPLA but allowed giant refugee camps to be set up just inside the Ethiopian border that provided a safe haven for up to 400,000 southern Sudanese civilians fleeing the fighting. Furthermore, these camps – largely provided for by the UN and foreign non-governmental organizations – also existed cheek by jowl with SPLA training camps, and there was plenty of cross-fertilization between the two. In particular, this is where about 17,000 southern Sudanese children fled to, the so-called 'Lost Boys of

A Dinka at war: John Garang leads the SPLA

Sudan'. Many of them became child soldiers in the ranks of the SPLA, some aged as little as twelve years old.[3]

Conversely, the time of greatest peril for the southern rebels came in the spring of 1991 when Mengistu's regime was overthrown by Ethiopia's own home-grown rebels, backed by Khartoum – the Ethiopian People's Revolutionary Democratic Front. When they swept into Addis Ababa, consigning Mengistu to exile in Zimbabwe, the rebels-turned-politicians swiftly repaid their debt to the Khartoum government by closing the SPLA training camps on Ethiopian territory and cutting off their supply of arms. The SPLA had to repatriate hundreds of thousands of their people to southern Sudan in a rush, in what nearly turned into a humanitarian disaster. The closing down of Ethiopia as a rear supply base also severely disrupted military operations and dislocated the SPLA leadership.

It was at this juncture that the SPLA split, almost fatally. In August 1991, three senior SPLA commanders, Riek Machar, Lam Akol and Gordon Kong Cuol, rebelled against the leadership of Garang and announced (prematurely, as it turned out) that he had been removed as leader of the rebel army. They published a pamphlet, *Why John Garang Must Go Now*, to justify their coup; in it they complained of his dictatorial, ruthless style of command. But they also outlined a separate vision for the future of southern Sudan in opposition to Garang's – the two competing 'manifestos' remained the most obvious alternatives for the future of southern Sudan up to the referendum on independence due in 2011.

Garang was a strong advocate of the unity of the Sudanese state, but only if *all* the oppressed peoples of Sudan, in Darfur and the east as well as the south, united together to oust the Islamic regime of Bashir from Khartoum and replace it with a federally minded government composed of representatives from all the tribes and religions of Sudan. This concept of a democratic and federal Sudan was often referred to as the 'New Sudan'. This led Garang to seek out alliances across the whole of the country, for instance with the Beja in the east and the Fur in the west, to create a coalition of opponents against Bashir's government. The political expression of this was the National Democratic Alliance, active for a while in the early 1990s. Economic disadvantage and marginalization were the most important factors for Garang rather than race and religion.

Machar, Akol and Cuol, by contrast, had given up on the idea of a united Sudan and argued instead for the straightforward independence of the south from the north. But as well as offering two competing visions of the south's place in Sudan as a whole, the rebellion of Machar et al. in 1991 signified something much graver and more visceral: the deep ethnic divides within the SPLA. Garang was a Twic Dinka; Machar, the leader of the rebellion against him, was a Nuer, and Lam Akol was a Shilluk. Many non-Dinka resented the preponderance of Dinka, the biggest tribe in the south, within the SPLA and suspected that their own rights would be trampled on by any Dinka-dominated government of the south. Machar's new rebel grouping, called the 'Nasir Faction' or SPLA-Nasir, was Nuer-dominated and it now went into battle against the Dinka-dominated SPLA, provoking two years or so of often bitter ethnic conflict. The Nuer invasion of Dinkaland in 1991 cost thousands of Dinka lives, including women and children. These so-called 'Bor Massacres', however, backfired on Machar as many southerners (as well as his numerous foreign sympathizers) were so appalled by the needless blood-letting that they refused to rally to SPLA-Nasir, however much they might have disliked Garang. By 1995, Garang was back in charge of the whole SPLA and winning battles in the field again. The wily and duplicitous Machar would only be fully reconciled with Garang in 2002.[4]

The split in the early 1990s revealed fully the ethnic differences within southern ranks. The consequent rivalries between the various southern leaders were, of course, fully exploited by the Khartoum government, which did everything it could to cleave the warring southern factions apart even further. Riek Machar's Nuer faction, for example, asked the Khartoum government for money and weapons to fight Garang, and these were readily given. For Bashir's regime, SPLA-Nasir thus acted as another sort of proxy force against the main SPLA; indeed, Khartoum signed a formal agreement with the SPLA-Nasir faction in 1992, making various vague promises on southern independence in return for continued hostility against Garang's forces.

Paying different rebel factions off to divide and weaken them was a tactic that was repeatedly used in the south and later in Darfur. The Khartoum government also used another local ethnic militia, the Lord's Resistance Army (LRA), led by the crazed Joseph Kony, against the SPLA. An Acholi insurgency based mainly over the border in northern Uganda, the LRA was given weapons by Khartoum and sanctuary on the Sudanese side of the border in return for fighting against the SPLA.

The Lord's Resistance Army was sustained by Khartoum for about twenty years to terrorize the entire region. At the time of writing (early 2010) it was still operating in the jungles of northern Congo and south Sudan, despite the deaths of some of its leaders.

IN THE GHOST HOUSES

In north Sudan, the brutality of the Islamist regime seemed to increase in direct relation to the people's general indifference or hostility towards it. Under Turabi, the great jurist and avowed legal scholar, the government quickly descended into a pit of merciless and arbitrary violence as the Internal Security Bureau and the army enforced its repressive policies. Torture, disappearance, extra-judicial killing and imprisonment all became routine. Much of this happened in the notorious 'Ghost Houses', where hundreds of 'political opponents' were detained for months, or even years. Many of the victims were the middle-class professionals deemed by the regime to be their most likely opponents. This was something totally new in Sudan, and shocking to many. It was the Red Terror of the Islamist revolution.

Human-rights organizations began to document the torture and mock executions that took place in the Ghost Houses, so-called because most of the brutality was inflicted at night – when ghosts walk. In one case, a journalist and his friend were arrested, blindfolded and then driven around Khartoum for hours. As the journalist later recounted for Amnesty International:

> We stopped at about 3 p.m., a gate was opened and we drove through. We were dragged from the car, told to stand against a wall with our hands up and against it, then we were struck by many people all over our bodies with electric cable, plastic water pipes and lengths of wood. This lasted from 3 p.m. until 8 p.m. – with an interruption at 6 p.m. for evening prayers . . . this is referred to as the 'reception party'.
>
> At around 11 p.m., I was blindfolded and taken . . . to an unknown destination . . . they said I should make a will. Then I was forced up some stairs and made to lie on what felt like a

leather couch. After a few seconds I began to feel small but painful cuts all over my body, as if they were made by razor blades. This went on for around two hours with some breaks . . . I was taken back to the Ghost House around 3 a.m. This pattern of being made to stand all night, sometimes being taken to the other place for the 'couch treatment' and sometimes just being taken outside and kicked and beaten continued until the next Wednesday, six days after my arrest.[5]

Salih Osman, a Darfuri, is a human-rights lawyer, an MP and one of the Bashir regime's most outspoken, brave and implacable foes. In 2008 I met him in his dingy office in central Khartoum, where he recalled his own experiences at the hands of the NIF.

After the 1989 coup, he had immediately been picked up by the NIF as a Darfuri activist. On that occasion, he was detained in prison for four months before being released. But in the summer of 1990 he was arrested again. This time he was taken to El Fasher, then all the way across the country to Port Sudan, and finally to Khartoum. In the capital he was taken to an unmarked house in the city centre, next to the central bank. The location was already notorious as the place where one of the doctors' union leaders, Dr Ali Fadoul, had been tortured and killed only three weeks before Salih arrived.

Salih was kept here for three months. No one outside knew where he was or what had happened to him. He was physically tortured, but, as he told me, it was the mystery of his whereabouts that 'was also a real torture to the family members'. There were seven other Darfuris with him, among a total of about thirty detainees in the house; they were crowded ten to a room with nowhere to sleep except the bare floor. He was routinely beaten with whips, punched and slapped. He was often deprived of rest by various means: the lights would be left on, guards would wake him up or water was poured on the floor to make sleep impossible. The inmates were often starved and subjected to a constant torrent of verbal abuse. He was frequently told that in the Ghost House no one would protect him if he disappeared, and that by opposing the government he was opposing the word of God. The inmates used to pray that they would be sent to Kobar prison, 'a paradise compared to the Ghost Houses'. Salih's wish was finally granted, and he spent the following three months in Kobar.

The people who did this to Salih were either from military intelligence, or they were internal security agents. In his case, religion was often invoked as a pretext for their actions. To Salih, a constitutional lawyer by training, '*Sharia* law was used as a weapon against political opponents. It did not have a religious dimension at all. Killings and tortures were justified by these laws . . . corruption, abuse of power, all justified by these laws.' At the beginning of the revolution, Salih argues, the introduction of *sharia* was quite popular in the north. People thought that it was going to be applied for the benefit of ordinary people in the name of justice and equality – but gradually, 'People came to see that *sharia* was just being manipulated.'

Many were outraged by what they heard and saw. The regime was particularly harsh on black-market money changers; one, a banker, was discovered with $1,000 in his house and summarily executed. In April 1990 the government announced that it had foiled an attempted coup. A day later, after a fleeting pretence of a trial during which the defendants had no legal representation, twenty-eight military officers were executed. Few believed the official story. According to an Amnesty International report at the time: 'Two of the men executed were reportedly arrested at least three days before the alleged coup attempt; some sources claim that they were executed before the date of the trial.'

Turabi, however, blithely carried on as though nothing untoward were happening in Sudan. He travelled to the West on several occasions, continuing to promote his very reasonable-sounding philosophy of political Islam. But sometimes his victims caught up with him.

On one famous occasion, in April 1992, he addressed an audience at the Royal Society for the Encouragement of Arts, Manufacturers and Commerce in London on the subject of nationalism and Islam. His enemies – dissident refugees – and his Islamist supporters had packed the hall, to barrack or to cheer. Turabi was listened to in silence as he gave a learned, philosophical disquisition on his subject, apparently arguing – as usual – for a modern and progressive Islam.

'Excessive fidelity to immutable principle may lead to historical irrelevance and visionary abstraction from reality,' he opined. 'The historical test for Muslims has always been to recover after every setback, seeking through the revival of faith (*iman*), the renewal of thought (*ijtihad*) and the resurgence of action (*jihad*) to salvage religion from temporal containment and ensure its progressive development, relevance and continuity in history.'

When Turabi had finished, a Sudanese man called Abdel Bagi, dressed in traditional *jellabiya*, caught the eye of the chairman and rose to speak. He asked to talk in Arabic and a former opposition parliamentarian, Mansur el Agab, agreed to interpret for him. Abdel Bagi then began, as Alex de Waal recounts, to tell his story:

> [Bagi] was arrested, tortured, forced to lie in freezing water. His leg became gangrenous and had to be amputated. At this point, Abdel Bagi took off his wooden leg, until then concealed beneath his jellabiya, and thrust it in Turabi's face, 'What does your Islam have to say about this?'
>
> The room exploded with the dissidents, refugees and exiles shouting 'fascist!' at Dr Turabi while the Sudan-government-sponsored students, embassy staff and sundry Muslims tried in turn to shout them down. After the hubbub had subsided, the chairman put the question to Turabi again. He gave a high-pitched laugh and answered: 'Islam does not permit such things.'[6]

Was Turabi simply in denial about the forces that he had unleashed, or genuinely ignorant? Probably more of the former, and a little of the latter. To his interlocutors at the time, like the US journalist Judith Miller, Turabi simply 'denied things' that she knew from first-hand experience to be true: 'Abuses that could never be defended by Islamic principles or any other moral standard.'[7] He had, for Miller, simply assumed a defence common to all dictators, that of flatly denying the obvious. Talking to me almost twenty years later, Turabi acknowledged that there were some abuses, but simply blamed everything on the army. It was the work mostly of 'soldiers . . . a few officers', he claimed.

But as even many of his previously devoted supporters now concede, Turabi himself must have known all too well what was going on. His increasingly feverish behaviour, his callousness and the apparent betrayal of many of the early principles of the Muslim Brotherhood began to worry his loyal cadre of acolytes, such as Sayid el-Khatib. It may have been an assault at Ottawa airport in 1992 that unbalanced him: Turabi was badly beaten by a karate-trained Sudanese dissident in the departure lounge and spent several months in hospital and afterwards at home recovering. Or maybe it was merely the intoxicating effects of power. El-Khatib argues that it was probably a bit of both. He says that Turabi's near-death experience in Ottawa reminded him of his own mortality, and thus of the need to force the pace of his Islamic revolution by any means. Turabi begged el-Khatib to return from the USA to work for him personally in 1992. He did so, for a year. But el-Khatib was appalled by what he saw up close: 'This was more than we had bargained for . . . this was power for power's sake, without regard to the national interest of the country.'

There was worse to come, far more detrimental to the 'national interest'. If the exact responsibility for the dreadful human-rights violations of the era is hard to pinpoint, there is no doubt that it was Turabi who was personally responsible for turning Sudan into the new centre of state-sponsored international terrorism.

SPREADING TERROR ABROAD: ENTER OSAMA BIN-LADEN

Just as the new Bashir/Turabi government moved quickly to parade its Islamist credentials at home, so it had an early opportunity to do the same abroad. In the late summer of 1990, Saddam Hussein's Iraq invaded Kuwait. Most of the Arab world supported the US-led coalition that was assembled to eject Saddam's forces. Some Arab armies actually fought in the coalition. Turabi, however, focused his outrage on the intrusion of US and other infidel troops onto Muslim soil, especially the holy land of Saudi Arabia. Determined to put Sudan in the vanguard of the radical Islamist revolution, he thus supported Iraq against Kuwait. The priority, for Turabi, was to rid Muslim lands of infidels and their apostate allies, those friendly, secular or overly moderate Arab governments.

One result of this policy was the foundation of the Popular Arab and Islamic Congress (PAIC) that met in Khartoum for the first time in April 1991. It was a sort of alternative Arab League, an organization derided as supine and collaborationist by the likes of Turabi. The Sudanese government waived visa requirements for all 'Arab brothers' at the time, so many known terrorists were able to enter the country. As Collins records, the government modestly described the PAIC gathering as 'the most significant event since the collapse of the Caliphate'.[8]

Over the course of the next few years, PAIC gatherings in Khartoum attracted Hizbullah from Lebanon, the Palestinian Liberation Organization of Yasser Arafat, the Islamic Salvation Front from Algeria, Somali Islamists and similar groups from Yemen, Egypt and elsewhere. It was a Davos in the desert for terrorists. The meetings also attracted many of the Afghan-Arab *mujahideen* who were now at a loose end after helping to oust the Soviet army from Afghanistan at the end of the 1980s. They too began to arrive in droves. Among these battle-hardened fighters was the already-famous *jihadist* Osama bin Laden. The wealthy scion of a powerful Saudi construction family, bin Laden had fallen out with the Saudi royal family over the basing of American troops in the kingdom to eject Iraqi forces from Kuwait in the 1990 Gulf War, to which, like Turabi, he strenuously objected. Casting around for another centre of operations, bin Laden was enticed to Khartoum by Turabi. The Saudi arrived in December 1991 as an honoured guest of Turabi and the Sudanese government. The Sudanese official assigned to liaise with bin Laden and help him during his time in the country was Salah Gosh, later the head of the Sudanese intelligence service, the Mukhabarat.

Turabi described bin Laden to me in 2006 as 'a warrior and a freedom fighter against the Russians', adding that he 'inspired the spirit of resistance and struggle against everyone'. Nonetheless, Turabi was also keen to downplay the connection. With his next breath, he added that bin Laden's role in Sudan was 'just blown up by the media'. The line that Turabi and other Sudanese Islamists came to adopt in the mid-2000s, by which time they were anxious to distance themselves from the activities of al-Qaeda, was that bin Laden was invited to Sudan merely as a 'businessman'. He was supposed to use his enormous wealth gained from the family construction business to build roads and farms. Turabi claimed to me that he had met bin Laden just three times.

In fact, their relationship was a great deal closer, as we shall see. There is no doubt that bin Laden was a good catch for Turabi and the Sudanese, with much to offer the impoverished country. He started up numerous companies and, as was expected of him, built several roads, including the much-needed main tarmac road from Khartoum to Port Sudan. As a financier and entrepreneur, bin Laden amassed an impressive portfolio of enterprises. Taba Investments and Laden International included a range of agricultural, food and export businesses. Bin Laden's main interest was in construction, but, according to the US journalist and historian of al-Qaeda, Lawrence Wright, it was farming that 'captivated his imagination' in Sudan. Acquiring farmland all over north Sudan, he became probably the biggest single private landowner in the country.

Like the British before him, and the Gulf Arabs of Numeiri's era, bin Laden also seems to have become gripped by the potential of Sudan as a breadbasket of the Middle East. He acquired about a million acres of land. Among his biggest holdings was the Al Damazin farms project in the Upper Nile region, near to the Ethiopian border, which employed about 4,000 people, as well as other farms in the most fertile part of the country in the eastern state of Gedaref. His agricultural company gained a near monopoly on some of the country's major farm exports, such as sesame, white corn and gum arabic. Indeed, at a time when the Sudanese economy as whole was contracting, resulting in great economic hardship, bin Laden's various enterprises must have constituted a significant proportion of the national economy – even if the Saudi did not make any money from them himself.

Bin Laden bought another big property near Soba, where he kept much of the heavy machinery he needed to build roads. He also had a large three-storey villa in the Riyadh district of Khartoum for himself and his immediate family, another house downtown for his offices, on Mek Nimir Street, and a separate guesthouse for visitors and entertaining, plus several other houses nearby for his bodyguards and entourage. Bin Laden enjoyed a comfortable, even pampered existence, devoting most of his time to his agricultural projects. To his friends and family, he appeared to be mainly absorbed by the challenge of growing large sunflowers.

As to the relationship between Turabi and bin Laden, accounts vary. Turabi's associates, such as his assistant Ibrahim Mohammed al Sanoussi, who, among other things, was in charge of indoctrinating the press-ganged militants of the PDF, like to paint a picture of a bucolically happy relationship, of two devout optimists doing their best for a new Sudan. Here is Sanoussi:

> Osama began to make canals and cultivating soil, and sunflower oil. It was very successful . . . at that time Dr Turabi and Osama were great friends. We used to sit together and were chatting about this agricultural schemes and how he made the roads and the kinds of stones [he used]. . . . At that time still we thought he was a religious man and not a politician because sometimes we would be meeting and he never speaks to us about politics. He asked Dr Turabi especially about his ideas about Islam, [and its view on] mortgages.[9]

To begin with, bin Laden must have looked up to Turabi as a mentor and teacher. After all, Turabi's fame had spread throughout the Arab world via his speeches and writings on Islam. But it must also be true, as Wright suggests, that bin Laden would have found Turabi's sophistry, contrariness and idiosyncrasies hard to take. For the two men were completely different in character: the Saudi 'terse and laconic', according to Wright, Turabi 'endlessly theoretical, a brilliant windbag'. As bin Laden confided to his friends, 'This man is a Machiavelli, he doesn't care what methods he uses.' He was neither the first nor the last to come to that conclusion.

Despite what was happening in Sudan, Turabi continued preaching his surprisingly progressive-sounding version of Islam at soirées in his house. He would talk of integrating sport and music into Islam, or of reconciling Sunni and Shia Arabs. Much of this must have been almost heretical to bin Laden, the strict Saudi Wahabbist. Certainly, bin Laden's son, Omar, enjoyed Khartoum most for its relative social and sexual freedoms, so different from the puritanical cocoon of their homeland, Saudi Arabia.

But Osama bin Laden was not in Sudan experimenting with giant sunflowers just out of a love of horticulture. According to the CIA, his sunflowers grew so large because they were genetically modified – testimony to his interest in biological warfare. For in return for his investment in Sudan, he was allowed a free hand by the Sudanese government to nurture his nascent terrorist organization, al-Qaeda. On arrival, one of his first acts was to hand over five million dollars to Turabi's PAIC and through that organization he had easy access to the knowledge and training of every other militant Islamist terrorist group in the Middle East. The construction machinery he kept at Soba served to build not just roads, but also the nineteen or so training camps he set up in the desert around Khartoum for the *mujahideen* flocking in from Afghanistan. Bin Laden also used the Sudanese government as diplomatic cover to move al-Qaeda operatives in and out of the country and to build his network.

Hundreds or possibly thousands of *mujahideen* arrived in Sudan to work for bin Laden or to train at the camps. Al-Qaeda itself may even have screened the credentials of incoming Afghan Arabs on behalf of Sudan state security. The links between bin Laden and al-Qaeda on the one hand, and the Sudanese government and the NIF on the other, were obviously extensive – which would later make Sudan such a potential treasure trove of intelligence for the CIA after the terrorist attacks of 11 September 2001.

In 1992, the presence of US troops on Muslim soil, up to then confined just to the Gulf, came much closer to al-Qaeda's home in Sudan with the US intervention in Somalia. This ill-fated expedition, the subject of the Hollywood film *Black Hawk Down*, was carried out in conjunction with the UN ostensibly as a humanitarian mission. It was designed to secure food supplies for the ravaged Somali population by defeating local warlords who had brought the government down in 1991. In fact, it served to galvanize al-Qaeda into its first attacks on 'infidel' troops. US soldiers in transit at a hotel in Aden in 1992 were targeted, as were, according to some sources, the US troops killed in Mogadishu.

According to Abdel Bari Atwan, a respected Arab source on al-Qaeda who interviewed bin Laden in 1996, al-Qaeda sent an operative to the Somali capital to co-ordinate the attack that brought down the two US Black Hawk helicopters. The bloody fighting in the Somali capital killed nineteen US soldiers. Atwan later wrote: 'The US swiftly withdrew its troops from Somalia, something bin Laden told me he greatly regretted, for he had been planning a war of attrition against them (something now apparently well under way in Iraq).'[10]

In 1993 bin Laden also started plotting the 1998 attacks on the US embassies in Nairobi and Dar es Salaam. If al-Qaeda was not actually born in Sudan, it certainly developed its modus operandi in the bosom of Turabi's Islamic revolution. And there were several other well-known terrorists in Khartoum besides bin Laden at the time. Ilich Ramirez Sanchez, also known as 'Carlos the Jackal', then the world's most wanted criminal, arrived in 1993. He stayed for a year before being snatched by the French secret service.

In 1995 the PAIC gathering was better attended than ever, and more militant in its language. This was the high tide of Turabi's revolution: the Islamic movement was vanquishing its opponents at home; the military of Omar Bashir was firmly under his control; the worldwide *jihad* under his direction was underway abroad; and he had Osama bin Laden's money to prop all this up.[11]

Most of Sudan's traditional allies – the USA, Britain, Egypt, Saudi Arabia, Ethiopia, even Libya – watched on with a mixture of bewilderment and frustration, and finally alarm, as the true nature of Sudan's Islamic revolution revealed itself. Indeed, Turabi seemed almost to court disaster with his careless boasts about how his Islamic revolution would sweep all before it.

He directly provoked a new war, for example, on the borderlands with Eritrea and Ethiopia in eastern Sudan. The NIF backed Islamist guerrillas in both Eritrea and Ethiopia, supposedly to protect the rights of suffering Muslim minorities. 'Ethiopia will self-destruct in the near future, thus paving the way for the establishment of an Islamic Oromo state and resulting in a chain of Islamic polities extending to the Indian Ocean,' proclaimed Turabi.[12] Far from it. The result, rather, was the beginning of a low-intensity but long and damaging conflict that broke out in the east as Eritrea responded to Turabi's threats by arming and backing marginalized Beja rebels against the regime in Khartoum. Ethiopia, feeling similarly threatened, backed the SPLA against Khartoum. Two could play at fighting proxy wars.

Farther from home, PAIC's plotting against moderate Arab regimes worried countries throughout North Africa and the Middle East. Yet for years Sudan was left alone – until eventually it became too dangerous to ignore. The turning point came with two terrorist attacks, both of which were traced back to Turabi's regime in Khartoum. In 1993, a small team of people exploded bombs in the basement of the World Trade Center in New York. The bombers themselves were tracked down fairly quickly, and the immediate ringleader identified as the blind Egyptian Sheikh Omar Abdel Radman; he evaded capture to attend the PAIC meeting in Khartoum in December of that year. Further digging, however, revealed the bombers' links to a hitherto unknown group called al-Qaeda, guests of the Sudanese government.

Then, in June 1995, assassins tried to kill the Egyptian president Hosni Mubarak when he visited the Ethiopian capital Addis Ababa for a meeting of the Organization of African Unity. The shooters riddled Mubarak's car with bullets and killed two bodyguards, but the president survived. The would-be killers were from an outfit called Islamic Group, but it was quickly discovered that they had trained in Sudan and that their weapons had been smuggled into Addis through the Sudanese embassy there. Moreover, Turabi himself praised the perpetrators of the attack in an interview, adding of his meetings with Mubarak, just for good measure: 'I found the man to be very far below my level of thinking and my views, and too stupid to understand my pronouncements.'[13]

This finally roused the international community into action. The US government, alarmed by PAIC even before anyone had heard of al-Qaeda, had first put Sudan on its list of state sponsors of terror in 1993 and had applied a raft of sanctions against the country, the first of many. Now, in 1995, an enraged Egyptian government led the Arab and Western charge against Sudan. Egypt took Sudan to the UN Security Council to punish the country for its complicity in the assassination attempt on Mubarak. The Security Council duly obliged, and more sanctions followed, especially when Sudan refused to yield anyone up for the crime. It was the first time that foreign countries had begun to turn the screw on what had become a rogue state, not only for the West but for many Middle Eastern and African countries as well.

THE HOLLOW DRUM OF POLITICAL ISLAM

It was at this point that many Sudanese started to reconsider whether Turabi's revolution was worth the cost. By 1996, Sudan had become isolated diplomatically and financially. Sanctions compounded the woes of an economy in free fall, since the revolution had forced many businessmen and financiers out of the country. Living standards were dropping fast and goods disappearing from the shops. Government and administration were in disarray; the civil service had been gutted of its best people. Many of Turabi's acolytes were dismayed by the rising level of human-rights abuses, as well as the increasingly barbaric war in the south, to say nothing of the armed insurrection by the Beja in the east. Was this really what they had signed up for in 1989?

Take Sayid el-Khatib, once Turabi's devoted assistant. From 1992 to 1997 he was growing 'gradually [more] disillusioned', he told me a decade later. Sudan was neither managing to build a democracy nor improving its relations with the outside world: 'We were losing our soul too.' El-Khatib recalls how most of Turabi's former supporters and disciples finally lost patience with him, at different moments and for different reasons. What he described as his own 'last straw' came on the eve of the holy *Eid* in 1996. Young recruits to the PDF in Khartoum wanted to spend the *Eid* with their families before being sent off to fight, but Turabi denied them permission to do so. El-Khatib continues the story thus:

> So they escaped from the camp and tried to get back to their families by crossing the Blue Nile on a boat. But the boat capsized, and fifty-nine drowned. I saw Turabi that afternoon and asked for some sort of official investigation. But Turabi just laughed and dismissed it. He quoted the Koran, about people deserting during battle being high treason . . . and all his acolytes [around him] laughed too.

For el-Khatib, Turabi seemed to have lost the moral bearings that had once guided him: 'That was the last meaningful conversation that we had.'

In general, the popular enthusiasm for Turabi's Islamic revolution was, in most respects, strictly limited. For all the Ghost Houses and *jihads*, the revolution was always shallow, even if it was broad. Nor should this be surprising. Turabi's brand of political Islam enjoined its adherents to denounce their enemies and to kill in the name of God, but it was an injunction thoroughly at odds with the traditional Sudanese Sufi strain of Islam, which is much more concerned with values of tolerance and compassion.

This distinction, between Sufism and the modern form of political Islam represented by Turabi, is vital to understanding Sudanese society, and with it the ultimate failure of the country's modern Islamic revolution. The Islamization of Sudan, dating back to the thirteenth century, happened slowly and gradually rather than by conquest, as was more often the case elsewhere. The Sufi orders, or *turuq*, first came to Sudan from the Middle East in the sixteenth century. They became the dominant form of Islam in Sudan, and to a lesser extent in Egypt as well. Indigenous *turuq* such as Majdhubiyah, the Idrisiyah and the Ismailiyah were founded in the Nile Valley. The Khatmiyyah was one such, albeit a much more organized *tariqa*, founded by Mohammed Osman al-Mirghani (1793–1853). The Mirghani family turned the Khatmiyyah into the Democratic Unionist Party (DUP), with its power base in the east.[14]

For a close observer of Sudanese Islam like Jerzy Skuratowicz, the manner in which Sufism slowly and softly spread across the country 400 or so years ago explains much about modern Sudan. Jerzy, a friend of the late Ryszard Kapuscinski, the renowned Polish journalist and writer about Africa, arrived in the new Sudan just after its birth in 1956; his father was the first Polish ambassador to the newly independent country. Jerzy has been coming back to Sudan, mainly with the UN, ever since.

The Islamization of Sudan, he explained to me, was achieved over time by wandering preachers, traders and nomads who lived with the indigenous Sudanese: 'So the Sufi Islam here absorbed a lot of the traditional practice of pre-Islamic Sudanese culture.' In the words of one scholar of Sufism, during this process the northern Sudanese 'exercised their genius for acculturation by moulding the religion of the Prophet to their own tastes rather than to the likes of the theologians. They sang in it, danced in it . . . paganised it a good deal, but always kept the vivid reality of its inherent unity under the rule of one god.'[15]

From the very beginning, Sufism evolved as a reaction against the more severe, legalistic strain of orthodox Islam that predominated in the Middle East. The principal insight of Sufism was that the individual could secure a more personal relationship with God through his own spiritual disciplines, which might often involve singing and dancing. The 'whirling Dervishes', who still perform every Friday afternoon in Omdurman, are a very tangible expression of this Sufi tradition. They work themselves up into a form of ecstatic trance through dancing.

Sufism has always been extremely worrying to orthodox Islamic scholars; some of them think that it cannot be counted as a genuine form of Islam at all. The only reason that it thrived in Sudan was because of the country's geographical isolation from the rest of the Middle East, out of orthodox reach. Yet eventually, home-grown Islamic scholars like Turabi caught up with Sufism, viewing it as a corrupt version of Islam. For the orthodox clergy, *marifa* (divine knowledge) was to be gained by the rigorous study of scripture and tradition rather than the chance outcomes of spiritual experience. Thus, in one sense, the Islamist revolution of the Muslim Brotherhood in 1989 was but another round in a longer struggle between two competing interpretations of Islam.

Nor was it a struggle confined only to Sudan. In Islamic northern Nigeria, for instance, an area with very strong links to north Sudan, the same confrontation was being played out between the traditional Sufi sects of the old caliphate of Sokoto, the Tijaniyya and Qadiriyya, and the younger, more Western-educated adherents of the Izala movement, whose founder Abubakar Gummi had been trained in Khartoum. The Izalas also wanted to return to the stricter interpretations of the prophet, yet combine this with more contemporary values.[16]

Turabi's Islam was a fighting religion, which sought to impose a stricter and more rigid interpretation of the faith on society. Sudanese Sufism, by contrast, is open, liberal (in the sense of accepting other religions and strains of Islam) and non-belligerent. A Sudanese imam explained to me how he saw the difference between his own Sufism (of the Khatmiyyah sect) and the government's brand of political Islam, as I spent the afternoon chatting with him in the eastern city of Kassala. He told me that he only preached on Fridays about 'things that bring people together across religions and within religions'. He wanted, he told me, for people 'to see the good in God, rather than the hatred and punishment of God. I want people to see the mercy and compassion of God.' The imam was as good as his word in his sermons, preaching openly about the need to show sympathy for people with HIV/AIDS, for instance. He also acknowledged the existence of, and talked openly and sympathetically about, prostitutes and homosexuals, often taboo subjects in Muslim countries.

Without using any specific names, he contrasted the 'true scholars' of Islam with the 'false scholars, those who preach without knowledge, using religion for their own glory, to divide people rather than bring people together in the name of God'. These, he told me, are not really 'fundamentalists', as the West likes to call them – 'they are merely ignorant of religion'.

His view of Islam was the majority view of the imams and sheikhs in Sudan, he assured me, and I think that is probably true. Nonetheless, he conceded that the minority had the louder voice in Sudan; he was part of a 'quieter majority'. He quoted me a Sudanese proverb to explain this distinction: 'A hollow drum makes a bigger noise.' Tellingly, the imam asked not to be quoted by name, for fear, still, of being squashed by those bigger noises.

Indeed, the values that the imam was talking about, of compassion, pluralism and tolerance, have always seemed to me to be much more in keeping with the natural gregariousness, curiosity and friendliness of ordinary Sudanese. The indigenous tradition of hospitality, above all, is taken very seriously; a Sudanese, regardless of wealth or poverty, is obliged to help to the utmost a stranger in distress. Any visitor to Sudan can testify to the strength of these values. Famously, for instance, and in total contrast to most Westerners' perceptions of Sudan as a whole, Khartoum remains the safest and most welcoming city in Africa, in harsh contrast to, say, Johannesburg or Nairobi. Khartoum's ease has nothing to do with the fear provoked by the harsh penalties in *sharia* for wrongdoers, as is sometimes argued. Everyone assures me that Khartoum was just as safe and relaxed even before 1989.

Ordinary foreigners in Khartoum have almost never been targeted by Sudanese, even when the government was doing its best to stir up anti-Western passions for political ends. The only serious incident against foreigners occurred when a Palestinian sympathizer lobbed a bomb into the restaurant of the Greek-owned Acropole Hotel in downtown

Khartoum, killing four people. But that happened in 1988, before the NIF came to power.

The many southerners who were forced by the *jihad* to flee their homes for the black belt of Khartoum were always surprised by how welcoming ordinary northern Sudanese were. Ring Kuol lived there during the most fevered days of the Islamic revolution in the early 1990s, and recalls, 'The Khartoumese were not really strong believers. Their heart was not really in it. The people were being manipulated for Islam.' As a vet, his job was to visit the villages in the north to tend to the cattle. He observed that the villagers 'did not have a real belief and . . . they did not really believe in any of [the new Islamic ideology]'.

Indeed, it is a remarkable testimony to the fundamental decency of the Sudanese people that even during the most intense years of Turabi's Islamic revolution, all the old Christian seminaries and churches in the heart of Khartoum carried on their work much as usual. In Nimule, in southern Sudan, I talked to two local Catholic priests, Joseph Mawa and Madramaa Andrew, both from the Madi tribe. I was surprised to learn that they had both travelled from the south to St Paul's seminary in Khartoum to complete their training as priests in 1990, at the most extreme point of Turabi's revolution.

Alarmingly, St Paul's was opposite Kobar prison, then filling up with all the opponents of the regime. Nonetheless, life went on much as usual for the 130 or so seminarians. They lived in the St Paul's compound, but they were expected to go out and eat with, and help, the local population. Neither Joseph nor Madramaa could remember any direct hostility from local people, with whom they mixed very happily throughout the early 1990s. Indeed, their presence tended to reassure people that southerners were not, in fact, 'very dangerous', as they had been led to believe. The two priests sympathized with those forced to go on *jihad* from the parts of the city that they worked in. 'The people who did *jihad* were very poor and they were being paid to do it,' they told me.

Indeed, the only time that the priests could remember any harassment at all was when the government security services were directly involved, especially on Sundays. Sometimes the priests would be followed to their services in the black belt and have their sermons recorded or videotaped. The goons were on the lookout for any occasion when a sermon might veer close to challenging the government's authority. My two priests were careful and nothing ever happened to them. One of their colleagues, however, was not so lucky. Lino Sebit was accused of 'inciting rebellion' and taken off to be tortured by the secret police. Sebit had died only three weeks before my encounter with Joseph and Madramaa, partly as a result of the long-term effects of the beatings he took in the early 1990s. He had lived only to his early forties.

Just as the seminary carried on much as usual, so did the work of the most prestigious educational establishments in the country: the Christian primary and secondary schools. The most important of these are the Catholic Comboni schools. Daniel Comboni was born near Lake Garda in Italy in 1831, and thirty years later started his first missionary journey to Africa. He founded the Comboni congregation in Khartoum in 1881 and eventually died there. The 'Comboni Fathers', as his missionaries came to be known, founded schools throughout the continent, but their work was concentrated in Sudan. Several secondary schools for boys were opened in the Three Towns as well as in El Obeid, Atbara and Port Sudan. A number of schools were also opened in the south, and the Comboni Sisters started one of the first girls' schools in the country.

Remarkably, despite being such a prominent and powerful symbol of Christian, Western influence in Sudan, the Comboni order was scarcely touched by the Islamic revolution. I learned more about how it survived, and even flourished, from Father Luigi Cignolini, a priest and teacher at the huge and very well-scrubbed Comboni School in Port Sudan, founded in the 1950s. He first arrived in the country in the early 1980s, then spent some time away, but later returned to his first love. He explained that throughout the Islamic revolution, the Comboni missionaries had had all the usual difficulties with visas and bureaucracy, but they had never been forced to close any church or school. Indeed, their schools continued to enjoy the legal privileges to which all religious institutions in Sudan were entitled. In Port Sudan, for instance, their school received free water and electricity, as did all mosques and churches. A degree of Arabization was imposed: lessons had to be in Arabic rather than English. But English was still taught, as was the history of Christianity.

Fr Cignolini attributed the survival of the Comboni schools precisely to the 'Sudanese Islam of Sufi'. This is the true *sharia* law, he told me, of 'respecting others. The Sudanese are devout Muslims, but not fundamentalists.' Indeed, Fr Cignolini seemed quite envious of how the local mosque filled up with worshippers, in contrast to his own church. 'You can't help admiring them,' he smiled. In many ways the Comboni schools are an exercise in the best of Sufi Islam in practice. In Port Sudan, 90 per cent of the parents and pupils at the Catholic school are Muslim, the rest a variety of Christians. All classes are taken together, except for religious studies where the pupils are separated – but Christianity and Islam are allotted equal time. It accepts both boys and girls, and although many classes are single sex, some are mixed. When I visited the school in 2009, the head teacher was a Christian from Juba, yet most of the staff were Muslim. After nineteen years of the Islamic revolution it was doing better than ever, with 848 pupils in the secondary school and just over 2,000 in the primary school.

However, the fact that Christian schools prospered under the NIF was not only a tribute to the strength of Sufism. There was a good deal of hypocritical self-interest involved too. The fee-paying Comboni schools were, and remain, among the best schools in Sudan. So, as Father Cignolini cheerfully admitted to me, in Port Sudan 'most of the sons and daughters of the governing elite send their children here'. Yet this was the very same elite that had trashed the public school system by reducing the curriculum, for ideological reasons only, to a narrow and educationally worthless range of government-inspired subjects. Thus, as with the universities, the members of the regime (or at least their children) escaped the adverse consequences of their own disastrous educational policies.

THE DOWNFALL OF TURABI

Just as the Muslim Brotherhood turned against Turabi in the late 1990s, so did the army leadership. Opinion began to build against Turabi's PAIC and al-Qaeda; they were now more trouble than they were worth. In 1996 the Sudanese government changed the visa rules for entering the country so that the PAIC could no longer function as it had, and in May of the same year Osama bin Laden quietly left the country on a private jet bound for Pakistan, after which he returned to Afghanistan.

The reasons for bin Laden's abrupt departure from Sudan are still hazy. The USA, which had only recently come to appreciate his importance, undoubtedly put pressure on the Sudanese to expel him – but the Americans also hotly deny the story that Sudanese intelligence offered him up for what is now called 'extraordinary rendition'. It was probably Turabi who finally persuaded the Saudi to go, warning him that he would no longer be able to operate freely in Sudan as there was now too much hostile interest in him there.[17]

What is certain is that bin Laden left in a hurry, and was forced to liquidate his businesses in double-quick time. The government confiscated his heavy equipment, worth about $12 million. In fact, he was fleeced to the tune of anywhere between $30 million and $160 million. Turabi's regime, bin Laden later recalled ruefully, had turned out to be a 'mixture of religion and organized crime' – rather an accurate description.

Meanwhile, as Turabi's erstwhile supporters grew more and more disillusioned, frustration and anger turned to action. In early 1998 Sayid el-Khatib and sixteen others from the Muslim Brotherhood finally confronted Turabi. El-Khatib spoke for about thirty minutes, as did thirteen more. They all said the same thing: there was now a lack of *shora*, or consultation, in the Brotherhood. Turabi had discarded his previous commitments to democracy and had become increasingly dictatorial. Turabi dismissed it all, and accused them of being an unrepresentative 'clique'. He challenged them to take it to the full *shora* council of the Brotherhood, which, perhaps to his surprise, they did.

The by-laws of the council ruled that for a matter to be discussed, ten people had to propose it. President Bashir was the head of the council. The formerly subservient army officer now definitively broke ranks with Turabi and proposed the motion against his former mentor. According to el-Khatib: 'He was fed up by then . . . there were too many things happening without his knowing.' Bashir, for instance, had been kept in the dark about his own government's role in the attempt on President Mubarak's life. El-Khatib supported the motion, as did Ali Osman Taha and Ghazi Atabani, among others.

The vital council meeting took place in the Friendship Hall, with about 500 people present, on 10 December 1998. El-Khatib read out the motion critical of Turabi, who was not told of it until thirty minutes before the meeting. Debate lasted from ten in the morning until midnight. When the motion was put to a vote, el-Khatib recalls, almost everyone stood up to support it. It was 'gratifyingly scary, and a shock'.

The motion that was approved was, on paper, quite a technical one: to make the leadership of the Muslim Brotherhood more accountable. But symbolically, of course, the vote was a clear repudiation of Turabi's leadership. It was probably his first real reverse since the failed coup of 1976, almost a quarter of a century before. As el-Khatib recalls, Turabi was 'in shock'. He claimed that the action was part of a CIA plot and even asked the Emir of Qatar to intercede on his behalf with Bashir.

There then followed a year-long power tussle between Turabi and Bashir and the latter's new allies in the NIF, which had now been renamed the National Congress Party (NCP). To people like el-Khatib, Turabi became 'vindictive', turning on his former acolytes. He still had power in the rank and file of the movement, and cleverly got himself elected as the chair of a new Leadership Authority at the top of the NCP. From this perch, he threatened to reduce drastically the power of the presidency. This was too much for Bashir. On 12 December 1999, two days before the National Assembly was due to vote on the matter, tanks and troops swarmed around the building to close it down. The national assembly was dissolved and Turabi was sacked as speaker.

A state of emergency was declared. Turabi was banned from all political activity and removed from his post as secretary-general of the NCP. The PAIC was shut down, and Turabi's money that had been funding it was sequestered. When he was arrested in February 2001 for treason, his downfall was complete. Foolishly, he had handed the government an excellent pretext for his arrest by trying to negotiate a deal with the SPLA to come to his rescue. He was put in prison, and then placed under house arrest for the next few years. A quiet purge was conducted of those who had stayed loyal to him in the government and within the security and intelligence services.

I met Turabi for two long interviews in 2006 and 2008. Then in his mid-seventies, he appeared as sprightly, talkative and forward-looking as ever. He still lived in the district of Riyadh, in a sprawling compound just around the corner from the huge Chinese embassy, close to where the bin Ladens used to live. It was very much a family compound; Turabi has had three sons, three daughters and fourteen grandchildren, and four of his children with their families were living on the upstairs floors of the main house when I visited him.

Contrary to his reputation, the once-aggressive Islamist had now become positively eager to meet Westerners. He flaunted his up-to-date knowledge of Western thinking and news, picked up from that day's CNN or BBC reports. It seemed a far cry from the days when he was shunned and isolated as the godfather of al-Qaeda. But then, by the time I met him he had a rather different story to tell about himself.

Trim and wiry in build, intellectually effervescent, he spoke faultless, sometimes colloquial English in an emphatic and often discursive stream of words, punctuated by high-pitched giggles as he complimented himself on another pithy epigram or witticism. Legend has it that in an official encounter with Jimmy Carter, the then US president grew increasingly furious as Turabi just talked over him. His head nodding furiously from side to side, dressed immaculately in his *jellabiya*, Turabi has an almost permanent grin on his face; the whole impression is of brain and body in perpetual motion. He can easily seem eccentric, even batty. The younger, more secular-minded Sudanese, who despair of what Turabi did to their country in his Islamic revolution, joke of going to have 'tea with the fruitcake'.

On the other hand, it is also easy to imagine how Turabi managed to mesmerize several generations of Sudanese students with his fluency of thought and word, laced with a great deal of charm. David Shinn, the deputy ambassador at the US embassy in Khartoum in the mid-1980s, recalled for me the Turabi of that era as being 'a very impressive guy . . . fun to talk with, so articulate and well read. He could tell you that you were all wrong, without really offending you.'

Certainly, he had always been adept at telling people pretty much exactly what they wanted to hear. In my interviews with him, he would dwell on subjects that would present himself in the best light to a Western journalist. But when I raised issues that might embarrass him – such as his association with al-Qaeda, or the brutality of his regime in the 1990s – he would flash his smile, actually wriggle in his seat and change the subject. And then, very occasionally, the genuine rancour would emerge: I would get a lecture about, for instance, the USA as the 'incarnation of the devil'. If Sudan has presented an almost schizo-phrenic confusion of identities and orientations to the outside world, poised between modernity and mediaevalism, between liberalism and barbarity, these were the confusions and contradictions of Dr Turabi. He died in 2016, aged eighty-four, of a heart attack. He attracted a loyal following right to the end: about 170,000 mourners attended his funeral.

BASHIR'S GOVERNMENT – THE GAP BETWEEN RELIGION AND THE STATE

So the Islamic revolution in Sudan had split, partly over the warped ambitions of one man. But it was also clear that the revolution had never won over the hearts and minds of ordinary Sudanese anyway – Sufism had proved too resistant. There was now a clear divide between those who would consider themselves to be pragmatic Islamists, and those, a much smaller minority, who would stay loyal to Turabi and the vision of his revolution. The latter group founded the

Popular Congress Party, with Turabi as its leader, in June 2000. The pragmatists, most of whom stayed on in President Bashir's government, were left to pick up the pieces of the Turabi decade. Above all, they wanted to end Sudan's diplomatic isolation, end the draining and apparently futile war with the south (as well as the insurgency in the east), and repair the economy.

It took some time for the character of the new Turabi-less government to emerge. Shorn of its erratic ideologues, the new government dedicated itself to nothing more noble than clinging to power. Dousing the flames of the Turabi years occupied much of their time, as did simply staying in office. One US diplomat described the modus operandi of Bashir's regime to me as 'brutal pragmatism'; it is a good description. The ruling clique of the NCP seemed ready to work with anyone from any party who would help them shore up their positions. Money was usually on offer, as were token positions in power – a vice-presidency here, a special advisership to the presidency there. Political alignments became comparatively fluid, at least in the north.

The ousting of Turabi also meant that President Omar al-Bashir could now finally slip the strings of the puppet master. More and more, the government bore his own personal stamp. Born in 1944 in the village of Hosh Bannaga in the far north of Sudan, Bashir was by training and temperament a military officer. He had distinguished himself in combat during the 1973 Israeli–Arab war, fighting alongside the Egyptians in the Sinai. He was thus a very different kind of man from those disputatious, highly educated and cosmopolitan politicians reared by Turabi, many of whom still filled the top ranks of the NCP in the 2000s after the fall of their mentor. Indeed, Bashir became adept at playing the role of the earthy populist against his subordinates' more low-key and cerebral approach. He has married twice, the second time to the widow of a fellow officer who was killed in a plane crash, but has no children.

The US diplomat who called the new system 'brutal pragmatism' was also prone to compare Bashir to Ronald Reagan in their styles of government. Both, he argued, were broad brush, big-vision politicians, most at ease on the streets or at rallies with their 'constituents', happy to leave

President Bashir waves his cane

the detail (and indeed much of the hard work) to their underlings. The comparison is a bit far-fetched (my interlocutor was no admirer of Republicans), but works up to a point. One of Bashir's hallmarks is the stick that he wields at public meetings; it is a traditional symbol of authority in Sudan among the tribal chieftains, and helps him to identify with people beyond his base in the rarefied world of the Muslim Brotherhood.

One of the main consequences of the new pragmatism was a modest withering of the Islamic revolution. This was a welcome development to younger Sudanese in particular. The religious police became less active. President Bashir had no specific strategic or political vision to replace the Islamist revolution, and instead some of the old patterns and traditions of Sudanese life became more evident again, emerging in the space opened up by a less ideological government.

Take the role of women, for instance. The country had long taken a lead in the Muslim world in asserting women's rights, partly a consequence, again, of the Sufi tradition. For example, Sudan had established one of the very earliest Muslim private schools for girls, in 1905, which later became the Afhad University for Women, among the first such institutions of its kind in the Muslim world. It was founded in Omdurman, despite this being the most traditional of the Three Towns, and the university continues to thrive there to this day.

The Sudanese Women's Union, affiliated to the Communist Party, was founded in 1951 and grew to become one of the largest and most effective lobby groups for women's rights in Africa. Its president, the celebrated Sudanese feminist Fatima Ibrahim, was the first woman elected to the Sudanese parliament, in 1965, the year that women won the right to vote and hold office.[18] During the following two decades or so, women continued to make great strides in occupying public offices and posts, at least in the Three Towns, more so than in most other Arab countries. Sudan appointed the first women justices in the *sharia* court legal system.

But the 1989 Islamist coup brought these advances to an abrupt halt. Mahmoud Taha of the Republican Brothers, himself a great advocate of women's rights, warned that the triumph of political Islam would set back the cause of women in Sudanese society, and he was right. For years Hassan al-Turabi had himself espoused women's rights, and a few women had been among the leaders of his own Islamist party, the NIF. Indeed, after the elections of 1986, the only two female MPs were from the NIF. But in apparent contradiction of almost everything that Turabi had preached in the past, women were particularly discriminated against under the new *sharia* laws after 1989.

Strict dress codes were now applied by the religious police and violators in 'immodest dress' could be flogged. Women were forced to wear the *hijab* if they worked in government offices or participated in any government-sponsored activity, like the PDF. As a sign of extreme piety, some women now wore the *khimar* or even occasionally the *burka*, the strictest possible interpretation of the veil.

Deploying 'cultural' arguments, President Bashir himself opined that the ideal Sudanese woman's place was now in the home, taking care of her children, her reputation and her husband. Thousands of women were arbitrarily sacked from their jobs, particularly if they were members of opposition parties. To give but one instance: by the mid-1980s 25 per cent of Sudan's diplomats were women, a very high figure for an Arab (or even Western) country. By 1993, there was none left.[19]

Many other restrictions discriminating against women were introduced. According to the new Public Order Acts of 1992 and 1996, the mixing of men and women in all sports activities was prohibited. The pioneering Sudanese Women's Union was closed down; Fatima Ibrahim was forced into exile in London. Men, however, fared rather better under the new Islamic laws. A 1991 law reiterated the right of men to polygamous marriage, allowing them to marry up to four wives, and also to divorce them at will.[20]

Yet, as in other aspects of Sudanese life, the revolution's adverse impact on women had its limits, and proved to be at least partly reversible. So strong was the existing institutional framework of women's participation in Sudanese life that they continued to go out and find jobs, even if their pious husbands did not want them to or the imams disapproved. Indeed, women found some innovative roles within the new Islamic society. Women preachers, for instance, began to appear, even in the more conservative regions of the country such as the east.

From the mid-2000s, the regime became more pragmatic. Women began to come back into the professions, as doctors, health workers, lawyers, civil servants and even police, although to a much lesser extent than before. New women's groups emerged, campaigning openly for changes in those parts of the penal code that were obviously discriminatory. The religious police were also forced to be less intrusive. In return, most women respected the outward forms of piety in dress and manners – up to a point.

Some younger women, on the other hand, especially after the mid-2000s, often rebelled against the conservative dress codes and morality of their parents. These girls are derisively called *banat almuda* –

'fashion girls' – by their scandalized peers. They subvert the dress code of the Islamic revolution by wearing the most brightly coloured head-scarves over the tightest, longest skirts (or even trousers or jeans) that they can find. A good spot to find the fashion girls in full flow is on the lower slopes of the Jebel Totil, the spectacular hill overlooking Kassala in the east. Here, at sundown, hundreds of young Sudanese gather in the open-air coffee-houses to look for a partner, even a husband, or to celebrate their marriage: it is a traditional rendezvous point for newly-weds. A lot of coffee is drunk and flirtatious glances exchanged. In this hormone-charged bazaar, the fashion girls will pose and strut for the cameras, little different from their Western peers.

In the hands of the fashion girls, a dress code that was specifically designed not to attract attention has thus been converted to capture as much attention as possible. In Khartoum, underneath the traditionally demure dresses that they wear in public, girls going to university or to parties will often (I am told) wear something much more revealing. One speciality is a small top that reveals the midriff; a space that is known, roughly translated, as 'the gap between religion and the state'.

For young men, meanwhile, the 2000s also saw a certain relaxation in the moral code. Indeed, certainly in terms of their vices, younger men seemed to rejoin the rest of Africa. In 2009, I spent a morning in New Halfa, in the eastern state of Gedaref, talking to the local police commissioner Colonel Amin Said Mohammed. He told me that by far the biggest problem he had to contend with was 'people who are drunk doing harm to others'. He had twenty-five to thirty cases a week, in a local population of no more than 200,000. Despite the *sharia* prohibition on alcohol, the boys got tanked up on a home-grown moonshine made out of dates, the commissioner told me, brewed for them by the women. This concoction was very cheap and easily available. With so little employment, and much of it seasonal in the rural areas, 'most of the year the youth have nothing else to do'. Locally grown cannabis was also a problem, the commissioner revealed, so the police were now running a drugs-awareness programme to educate people about the damaging effects of both cannabis and heroin.

EASIER AT HOME, EASIER ABROAD?

Just as the new post-Turabi regime eased off on its own citizens a little, so another benefit of the new pragmatism was that the government looked to end its isolation abroad, if only to reduce the dizzying number of international enemies that Turabi's regime had collected by the turn of the millennium. However, this was not to be as easy as some had imagined. For a more immediate legacy of Turabi's rule was that he had pricked the collective conscience of what had formerly been Sudan's closest ally, now the world's sole surviving superpower – the USA. During the 1990s, 'abroad' had come to form some very strong opinions about Sudan.

CHAPTER FOUR

SUDAN AND THE WEST: SLAVERY, CONSCIENCE AND AL-QAEDA

Like most others in the West and the Middle East, US diplomats had been confused at first as to the exact nature of the regime that took over in Khartoum in June 1989. Numeiri, in the second half of his presidency, had been a good friend to the USA, and, in return, by the mid-1980s Sudan had become the biggest recipient of US aid in sub-Saharan Africa. The relationship had even bumbled along without much change under Sadiq al-Mahdi. The coup of 1989 obviously marked a rupture – but how serious a rupture?

Over the next few years, as we saw in the last chapter, the truth about the nature of the new Islamist government in Khartoum emerged. Sudan actively promoted itself as a state sponsor of terror, much of it directed specifically against the USA and its closest allies, such as Egypt. Thus the previously close US–Sudanese partnership degenerated into what Charles Snyder, the man in charge of Sudan at the State Department under President George W. Bush, later described for me as a 'Cold War relationship'.

The CIA maintained a significant presence in Khartoum in the early 1990s, as the Sudanese capital was an excellent location from which to observe and monitor the contemporary terrorist threat from Islamist radicals. The CIA station chief between 1993 and 1995 was a career intelligence officer called Cofer Black; he and his team spent long hours keeping track of all those who gathered in Khartoum for Turabi's Popular Arabic and Islamic Congresses. The threat that these groups posed to the US became much clearer when Black's team uncovered a plot to kill or kidnap their boss. The would-be assassins were probably bin Laden's *mujahideen* who had detected the CIA surveillance.[1] The danger from Sudan seemed to be even more clear and present when the National Security Adviser in the Clinton administration, Tony Lake, received death threats from one of the terrorist groups now based in Khartoum, although in the end it turned out to be a false alarm. In response, the USA's once-formidable presence in Sudan was gradually scaled back for security reasons. The number of staff at the embassy was reduced and dependents were evacuated.[2] In 1996, as al-Qaeda training camps sprang up in the desert around Khartoum, all the remaining embassy officials left for their own safety. A full ambassador has yet to return, and US interests were still being presided over by a mere chargé d'affaires at the time of writing in 2010.

All in all, it was clear by the mid-1990s that Sudan had become a very serious problem. Not only did it appear that the Islamist regime was waging what some now called a 'genocidal' war against the southern Christians, but Islamic *jihadists* from Sudan were turning up all over Africa and beyond: in Ethiopia, Eritrea, Lebanon, Somalia and Kenya. The country had become a serious menace to regional security. Moreover, the intimate connections between the Sudanese government and al-Qaeda were beginning to emerge. The trials of the 1993 World Trade Center bombers revealed a little, and the investigations into the bombings of the US Embassies in Nairobi and Dar es Salaam in 1998 even more. Reviewing the evidence from these atrocities, it was clear to the US authorities that members of the Sudanese regime had been heavily involved. Khartoum's fake passport operation, which had helped bin Laden, was exposed, as were other links that convinced the Clinton administration that the Sudanese government was involved directly in terrorism. Although the true threat of bin Laden's network went unappreciated at the time, as we have seen the USA did exert pressure on the Sudanese government to expel him from Sudan, which they effectively did in 1996.

The obvious security threat as well as the mounting anger in Congress over Khartoum's war in the south meant that the few meagre attempts in 1990–91 at constructive engagement with Turabi's government were abandoned, to be replaced by an attitude of outright hostility. Stephen Morrison, then the head of the Africa section of Madeleine Albright's policy planning shop at the State Department, described the new policy to me as a mix of 'containment, aggression and regime change'. Sudan's former role as a Cold War bulwark against Marxist Ethiopia in the 1980s was over. In a neat reverse, the neighbours were now all enlisted as 'frontline states' by the USA in a new strategy *against* Sudan. The new alliance reflected the political changes in the neighbouring states in the USA's favour: Ethiopia was now led by the new president Meles Zenawi, Eritrea by Issayas Afewerki and Uganda by Yoweri Museveni. Their job was, in Morrison's words, to 'take the Sudan government down'.

The 'covert' side of this strategy involved funding these frontline states to hem Sudan in, while also helping the southern rebels. John Garang and the SPLA had previously been cold-shouldered by Washington because of their close links with Marxist Ethiopia, but once Mengistu had been ousted and replaced by Zenawi, relations became very close. 'Non-lethal help' was given to the southern guerrillas, according to Morrison. This included the considerable boost of providing C-130 transport planes to help the SPLA get around what was a massive southern battlefield. The National Security Council received about US$20–30 million to pay for the general strategy against Sudan, including the covert operations. However, as Morrison admits today, it was all 'quite amateurish . . . We never enlisted the support of the Pentagon or had a large covert budget.' The 'frontline state' strategy fell to pieces anyway when Eritrea and Ethiopia went to war with each other in 1998 over a disputed border, ending any hope of coherent regional pressure against the regime in Khartoum.

There was one very overt show of force against Sudan, though. This was the firing of thirteen US cruise missiles into the Shifa chemical factory in 1998 in direct response to the Sudanese government's involvement in the US embassy bombings. As it turned out, the Americans had picked the wrong target. But the attack nonetheless demonstrated Sudan's extreme vulnerability to attack, and brought home very physically to members of its government how regime change might start. It was an excellent demonstration of the big stick, and certainly stayed in the minds of Sudan's politicians.

A CONSTITUENCY OF CONSCIENCE

Quite apart from the disintegration of Sudan's once close official relationship with the USA because of terrorism, the bloody and brutal civil war between north and south Sudan also began to attract the passionate interest of a small group of human-rights activists, mainly from the US.

It was principally the use of slavery by the Arab militias that now rallied opinion against the north Sudanese government. Back in General Gordon's time, the slave trade might have been morally repugnant to the British, but its existence in parts of the world like Sudan was hardly a revelation. For Western liberal democrats of the late twentieth century, however, to discover that slavery continued in Sudan – until recently a close ally of the USA – was surprising and truly shocking. The discovery attracted an unusually diverse coalition of men and women against the Islamist regime in Khartoum, who were to exercise an enormous influence on the USA's official relations with Sudan thereafter. Above all, they succeeded in elevating Sudan, hitherto an obscure bit of sand somewhere in east Africa, into a hot domestic issue.

This part of the story begins with John Eibner of Christian Solidarity International (CSI), a Swiss-based evangelical church organization. A softly spoken man, the grandson of Hungarian immigrants, Eibner was born and raised in upstate New York but has lived most of his adult life in Britain; he married a Briton after graduate school in the UK. A

Baptist by faith, Eibner was first drawn to Sudan by the plight of the Christian churches in the south. CSI, described by Eibner himself as the 'Christian Amnesty International', was set up in the 1970s to campaign for Christians in prison or suffering abuse or torture. In that era, CSI's services were primarily in demand in Latin America. But in 1992 Eibner read of an appeal for help by the New Sudan Council of Churches (NSCC) a freshly formed organization that claimed to represent all the Christian denominations of southern Sudan. The NSCC warned that Christians in the south were under imminent threat from the *jihad* that had just been declared against them by the National Islamic Front (NIF) in Khartoum. It was the start of the onslaught by the brainwashed teenagers of the Popular Defence Forces.

Eibner, together with a British CSI campaigner and member of the House of Lords, Caroline, Baroness Cox, set out to see for themselves how real this threat to the southern Sudanese actually was. Cox had originally trained as a nurse but later became an academic. By the early 1990s, however, her main interest was in human rights. Ennobled by Prime Minister Margaret Thatcher, with whom she was often compared, Cox was also a devout Christian; hence her work for CSI at the time she became involved in Sudan. Together, Eibner and Cox were to form a fearless and intrepid partnership.

The link between the churches of southern Sudan and Christians of all denominations worldwide was to play a vital role in the Sudan story from now on. After 1956, even during the worst days of the civil war with the north, a strong Christian church presence had survived. Thus priests and bishops were usually the best placed to keep the outside world, and particularly their fellow congregations, informed of the worsening situation in the south. Gradually, their fellow churchmen and women in the West responded.

On their first trip to Sudan in 1992, it was immediately clear to Eibner and Cox that there were some dreadful atrocities being carried out in the south. Furthermore, as Eibner recalls, 'there was almost nobody there' to report on it. Operation Lifeline Sudan, a food-supply chain run by Western aid workers from Kenya into Juba, provided some connection with the outside world. But the Operation Lifeline people could only work within geographical restrictions set by the Khartoum government. Eibner and Cox, however, flew to more remote districts and heard the terrible stories of what seemed to be an organized campaign of ethnic cleansing.

Particularly striking was the testimony of Makram Max, Bishop of El Obeid, the capital of Kordofan. By that time he was in exile, but he told Cox and Eibner about the massacres in the Nuba Mountains in 1992 by Arab mounted raiding parties – a continuation of the aggression that had been going on since the mid-1980s. It was also clear that the Arab militias had abducted people to be enslaved in the north. Slaving was most common in the border area between the Muslim north and the Christian south – in Kordofan and Bahr al-Ghazal. Eibner and Cox were to focus most of their campaigning efforts on the latter area.

To a degree, the revival of slaving in the 1980s in Sudan was a particularly barbaric aspect of the Sudanese government's counter-insurgency strategy to defeat the southern rebels. Slaving was employed as a policy of terror against the southerners by the Arab militias, the so-called *murahileen*. The Arab raiding parties would destroy whole villages, killing many of the men, before abducting the women and children. The Nuba or Dinka captives would often be raped and the children reared as Muslims. The slaving campaigns increased in intensity in the Turabi years of the early 1990s, when Eibner and Cox first arrived in Sudan. Outwardly respectable middle-class families in Khartoum were supporting their comfortable lifestyles on the forced labour of twelve-year-old girls.

Slaving was not only directed against southern Christians. Arab raiding parties also attacked what they regarded as 'African' Muslims, in a precursor of the later conflict in Darfur. A particularly detailed and graphic account of enslavement has been given by a Nuba woman, Mende Nazer. Her awful experiences were recounted to a British journalist, Damien Lewis, and published in their book *Slave*. Taken from her village in the Nuba Mountains south of Kordofan by a mounted raiding party sometime in the mid-1980s, aged twelve, Mende was forced to work for years for a well-off Arab family in Khartoum. Constantly beaten and racially abused in the capital, she was then sent to work for a relation of the family in London, a diplomat in the Sudanese embassy. By then in her late teens, she eventually managed to escape and gained asylum in Britain. As a Muslim herself, Mende could not understand how another Muslim, her mistress, could mistreat her so; but her crime in the eyes of her abductors was to be African, rather than Arab. In the eyes of her owners this made her, as she was often reminded, little better than a dog.

In 1995, Eibner and Cox managed to travel to the village of Nyamlell in northern Bahr al-Ghazal just after a massive slaving raid, despite government attempts to prevent anyone getting there. Eibner remembers: 'The whole place had been burnt down and everyone was wandering around like zombies.' Eibner and Cox managed to speak to the wounded victims of the raid as well as some young girls and boys who had been taken as slaves to the north, but who had escaped and returned. In their report for CSI, Cox and Eibner wrote up one of the first detailed accounts of slaving as a weapon of counter-insurgency. Part of it was based on the eyewitness account given to them of the attack on Nyamlell by the Civil Commissioner of Awiel West Country, Akechak Jok:

The most recent raid took place on the morning of March 25. About 3,000 Arab tribesmen and soldiers arrived with no warning. They burnt most of Nyamlell's *tukuls* [huts] and destroyed the brick structures, including the church. All the stores of the German NGO, Agro-Action, were looted. Eighty men and two women were murdered. 282 were enslaved, among them forty-eight children. The hands of the captives were tied behind their backs and they were marched northwards. Some of the children have been sold off at the markets in Meiram and Daien. Others have been brought to the cattle market at Manyeil, eight miles to the west. Arabs and Dinkas go there to trade. There is one Arab trader who regularly turns up at this market with local children for sale. Some families have been able to buy back their children here. Some of the slaves have escaped and returned home . . . The slaves are usually forced to perform agricultural and domestic labour. All they receive from their masters is shelter and enough food for survival. When children are abducted they are often forced to become Muslims. Many women and children are sexually abused. It is not unusual for women to become the concubines of their masters.

A fifteen-year-old girl called Aguawai Akot told Eibner and Cox how she had been enslaved from the age of seven:

I was alone at home when the raiders captured me. A man called Abmadam became my master. I lived with his family in a village called Nyichol in Darfur. I was given only millet and milk for survival. When Abmadam was angry, he would beat me with a stick all over the body and call me ugly names. He gave me a Muslim name, Awah. I had no choice but to observe Muslim rituals. I was treated like a dog and was called slave. They made me work seven days a week. I never had a free day. My two brothers came to find me, but the Arabs shot dead the older one. My younger brother had to go back without me. My mother died while I was with Abmadan. Abmadan had many offers to buy me, but he refused them all until last month. He took me to the cattle market at Manyeil. Other children were taken there and sold back to their parents but I had no family left. But a man named Butrous Bol Bol saw me and could tell I was a local Dinka. He had to pay one [Kalashnikov] rifle and a cow to set me free.

From 1995 on, Eibner and Cox felt that they had to focus on the issue of slavery, particularly, as Eibner told me, because 'people knew what was going on, but nobody wanted to talk about it'. Western diplomats and others in Sudan were vaguely aware of the slave raids, but seemed reluctant to take any action.

Even as early 1992, after his first visit to southern Sudan, Eibner was convinced that the slave raids were all part of a wider strategy to undermine and displace those communities that Khartoum thought were harbouring SPLA rebels. For Eibner, in effect this amounted to a 'genocide', a term he used to describe the *murahileen* raids in the south in an article for the *Wall Street Journal Europe* in October 1992. It was the first time, as far as I can tell, that anyone had used the word in relation to events in Sudan.

CSI devoted considerable time and thought to publicizing the issue, regularly getting journalists into southern Sudan to report both on slavery and on the more general incidents of ethnic cleansing. Controversially, Eibner pioneered 'buy-back' schemes, whereby sympathetic southerners would travel to Khartoum and elsewhere to buy slaves back for their families, sometimes for as little as $33. Some, however, argued that this merely created a fresh market for slaves, incentivizing raiders to go out and capture still more.

John Eibner buys back slaves

The persistence of slaving in Sudan shocked everyone, but it was particularly disturbing to black Americans, themselves the descendants of slaves. As the news of the existence of slavery in Sudan spread, John Eibner found himself returning to southern Sudan time and again with an increasingly heavyweight array of black American journalists, activists, preachers and politicians, mostly with a background in the US civil rights movement. One particularly effective campaigner for CSI was Joe Madison, a prominent talk-show host. On his second CSI trip to southern Sudan, Madison took along with him the Reverend Walter Fauntroy, who had once been a close associate of Martin Luther King. The Reverend Al Sharpton was another big name flown out by the organization.

The black churchmen and activists were followed by the politicians who made up the 'black caucus' on Capitol Hill in Washington DC. Donald Payne, first elected as a Democratic congressman for New Jersey in 1988, was both a Christian (a Baptist) and a radical black politician, schooled in the protest politics of the 1960s. He called Sudanese slavery 'a stain on modern times', and started gathering political support in Washington for the southern Sudanese rebels and in particular for John Garang. Payne became the leader of the black caucus in Congress on all matters relating to southern Sudan, and later Darfur. Eibner helped Payne by arranging for visits to southern Sudan for other Democrats, such as Tom Lantos.

Payne later told me that at first it was difficult to interest people in southern Sudan, let alone provoke much of a reaction. In Payne's view, attitudes in the USA had hardened against any official involvement in Africa (such as Rwanda in 1994) after the US intervention in Somalia in 1992–3: 'US soldiers were killed by black soldiers in Africa . . . This had a lot to do with it. There is still a lot of racism in the world. It all changed after Somalia . . . There was a reluctance to go in anywhere.'

Ironically, however, all this began to change with the 'Gingrich revolution' of 1994, when the Republicans swept to majorities in the House and the Senate after two years of a faltering Clinton presidency. In theory, perhaps, the arrival of the abrasive Gingrich's new conservative army on Capitol Hill might have been expected to kill off a nascent Democrat-led congressional campaign based on human rights in a far-off country about which most people knew nothing and cared even less. In practice, however, the very opposite turned out to be the case.

For as well as being a black radical issue, slavery in southern Sudan and the persecution of the Christian churches also became a key issue for Republican-voting white Christian evangelicals. John Eibner had started off his human-rights career by campaigning for Christian liberty and freedom of conscience behind the Iron Curtain in the Soviet bloc – a big cause for conservatives and Reaganites in the 1970s and 1980s. For Eibner, who got to know many of them, the new generation of Republican congressmen and senators who entered office in the mid-1990s also 'wanted a human-rights agenda, and needed somewhere else now that the USSR had collapsed'. Southern Sudan fitted the bill. To Eibner, they wanted to show that 'Republicans cared about Africa and human rights'. In the late 1990s a Republican political strategist, Karl Rove, would parlay this general theme into a campaigning phrase, 'compassionate conservatism', for a new and at first unlikely Republican presidential candidate, George W. Bush. Among evangelical Republicans this strand of activism was also known as the 'Wilberforce agenda', in honour of the British parliamentarian who had played a large role in the abolition of the slave trade at the beginning of the nineteenth century.

These new, younger Republicans were mainly motivated by their faith. They were drawn to southern Sudan as much by the more general defence of Christianity against Muslim aggression as by the single issue of slavery. Take Andrew Natsios, for instance, who first took an interest in Sudan in 1989 as the director of emergency disaster relief for the overseas relief agency USAID. He was also a committed member of the United Church of Christ, and would be President Bush's choice to head up the whole of USAID in March 2001, after which he became Bush's special envoy to Sudan. As he recalled for me in 2008, even in 1989 the 'atrocities in the south [of Sudan] were so egregious' that it was almost impossible not to get involved. Natsios remembered the first cable that landed on his desk as the new director of USAID's disaster recovery programme in 1989. It simply said the 'Arabs had crucified Dinka' – literally.

Natsios, like many other influential US churchmen and politicians, got to know the southern rebel leader John Garang and his deputy Salva Kiir well. Natsios was impressed by their insistence that the war in the south had become what Garang described as a 'cultural' war; Christianity thus became, in Garang's words, a means to 'build a cultural wall against Islamization'. These arguments resonated powerfully in the church/political circles of the 'Bible Belt' of the USA in the late 1980s and 1990s; Billy Graham, the most famous tele-evangelist of the era, became a frequent visitor to southern Sudan. His son Franklin Graham was even more committed, using his NGO Samaritan's Purse to set up and supply rudimentary hospitals in the south.

These men also had impressive political connections at the top of the Republican Party. One of the most important of these was Bill Frist, the leader of the Senate majority in the middle years of George W. Bush's presidency and a one-time Republican presidential hopeful himself. A surgeon by profession and also a Christian evangelical, Frist did pro-bono medical work for Samaritan's Purse in southern Sudan during his holidays. But the senator who became the most influential voice on Sudan during the Bush era was Sam Brownback of Kansas. Born and bred in the state, which had its own significant history of slavery and emancipation within the Union, Brownback was a prime mover in raising the consciousness of Republicans on Sudan, together with Congressman Frank Wolf from Virginia. There were even hearings in Congress on slavery in southern Sudan chaired by Jesse Helms, the most right-wing of Republicans, but also, again, an evangelical Christian.

Brownback and Wolf were important in reaching out across party lines on Sudan; they were early builders of the unique political alliance that later become the SaveDarfurCoalition. Thus, in an extraordinary moment of cross-party co-operation, the white, conservative, southern Republican Brownback joined the black, radical Democrat Payne for a trip together to southern Sudan in 1998, along with another very active Republican congressman, Tom Tancredo. Quite possibly, men like Brownback and Payne would have found it almost impossible to agree on anything except Sudan.

With this strong bipartisan political encouragement, during the late 1990s Congress passed legislation to direct a massive $1.2 billion towards the south in humanitarian aid, mainly through Operation Lifeline Sudan. Technically, to get the permission of the northern government to fly anything in at all, the aid was supposed to be made available to all the Sudanese, not just the southerners. But most of it, particularly the grain, vegetable oil and beans dropped by the World Food Programme (WFP), went to the south. In fact, according to one source, a leaked internal WFP report acknowledged that 80 per cent of it went direct to the SPLA, to keep the peasant army going.

The gathering interest in Sudan on the right and left of politics in the USA stood, however, in increasingly abject contrast to the continuing lack of interest in the subject in Britain and the rest of Europe. Caroline Cox took every opportunity offered by her privileged position to ask questions in the House of Lords, the upper house of Britain's Houses of Parliament, and to make speeches about the persecutions and killings in southern Sudan. But, as she is the first to admit, she had little effect. Why?

For a start, the issue of slavery had a resonance in the USA that it did not have elsewhere. But the differing levels of interest on the two sides of the Atlantic also reflected divergent attitudes towards religion. The Christian dimension of Cox's and Eibner's campaigning attracted overtly religious Americans in direct proportion to the numbers of secular British and Europeans who were put off by it.

Cox also came up sharply against what she regarded as the innate bias of British officialdom in favour of the northern Sudanese Arabs. She felt that she received only superficial sympathy for her campaign on behalf of the southern Sudanese because of the wider and historic 'Arabist' sympathies of the British Foreign Office, again in complete contrast to US attitudes.

Another good reason for the comparative lack of attention that British and European governments, politicians and journalists paid to southern Sudan in the 1990s is that they were absorbed by war crimes nearer to home, in the former Yugoslavia. The political classes were focused on events in Bosnia and then Kosovo, wrangling over whether to intervene militarily in a region that was very much within the boundaries of Europe itself. There was little sympathy or political resolve left over for a seemingly intractable conflict in Africa.

NEW APPROACHES: MAKING PEACE WITH THE SOUTH AND THE BIN LADEN FILE

If, during the 1990s, Turabi's Sudan and Clinton's USA had became blood enemies, so by the end of the decade both sides were ready for a change of course. In Sudan, there was internal regime change when Turabi was thrown out of power and imprisoned. Close Sudan-watchers in the USA like Stephen Morrison saw this as a 'key moment'. His argument was that the USA now had an opportunity to 'engage and test' the new regime. Furthermore, with the collapse of the regional frontline strategy, the USA had few options left but to re-engage with Khartoum. As Morrison put it in a paper for the Center for Strategic and International Studies in February 2001, shortly after he left government:

> Ultimately, however, US policy [of the late Clinton years] did not significantly weaken Khartoum, strengthen southern and northern opposition, moderate the conduct of Sudan's war, enhance humanitarian access and deliveries, or promote a process of genuine peace negotiations. Instead . . . as neighbouring states and European Union member states steadily normalized relations with Khartoum, the United States found itself in conspicuous self-isolation with effectively no partners.

The new Sudanese government after Turabi was also interested in ending its isolation. Most importantly, it wanted to normalize relations with the USA. Other countries, such as Britain, had maintained a policy of what could be called pragmatic engagement with Khartoum throughout the USA's cold war against the regime there. But European countries were not considered much of a prize – the superpower still mattered as no other country did. The northern Sudanese ruling class had always seen themselves as cosmopolitan players, and isolation from the USA, where many had been educated, was very wounding. Economic sanctions hurt, and the USA also ensured that Sudan was cut off from the international finance system through its influence over the IMF and the World Bank. Many northern Sudanese were also exhausted and frustrated by the endless years of war with the south and were therefore anxious to end the conflict – something they hoped the USA could help them achieve.

There was thus plenty for the two sides to talk about at the onset of the new millennium. Furthermore, in exchange for favours from the West, the Sudanese knew that they had something to give that the USA would prize above all else – the inside brief on all the *jihadist* groups that had made Sudan their home in the 1990s. Some have argued that, to this end, the Sudanese government was offering the Americans a few gems from its files as early as 1997–8. Either way, it was time for the Clinton administration, even in its dying days, to 'test' Khartoum's new government.

A team from Washington therefore flew out to Khartoum in March 2000. Significantly, it was entirely a defence- and security-orientated group, from the CIA, the Pentagon and the State Department. From now on US governments were mainly to see the government of Khartoum through the prism of international terrorism. This was not unreasonable, given Sudan's turbulent and violent history since 1989, but it had important consequences for the later conflict in Darfur.

However, by 2000, along with the renewed interest in Sudan on intelligence and security matters at an official level, American policymakers now also had to take account of the new 'constituency of conscience' that had built up over slavery and ethnic cleansing in the south. Sudan was no longer just an inner beltway subject; there was a broader and very powerful political coalition pressing the White House to take action on Sudan, with a very different agenda from that of the spooks and professional diplomats. In January 2001 the loose arrangements and connections between Democrats and Republicans on Capitol Hill over Sudan were formalized when Senators from all sides joined hands to support the Sudan Peace Act, sponsored by Tom Tancredo. This bill denounced the Sudanese government's war in southern Sudan and the tactics that it employed there, including what were referred to as 'acts of genocide'. The legislation called for the full engagement of the US government in ending the north–south war and an inquiry into war crimes. For the first time this meant that there was now serious pressure from the world's superpower to end the long, brutal and almost forgotten war in southern Sudan. Turabi's *jihad* had provoked the strongest of responses.

The USA's legislative branch had done its bit. The onus was now on the new occupant of the White House, the head of the executive branch and the principal beneficiary of the Gingrich revolution in US politics: President George W. Bush. The new president, however, needed little prodding on Sudan. Bush might have entered office with an almost boundless ignorance of the world beyond the USA, but the one place he did know something about was Sudan. His father had been involved in two crucial events in Sudan as vice-president: the famine of 1984–5 and the evacuation of the Falasha Jews out of Ethiopia. The new president was also deeply influenced by the Republican evangelical lobby that had coalesced around slavery and southern Sudan. Franklin Graham was a crucial conduit between the lobby and Bush, together with a Texan evangelical called Deborah Fikes. As Karl Rove, Bush's political brain, conceived it, the Christian evangelical movement was crucial to Bush's chances of succeeding Clinton in the White House. So what mattered to the Christian right – Sudan – mattered a lot to Rove and Bush. There are, after all, probably as many as 100 million evangelicals in the USA (out of a population of just over 300 million), representing a huge slice of the country's voters. Sam Brownback recalled that for the new president, the issue of

Sudan thus 'fit perfectly . . . because we had matured the issue to a point where it was ready for a president to grab it . . . it was perfect timing for Bush to grab it.'

Michael Gerson, who became the head of Bush's speechwriting team in 2001, shared Bush's faith background and saw one of his principal jobs as reflecting the evangelical movement's 'tradition of social engagement in the White House'. Gerson thus became the president's eyes and ears on the Sudan issue throughout the Bush presidency. He also wrote Bush's notorious State of the Union address in 2002, in which he described Iran, Iraq and North Korea as an 'Axis of Evil'.

Gerson observed how Bush, conscious of the debt that he owed the evangelicals in an extremely tight contest with the Democrat Al Gore, began to pay them back as soon as he entered the White House. In interviews with me, Gerson and Andrew Natsios agreed that Bush's very first order to his new National Security Council (NSC) was to re-examine and reinvigorate the USA's Sudan policy. The National Association of Evangelicals swiftly presented a list of very specific concerns and recommendations for action and legislation to the new president, with Sudan pretty much top of the list. They pushed for presidential support of the Sudan Peace Act and asked for an international commission on religious freedom, to expose and publicize the persecution of Christians and others in Sudan and elsewhere. They also asked for sanctions against a Canadian oil company, Talisman, part of the Sudanese government's consortium to exploit the country's oil reserves. Already in 2001, such companies were thought to be unduly propping up the Sudanese government's war machine.

The evangelicals got much of what they asked for, and quickly. Bush appointed a special envoy to Sudan, a former senator and another evangelical Christian called Jack Danforth. The administration now threw itself into supporting the ongoing attempt, started by other east African countries such as Kenya, to try to achieve a peace settlement between the southern rebels and the government in Khartoum to end what was, by then, Africa's longest running civil war. In 2002 Bush signed the Sudan Peace Act into law.

Michael Gerson recalls that he regularly arranged meetings between Bush and those lobbying on southern Sudan. One such encounter he witnessed was between Bush and Simon Deng, a Christian former child slave from southern Sudan who had escaped to become a powerful and moving critic of the northern Sudanese government. The meeting started awkwardly, as Deng seemed reluctant to talk. But then, Gerson remembers, Deng 'teared up', and said: 'Here I am in this beautiful building and I was once owned by another human being.' Bush, Gerson recalls, was very 'affected . . . he was emotionally engaged by these meetings'.

Bush's full presidential commitment to the north–south peace process gave an enormous fillip to negotiations that had previously only limped along. The USA could bring some big sticks to the table to bully the northern Muslims into making concessions. But they also brought along some tempting carrots too, billions of dollars worth of aid for both north and south if a peace agreement could be signed. Any deal, however, would now have to be heavily in favour of the southerners if it were to satisfy the US evangelicals – this was the political price of the new administration's engagement.

Fortunately, by the end of 2000 and the beginning of 2001, the Bush administration found the newly Turabi-free administration in Khartoum in a receptive mood. Charlie Snyder, now installed as acting assistant secretary for African affairs and in charge of the Sudan brief at the State Department, recognized that there was a 'perfect storm' of circumstances for fixing the Sudan problem. Bush was highly motivated to end the war in the south; the evangelicals and the Christian right were in full cry about slavery; and the Sudanese seemed anxious to come in from the cold and renounce terror. Could a deal be done? Snyder and others certainly thought so.

The first (clandestine) meeting between the new Bush administration and the Sudanese government took place in the Windsor Country Club in Nairobi in May 2001. Representing the USA were Snyder and his political boss Walter Kansteiner, the new assistant secretary of state for African affairs. The US line, according to Snyder, was that if the Sudanese could 'get things right on terrorism' (the '*sine qua non*' for the Americans) in exchange the USA would facilitate negotiations with the southern rebels to end the civil war and support efforts to normalize Sudan's relations with the outside world. Snyder suggested at this point that the USA should formally come together with Britain and Norway to shepherd the north–south negotiations along. The Sudanese reply, from Foreign Minister Ali Osman Taha, came within forty-eight hours. It was an unequivocal 'Yes'. The deal was there to be done.

Looking back on it in 2008, Snyder explained to me his thinking at the time: 'We thought practically speaking they [the Sudanese] were looking for a way back into the game. They were under US and UN sanctions . . . Our experts thought they were exhausted.' The incentive was clear – Sudan would be allowed back into the international community. But even at this stage, the big stick was brought out too, as Snyder continued: 'Bush came to power as a cowboy . . . and there was an implied threat of military action as well . . . We used the reputation of Bush to threaten them . . . but said to the Sudanese that we could restrain them [the Bush conservatives and evangelicals] if we [Snyder and his Sudanese co-negotiators] threw them some red meat . . .' The 'red meat' would be a deal to end the war with the south.

Much to some people's surprise, it all moved forward much as Snyder and Kansteiner wanted. Sudan began to give up its intelligence secrets, although at first only slowly. Snyder described it to me as passing tests: for the rest of 2001, up to September, the Sudanese were 'giving us C grade stuff . . . to prove that they were serious. They just wanted to pass.' As well as divulging intelligence, the Sudanese government also had to prove that it was sincere about ending its aggression against the south. So the Sudanese were set what Snyder called various 'show me' tests. In the Nuba Mountains, for example, aid agencies asked for a ceasefire so that a polio vaccination programme could be carried out. Snyder was encouraged by the Sudanese response; they 'played it as straight as they could'. The Nuba Mountains ceasefire was respected, and the vaccination programme was carried out without hindrance.

In return, the Bush administration quietly began to give the Sudanese some of what they wanted in return. The USA did not oppose the UN's lifting of the sanctions imposed on Sudan for the attempted assassination of Hosni Mubarak in 1995. The new special envoy to Sudan, Jack Danforth, started work on 6 September 2001 with the specific brief to encourage peace negotiations between the north and the south. He began to co-operate closely with the east Africans, particularly the Kenyans, who had been attempting, on and off, to get John Garang and the northern government to talk seriously to each other for years. The Kenyan president, Daniel arap Moi, appointed the head of the army, General Lazaro Sumbeiywo, to chair a new round of negotiations.

The 'troika' of the USA, Britain and Norway was duly formed to support the negotiations and steer them along. The USA could provide most of the money to buy a peace deal with promises of post-war reconstruction; the Americans were also considered to have the most influence with the south. The British, on the other hand, were thought to have the most influence with the northern government in Khartoum. The Norwegians were chosen because they were big donors to the south and a relatively neutral country. After some early posturing all the parties – the SPLA, the Sudanese government, the troika and the Kenyans – met for the first round of substantial negoti-ations in the Kenyan town of Machakos in May 2002.

The terrorist attacks on the USA on 11 September 2001, five days after Danforth's appointment was announced, intensified the USA's engagement with Sudan but did not fundamentally recast the relation-ship, as has sometimes been alleged. Because of al-Qaeda's close links with Sudan, President Bashir's regime now came under closer US scrutiny than ever before. But the intelligence flow from Sudan to the USA had already begun, and the US role in the north–south peace negotiations continued as before. After 9/11, however, the USA demanded to see *all* the intelligence on al-Qaeda that the Sudanese had – and immediately. Furthermore, given the scale of the attack on their country, US officials were now prepared to make much more naked threats to get what they wanted.

As a result the Sudanese regime was 'suddenly', as Snyder remembers, 'really scared'. With good reason. The Bush administration invited every country to be with it or against it after 9/11 and the swift decapitation of the Taliban regime in Afghanistan in the winter of 2001–2 demonstrated what would happen to countries that gave the wrong answer. Would Sudan be next? It had already been hit by a cruise-missile strike only three years before. And, second only to Afghanistan, it had been Osama bin Laden's longest-lasting base of operations.

The USA played on this fear. Snyder, after a drink or two with his Sudanese interlocutors, would warn them that 'the boys are out'. From a diplomat, that was a none-too-subtle hint. But the 'boys' themselves – the CIA and the military – were much more direct at a meeting with the head of Sudanese intelligence General Sala Gosh and Foreign Minister Taha at a meeting in a London hotel in early 2002.

There, according to Stephen Morrison, the two Sudanese were confronted by several senior CIA officials. The former were 'told exactly what could be taken out' if the USA did not get more co-operation on the bin Laden file. Specifically, the US team warned that they would hit the Port Sudan oil refinery, the port itself, the oil pipelines leading from the oilfields up to the refinery and the Sudanese air force. And all that, the CIA men said, could 'be done in an afternoon with cruise missiles or a few aircraft'. In effect, such a co-ordinated attack would have destroyed the oil industry, almost the sole source of income for the Sudanese government.

This certainly seems to have concentrated minds. The year or so after 9/11 saw what Morrison calls the 'highpoint of American leverage' over Sudan, and it was used to the full. Snyder, reverting to his exam metaphor about the intelligence flow from Gosh and his fellow Sudanese spies, says that from the 2002 on they were 'solid A-hitters . . . giving us genuine goods'. The intelligence, he claims, was 'saving Americans where we did not even know that they were in danger'.

Indeed, given the extent of bin Laden's huge financial investment in Sudan, the government must surely have had a huge trove of information to yield up. Hundreds, if not thousands, of people had worked for bin Laden's various enterprises in Sudan and some of these, according to locals to whom I spoke, were now suddenly likely to 'disappear'.

Presumably they were picked up by their one-time allies in the Sudanese security services.

According to one journalist who wrote about the intelligence links between Sudan and the West in this period, Ken Silverstein of the *Los Angeles Times*, the CIA reopened its office in Khartoum towards the end of 2001. Officials would fly over from headquarters at Langley to interview al-Qaeda suspects held by the Sudanese; other suspects might well have been rendered to 'third' Arab countries for interrogation. The links at the top between Gosh, other Sudanese intelligence officials and the CIA and Britain's intelligence agency MI6 became very close. Gosh, of course, was particularly valuable as a source to the Western spies because he himself had been the Sudanese government's official linkman to bin Laden and al-Qaeda when the Saudi had lived in Khartoum in the early 1990s. Now, however, to the wry amusement of some, Gosh worked his passage back into the CIA's favour by apparently offering his fullest co-operation with the agency. Indeed, his help was considered to be so useful that he was feted at CIA headquarters in Langley, Virginia, for a whole week in 2005. Flown over in a private jet, he was extended the same courtesies usually reserved for the intelligence chiefs of close allies.

Occasionally, the world would be afforded some accidental insight into the new intelligence relationship. British journalist Jonathan Steele attended a two-day conference on African counter-terrorism in Khartoum in October 2005. The British and Americans had been invited along as observers. But at the closing dinner, in the garden of the Sudanese security ministry close to the Nile, they were called out of the crowd so that the Sudanese could show off their new friends. Steele wrote:

> Up stepped a senior CIA agent. In full view of the assembled company, he gave General Salah Abdallah Gosh, Sudan's intelligence boss, a bear hug. The general responded by handing over a goody-bag, wrapped in shiny green paper. Next up was a senior MI6 official, with the same effusive routine – hug, hand-shake,

bag of presents . . . The western spooks were less than happy to
have the press on hand, especially as their names were called out.
But loss of anonymity was a small price for the excellent cooper-
ation [they were getting].

All this was happening, of course, at the same time as the peace negotiations were proceeding with the southern rebels under the chairman-
ship of the Kenyan General Sumbeiywo. In the autumn of 2008, I
interviewed the general, a tall, erect man in blazer, check shirt and tie
in the grounds of the Serena Hotel in Nairobi. He would explain to me
how the al-Qaeda file and the search for peace in southern Sudan
became dangerously intertwined.

The general's sartorial appearance, instantly familiar to me, was no
accident; he had learned his trade partly in the British army. He had
won the coveted Silver Bugle as the best athlete at Sandhurst, Britain's
officer training academy, in 1970. He proudly recalled for me how he
had excelled at the 440-yard hurdles and the long jump. He had then
risen to the top of a Kenyan army that was highly influenced by the
military traditions of the former colonial power. Indeed, the links
between the two armies, British and Kenyan, remain close; units of the
British army still train in central Kenya.

But the general was more than just a soldier; he had also been head
of Kenya's external intelligence services, the equivalent of MI6 or the
CIA, for five years in the office of President Moi in the 1990s. Indeed,
in a glowing biography written about him to celebrate his role in the
Sudanese peace process, there is a throwaway line that suggests he not
only headed Kenya's espionage service but actually founded it.[3]

Whatever the case, this gave him intimate links with the Western
intelligence services. In particular, he was close to MI6, which had
presumably helped him set up the Kenyan intelligence agency, a
service that MI6 had performed in several other former British
colonies. He thus knew personally many of the 'friends', as Britain's
spies are euphemistically called. And he now observed them at work,
as his own negotiations for peace between north and south Sudan

quickly got wrapped up in Britain and the USA's larger post-9/11 anti-terrorism agenda.

General Sumbeiywo told me that it was in fact MI6 who did most of the running at first with the northern Sudanese government on extracting information on bin Laden, because the northerners were much more trusting of the British than of the Americans. This conformed to what was expected of the British in general; because of their historical connections they would serve as a better conduit to the northern Arabs. In particular, 'the British did the initial contacts . . . and gave assurances to the GOS [government of Sudan] that they just wanted to get al-Qaeda terrorists', not bring the whole regime down. Sumbeiywo says that the negotiations in Kenya on the north–south peace deal, what was already being termed the Comprehensive Peace Agreement (CPA), thus became a chance for the British and Americans to cultivate their intelligence connections with the Sudanese government. 'Quite a number of "friends" of mine came over during the negotiations,' the general remembered, 'to see Sudanese delegate members on the side, and then go on to Khartoum.' The US also had CIA officials on their observer team.

Thus the Anglo-US collaboration with the Sudanese government on intelligence about al-Qaeda began to colour all the negotiations about a north–south peace deal that started before 9/11. After that date, the Sudanese certainly felt the pressure of US threats to co-operate on terrorism and the CPA. But they also knew that they now had a very valuable chip of their own – the al-Qaeda file. Charles Snyder, as we have seen, judged what the Sudanese delivered up to be impressive. But General Sumbeiywo, looking on from Kenya, was not so sure. To him, the Sudanese 'just strung the British and Americans along', volunteering stuff that was relatively inconsequential. 'The people they gave them were set-ups . . . they were indoctrinated people.'

We will probably never know exactly how genuine or even useful the intelligence that the Sudanese gave to the Americans and British was during those years. Either way, the intelligence exchanges meant that during the period 2002–4 the British and Americans had, by their own lights, good reason to go soft on the Sudanese government. It seemed to have become a solid partner in the 'War on Terror'. Furthermore, the Bush administration needed the co-operation of Khartoum to get a north–south peace deal in order to satisfy the important domestic political constituency that had formed around slavery and the persecution of Christians in the south.

For their part, the Sudanese government, in General Sumbeiywo's words, had 'a simple aim – to stop the war with the south. It was draining the economy . . . and they were isolated and wanted to be reconnected with the West.' Thus all sides had a vested interest in getting the comprehensive peace that Sudan needed, and which now looked within reach. It was at this crucial moment, in the early summer of 2003, that the first reports came in of fighting in Sudan's western region of Darfur.

CHAPTER FIVE

DARFUR: HOW THE KILLING WAS ALLOWED TO HAPPEN

On 1 April 2003, Dr Mukesh Kapila stepped off the plane at Khartoum airport to take up his new post as the UN chief in Sudan. Kapila was in an optimistic mood. He knew Sudan reasonably well; he had spent a year at the University of Khartoum as a medical student and had also dealt with the country as a career official for Britain's overseas development ministry, DfID. And like almost everyone else in Sudan at the time, after decades of civil war he was anticipating the signing of a peace deal between the northern Islamic regime in Khartoum and the southern rebels, the Sudan People's Liberation Army (SPLA).

Kapila seemed to be a lucky man. These were the years of a much-hyped 'African Renaissance', in the words of the South African President Thabo Mbeki. As Resident and Humanitarian Co-ordinator for Sudan, Kapila was looking forward to playing his own modest part in this renaissance by setting up a permanent UN presence in south Sudan (to add to the existing UN structure in the north) so as to begin the region's reconstruction. He was expecting to preside over a new era of peace in Africa's largest country – accolades would surely follow.

The Sudanese government seemed to go out of its way to welcome him too, albeit mostly, he later realized, because of his skin colour. Yes, he carried a British passport, and the British government was still paying his salary. But he had been born in India to Indian parents, and had only come to England at the age of sixteen on a scholarship to a public school, Wellington, before going on to study medicine at St Peter's College, Oxford. The nuances of skin colour were, as he was to learn all too well, extremely important to the Arabs in Khartoum. They hadn't wanted a 'neo-imperialist' white; a brown-skinned man who was also linked to one of the great powers suited them well enough.

The omens for Kapila's mission seemed to be very favourable. In 2003 the intelligence and security co-operation between Washington and Khartoum was in full flow and the Bush administration was forcing the pace on a north–south peace deal, to be known as the Comprehensive Peace Agreement (CPA). Gradually, also, the post-Turabi regime in Khartoum was relaxing its guard. Exiles were being allowed back, more foreigners were being allowed in and the previously strict application of *sharia* law was relenting a little too. A slow, cautious normalization of Sudan's relations with the West seemed to be underway.

However, a few days after landing in Khartoum, Kapila began to hear stories of fighting in a region of Sudan that he had scarcely heard of – Darfur. At first, he discounted them. After all, as he told me in 2008: 'There were lots of little fights going on all over Sudan.' At that point there were no international UN staff in Darfur, only locals, so reporting was very sketchy. He set up a Darfur Contact Group to collate what reports they could get hold of from the region, and in June he sent some people there on a reconnaissance mission. But they didn't see much as access to the areas where there was meant to be fighting was limited by the government. Kapila tried not to worry. By September 2003, however, people were talking of burning villages and of refugees pouring over the western Darfuri border into Chad.

With growing alarm, Kapila talked to John Garang, the leader of the SPLA. He too was 'very concerned' about Darfur. In particular, Garang worried that if he signed the CPA with the Khartoum regime and thus joined a new national unity government for the whole of Sudan, as was proposed, he would be held jointly responsible for what was going on in Darfur. He wanted whatever was happening there to be stopped before he signed any deal.

Kapila visited Darfur himself for the first time with another UN official in September 2003. The Sudanese government officials who accompanied them kept the UN men on a tight leash, but they still managed to hear accounts of bombed villages and mass rape. The hospitals seemed to be full of gunshot injuries, often to children. Back in Khartoum, Kapila then went to see an ostensibly friendly contact in President Bashir's office. This man reiterated his commitment to peace and the CPA, as all of Sudan's politicians were wont to do. But then he added, chillingly, that he also wanted 'a final solution in Darfur'.

Was that the exact phrase he used? I asked Kapila. Yes, he replied, he remembered it very clearly. And the Sudanese official also seemed to know exactly what the implications of the phrase were. He said that they were determined to 'crush' the rebels in Darfur before signing the CPA. He seemed proud to tell Kapila this.

For the UN man, this encounter provoked an abrupt reassessment of his role in Sudan. Rather than complacently looking forward to presiding over a new era of peace, Kapila was now faced with the prospect of dealing with what many would later call a genocide.

THE ROOTS OF CONFLICT IN DARFUR

What brought Darfur to open conflict in April 2003? As we saw in the first chapter, the Darfuris shared all the resentments of other regional Sudanese against the riverain Arab elite in the centre of the country. Since independence, however, the Darfuris had not taken up arms like the southerners, or the Beja in the east. Indeed, with plentiful cattle and other resources, Darfur was actually regarded as one of the wealthier and more peaceful parts of the country.

This, however, had begun to change in the 1970s, largely out of sight of the rest of the country and of an international community focused, as everyone else was, on the awful war in the south. The western region was afflicted by a succession of droughts that affected

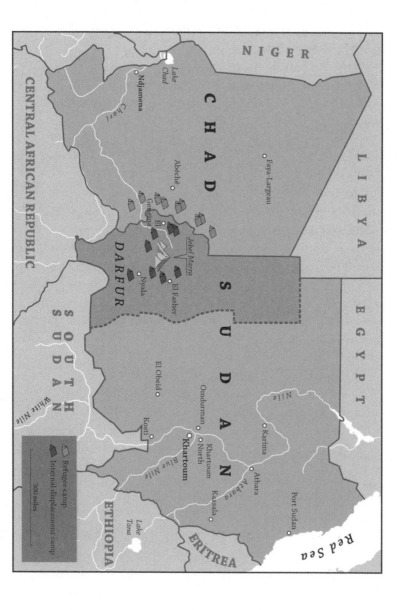

the traditional balance of life between the nomadic Arab tribes (pastoralists) and the settled farmers.

Those who have lived their whole professional lives in Darfur dealing with the consequences of these droughts can reel off the key years without pausing. Mohammed Sadiq, who returned to Darfur after his studies in the University of Khartoum in 1987 and now advises several NGOs on agriculture in Darfur, could, without any difficulty, name seventeen of them for me, beginning in 1972–3. The worst ones were in 1984–5, 1991, and then every year from 2001 to 2004.

The Arab pastoralists normally moved from south to north to follow the rain, but from 1990 onwards, because of the lack of rainfall and the subsequent shortage of grass, they would cut short the time they spent in the north from seven months to just two or three. Instead, they started encroaching on the more fertile areas in the centre and south of Darfur, particularly around the Jebel Marra, the mountainous heart of Darfur (*jebel* is the Arabic word for hill). This area was mainly populated by the African Fur, Masalit and other tribes. Thus the Arab nomads began attacking the settled farmers to claim a share of the available water and grazing land.

This dangerous situation was exacerbated by several other factors. For a start, there was a massive increase in population, putting more strain on diminishing natural resources. Abduljabbar Abdellah Fadul, who told me all about the educational vandalism of the Turabi years,[1] is another Darfuri who has lived with these problems all his life. He was born near El Fasher, and when I met him he was teaching at the town's university in the Faculty of Environmental Science.

He, too, could recite statistics off the top of his head. In 1955, in the first census of Darfur, there were 1.12 million people. By 1973 this figure had more than tripled to 3.6 million, and twenty years later it had increased to 5.4 million. The estimate for 2002, the last year before the modern conflict blew up, was 6.5 million. Within fifty years, the population had increased fivefold. In particular, Arab tribes from across the Sahel, especially from neighbouring Chad and Libya, had been arriving looking for land. Successive governments in Khartoum, however, obsessed by the development of the riverain centre, did not seem to be paying much attention. Thus in Darfur, despite the mounting human pressures, according to Abduljabbar: 'The strategy for livelihoods remained the same, based on small farmers and livestock.'

None of this necessarily had to lead to disaster. The migrations of Arab pastoralist tribes through the farming lands of the more fertile central Darfur region had often provoked disputes. But they had always been reasonably well managed by the traditional inter-tribal dispute mechanisms, meetings and *palavers*. These were the same mechanisms that the Dinka in Kordofan, for instance, had used to negotiate their own very similar disputes with the Arab Baqqara tribes.

But this is where politics intruded. From the 1970s onwards Khartoum's politicians, beginning with President Numeiri, began to dismantle the traditional tribal structures in the name of modernization and reform – a cover, in fact, for the more ignoble aim of destroying the political opposition movements that were sustained by those traditional structures, most notably the Mahdists of the Umma party.

This assault began in 1971, with the People's Local Government Act. It sounded innocuous, but its new boundaries of local control were, in the words of one historian, 'drawn deliberately to cut across rather than incorporate tribal *dars* . . . The rationale for attacking tribal authority – that it was undemocratic, corrupt, and stood in the way of development – soon became a fig leaf for politicisation of administration, first by loyalists and then mere cronies.'[2] While the old inter-tribal structures withered, there was never remotely enough money to fund the new structures; authority largely collapsed, and with it any hope of managing the growing conflicts over the immigration of outside tribes and the increasingly fierce competition for water and food.

After the coup in 1989, the National Islamic Front (NIF) government, like Numeiri's before it, set out to destroy further the base of Umma party support in Darfur. For one of the Umma leaders, Mubarak al-Mahdi, what happened next was little more than crude 'revenge' for the comprehensive defeat of Turabi and the NIF in Darfur in the elections of 1986. Divide and rule was now the order of the day. The NIF accentuated the tribal differences in Darfur, in order to emphasize the divisions within the region and break down support for the Umma. As we have seen, the region was administratively divided up again, this time into three separate states; the Fur, once a majority in Darfur, now became a minority in each of the three new states. The smaller tribes were encouraged to claim more land from the big tribes.

There was another, more brutal, aspect to this political vandalism. This was the policy of 'Arabization' or 'Islamization', mostly attributable to Ghadaffi and his attempts to create a new cross-border, transnational Arab state through the Sahel and Sahara in the 1970s. In the heavily militarized town of El Fasher in 2008, I spoke about this to several of the rebel 'commanders', the men who had started the Darfur rebellion in the early 2000s. We talked in the forlorn 'peace secretariat' building near to the base of the newly installed United Nations and African Mission in Darfur (UNAMID). Sadly under-used, with the plastic wrapping still clinging to most of the computer equipment, this US-funded peace secretariat represented the UN's lost hopes for a Darfur peace deal.

The commanders were eager to tell me why they had taken up arms in 2003 against the Sudanese government. By the time I was talking to them, they had little in common politically, the rebel movements having splintered into many different factions. The one thing they could all agree on, however, was that their reason for rebelling in 2003 was not primarily about economic marginalization or a shortage of land or water. It was because as Darfuri tribes – Fur or Zaghawa – they were already being attacked by Arabs who would target them due to their identity as 'black' and 'African'. Colonel Mohammed Adam of the Sudanese Liberation Army (SLA) was quite specific about this: 'The government of Sudan only attacked villages of the black people ... we were witnesses to that.' He insisted, as did other rebel commanders, that Darfur was thus primarily a 'political war'.

Another commander, of the Justice and Equality Movement (JEM), argued much the same. This conflict was 'not a problem of land', he told me:

We have everything, and our own rule to solve our problems among civilians. But Arabization was the new policy that created this conflict . . . the policy of Arabization and Islamization of Darfur, which has affected us very much. The Arabs had lived with us side-by-side for years . . . and then started attacking us. We had been surrounded by the Arab militias in our village . . . we decided to protect ourselves by any means. The government is giving the arms and weapons to the Arab tribes only . . . We asked for protection from the government but unfortunately they did not give the same weapons to us.

So they formed their own self-defence groups, which would later become the guerrilla rebel movements of the JEM and SLA.

It was mainly the smaller Arab tribes, who had been promised land and money, who carried out these attacks. But, as with the Baqqara and Misseriyya Arabs in Kordofan in the mid-1980s, the northern Rizeigat and Chadian Arabs of Darfur were themselves also victims of droughts and famines. Their desperate search for more land and better pastures became politicized and then militarized. Just as the government of Sadiq al-Mahdi had armed and let loose the Baqqara nomads against the civilian populations of the Nuba Mountains, so the Darfuri Arab tribes were similarly encouraged to believe that they too had impunity to loot and pillage their African tribal brethren.

From the mid-1990s onwards, therefore, there was a low-intensity conflict going on in Darfur, the consequence of a combination of domestic political warring, ideology, regional meddling and natural disaster. It was the Arabization of the struggle, however, that brought the taint of racism and ethnic cleansing that would shape the conflict from the late 1990s onwards, leading many to characterize it later as 'genocide'.

GETTING A GREEN LIGHT FOR KILLING

In 2002, however, the relatively low-key fighting of the 1990s morphed into a much wider, more serious civil war as those self-defence groups formed themselves into military organizations – 'rebels'. They carried out the first direct attacks on Sudanese government targets, notably the airbase at El Fasher, in April 2003. The conflict had entered a new phase.

Unfortunately for ordinary Darfuris, however, this also happened at a crucial moment in the country's wider history. It was at this point, as Kapila stepped off his plane ready to take up his new assignment, that the Sudanese government was locked in intense negotiations with the southerners and their foreign interlocutors, mainly the Americans, British, Kenyans and Norwegians, over making peace with the SPLA. The 'Naivasha accords', an important milestone in the negotiations, had already been signed. The eventual Comprehensive Peace Agreement was in sight.

This was the holy grail for the Europeans, the British and the Americans. As its name suggests, the CPA was designed to be just that – 'comprehensive'. It was supposed to solve all of Sudan's problems, at least to the satisfaction of Western donors, at one stroke. It held out the prospects of an entire constitutional overhaul of the country, including general elections (eventually held in 2010). It proposed a new upper chamber of parliament for greater regional representation, thus attempting to resolve the historical under-representation of the regions in the central government. By the same token, the leader of the Sudan People's Liberation Army/Movement (SPLA/M) would automatically become vice-president of the whole country in a new Government of National Unity in Khartoum. The personnel of this transitional government would be split 70/30 percent in favour of the northern government. Furthermore, the south not only gained a great deal of power over its own affairs, becoming practically a semi-autonomous state, it was also promised a referendum on complete secession in 2011. Full independence from the north could follow.

The destiny of the middle belt of the country, where the Muslim north met the south, was dealt with in a series of separate protocols. These were the areas of maximum friction between the two sides, as we have seen: the Abyei area, the Nuba Mountains and the Southern Blue Nile state. Abyei, and to a lesser extent Blue Nile, contained the vital oilfields, while the Nuba Mountains had been turned into a battlefield by the assault of the Baqqara militias on the local Dinka. Under the CPA, Abyei was allowed a separate referendum in 2011 of its own so its people could decide whether to join the south, maybe as a new country, or stick with the north. The other two 'transitional areas', as they were called in the CPA, were also promised separate popular consultations to decide their fate. Meanwhile, they were to be administered jointly by the SPLM and the north, 55 to 45 per cent in favour of the north. *Sharia* would not be applied in the south.

Some observers saw all this as a total capitulation by the north. The CPA seemed to embody much of the vision of the 'New Sudan' espoused by John Garang. The north's negotiators, however, thought that they got a good deal too, in the shape of a full 50 per cent of all of the south's oil revenues, at least up to 2011 – this was part of an 'Agreement on Wealth-Sharing' signed in 2004. Nonetheless, on paper, at least, it looked much like a total vindication of the south's long struggle with the north. Little wonder, then, that the northern government was expecting quite a bit in return for what many National Congress Party politicians saw as the dismemberment of their country.

The US government, feeling the weight of years of congressional and church campaigning over the south, desperately wanted to achieve a peace deal. Mired in Iraq after the spring of 2003, the Bush administration needed a foreign-policy success. The White House also wanted something tangible with which to reward its most faithful supporters, the Christian evangelical and conservative lobbies, before the presidential election due in November 2004. Lazaro Sumbeiywo, the Kenyan chair of the peace process, thus came under increasing pressure from the US team on the troika to get a deal before that date, apparently at any cost to the lasting strength of such an agreement. 'I was pushed to sign an agreement . . . in May 2004,' he told me; but he 'pushed back', arguing that many of the details of the proposed peace deal had still to be clarified.

The urgency of the Bush administration's political timetable 'was clear', the general told me, 'although I was never told explicitly'. Other diplomats from the troika were also made fully aware of the American need for haste. In fact both the negotiating parties to the agreement, the northern government and the southern rebels, asked the general to 'protect' them from the overbearing US insistence on clinching a deal. The general also had to cope with the US desire to claim as much visible credit as possible for the success of the negotiations. At one point, he told me: 'The US had ordered a special plane to take all the delegates to Washington.' When that didn't happen, the US special envoy, Jack Danforth, went as far as flying the entire UN Security Council over to Kenya in November 2004 to put some extra pressure on both sides. In the end, the CPA was signed in Kenya in January 2005, just too late to boost President Bush's slender re-election victory over his Democrat challenger, John Kerry.

Nonetheless, this political and diplomatic context conditioned the way that everyone reacted to the Darfur insurgency when it first blew up in April 2003. In particular, all sides were anxious that nothing should jeopardize the measure of trust that was building up over the north–south negotiations and the intelligence sharing on al-Qaeda.

For the northern Sudanese side of this story, I went to visit Dr Ghazi Atabani in his offices next to the presidential palace in Khartoum in 2008. Wiry, ascetic, intelligent, bearing a superficial likeness to Iran's President Ahmadinejad in appearance, he was now an 'adviser' to President Bashir. In the Sudanese government's byzantine pecking order, that gave him unusual importance; all the more so as he was also the leader of the ruling party's caucus in Khartoum's largely ornamental parliament. He had been the lead Sudanese government negotiator on the CPA for several years, as well as one of the Muslim Brotherhood who had split with their former mentor-turned-tormentor Turabi.

Atabani got straight to the point. As a reward for signing the CPA, and apparently giving up so much in the process, the Sudanese were expecting to be accepted back into the international community. This had been their primary policy goal since throwing over Turabi in 2000, and by this stage it seemed to be the best way of restoring the country's precarious finances. Billions of dollars were on offer from foreign donors to reconstruct the south and the rest of Sudan if they signed a peace deal. By default Sudan would therefore have to be reintegrated into the world's financial and economic institutions after enduring a decade's worth of sanctions from the USA.

The Sudanese government was also anxious to come off the US State Department's list of state sponsors of terror. The post-Turabi government bitterly resented its inclusion on this list, particularly as it now thought that it had established a good working relationship with both the CIA and MI6. Thus the Khartoum administration sought specific assurances from the USA that they would be taken off the list if they agreed to make concessions to secure the peace deal with the south. Those assurances were duly given.

This was confirmed to me later by US State Department officials. They pointed to a subsequently notorious meeting in London in about 2003 between Ali Osman Taha on the Sudanese side and Walter Kansteiner for the USA. Taha pressed the Americans yet again, as he had several times before, on their promise that Sudan would come off the terrorism register in exchange for signing the CPA. Kansteiner (again) said yes, and then, to reassure his interlocutor, he put a call through there and then to Cofer Black in Washington. Black had been CIA station chief in Khartoum in the mid-1990s, so he was well known to the Sudanese. From 2002 to 2004 he was head of all the US government's counter-terrorism efforts. Black spoke directly to Taha, and asserted that Sudan would be removed unconditionally after the deal was signed. This seemed finally to be good enough for Taha, who thought he had all the guarantees his government needed. However, critically for the future of US–Sudanese relations, their faith was misplaced.

The first rebel raids on government forces in Darfur erupted during these negotiations on the CPA, approximately when such pledges were being made. The government was surprised by the ferocity and sophistication of the rebel attacks and began to respond only haltingly. With their promises from the USA in the bag, they did not want to jeopardize the progress on the CPA by getting entangled in anything big in

Darfur. 'The CPA is, objectively, a much bigger and more important agreement than a Darfur Peace Agreement,' Atabani told me.

But the Sudanese government did get dragged into Darfur and to a degree that it probably did not at first intend. After recovering from the initial shock of the rebel attacks, the government quickly started to plan a strong and brutal counter-insurgency operation to put down what it viewed as an armed rebellion. Crucially, officials also claim that they had at least the tacit acceptance of the USA to carry out such an operation. Atabani says that the Americans were consciously 'looking the other way on Darfur' because they were as eager as the Sudanese, if not more so, to clinch the politically valuable CPA and to get more intelligence on al-Qaeda. The Americans, he argues, were therefore 'ready to accept a military solution [in Darfur], if it was a quick, surgical approach'.

Other members of the Sudanese government, not necessarily so sympathetic to President Bashir and the army, were also under the same impression. Mubarak al-Mahdi of the Umma party was doing a spell as a special adviser in the government from 2002 to 2004. Urbane and well connected, a fluent English speaker after nearly a decade of political exile in Britain, he was being used as a go-between with foreign countries at that time. Soon after the Darfur crisis started spiralling out of control, a senior US diplomat, whom he would not name for me, told him: 'We warned them [the Sudanese government] . . . and they messed it up. We said deal with it quietly and neatly. But they messed it up . . .'

What the Americans negotiating the CPA did not anticipate, according to Atabani, were 'the ramifications that arose subsequently' after the Sudanese army had indeed messed it up. These 'ramifications' were the huge activist campaigns in the USA that arose over the bungled military action in Darfur and the swift labelling of events there as a 'genocide'. As a result, when the Sudanese did eventually sign the CPA on 9 January 2005, far from being welcomed into the world community, their international pariah status merely deepened because of what they were doing in Darfur. The Bush administration felt politically unable to honour its pledge to take Sudan off the terror watch list.

Not surprisingly, as Atabani told me, the Sudanese 'felt betrayed by the Americans' over this. The Sudanese were 'made promises that were never honoured', and in private US officials admit as much. In the following years, the Sudanese would often bring these broken promises up as one of their main grievances; new US officials or ambassadors would have to be quietly briefed to expect this. For the Sudanese, there had been no asterisks or codas attached – Darfur should not have made any difference to the pact.

So, at least part of the Sudanese government's subsequent stubbornness and resentment over the Darfur issue stemmed from this sense of betrayal. In their view, the West had allowed them to attack the Darfur rebels, who posed the regime a mortal threat, and had then punished them for having done no more than what they had said they were going to do. That is Khartoum's side of the story, anyway. But how credible is this version of events?

Certainly, for the Sudanese government the timing of the insurgency that began in the spring of 2003 with the major attacks on army and air-force bases in Darfur was no coincidence. It looked like a blatant attempt to sabotage the new, more moderate government's attempts to make peace with the south and genuinely to reform the country. The rebel JEM, to their mind, was nothing more than a vehicle for the political ambitions of the endlessly scheming Hassan al-Turabi, now out to gain revenge against President Bashir. Once again, domestic elite politics intruded fatally on Darfur.

For, as Atabani was keen to emphasize to me, the government of 2003–4 was a very different creature from the one that had come to power in the coup of 1989 – the Turabi government that had declared a *jihad* against the south and which had sponsored bin Laden and other terrorists in the 1990s. When I asked Sayid el-Khatib, the director of the government's main think-tank, the Centre for Strategic Studies, about this in 2008 he told me that he had 'no doubt' that the Darfur insurgency in 2003 was at least partly an 'opportunistic' attempt by Turabi and his embittered followers to derail the CPA talks and the general rapprochement with the West.

There must be some truth to this. Sayid argued that the leaders of the JEM, the authors of the 'Black Book' of Darfuri grievances against Khartoum, were mostly Islamists who sided with Turabi when the Brotherhood split. Indeed, Sayid told me that Khalil Ibrahim, the leader of JEM, 'started JEM on Turabi's instructions . . . and went abroad on Turabi's instructions as well'.

Sayid was aligned to the government, so that might be special pleading. Perhaps a better witness is the Darfuri lawyer Salih Osman, certainly no friend of Bashir's regime. Although himself a member of the Communist Party, Salih had been at school with, or was closely acquainted with, many of the JEM leaders. 'They were disciples of Turabi . . . they knew Turabi', he told me. He was in no doubt that the armed group operated closely with Turabi and his Popular Congress Party (PCP). Turabi himself, often cagey about his connections with JEM, was only too happy to confirm the connections when I talked with him in 2008. He expressed his admiration of the JEM leaders. 'They were all with my wing of the NIF . . . our base was expanding in Darfur. They joined us . . .'

Indeed, Khalil Ibrahim, the leader of JEM, was a very visible assistant to the first and extremely nasty NIF governor of Darfur, El Tayeb Ibrahim Mohammed Kheir, the 'Iron Bar'. One of his jobs, according to some Darfuris, was to recruit *mujahideen* to fight in the south; Turabi's middle son, who shared a passion for fine horses with Osama bin Laden in Khartoum, probably provided some of the steeds for the *mujahideen* that fought there.

Thus the Darfur rebellion of 2003, viewed through the prism of the post-Turabi government, was seen primarily as an attempt at regime change by the extreme Islamists. This was certainly the impression that JEM left with one of their first Western interlocutors, Andrew Marshall. A professional mediator from the newly founded Centre for Humanitarian Dialogue, based in Geneva, Marshall was asked to go into Darfur in the autumn of 2003 by the UN's Mukesh Kapila to identify the unknown rebel leaders and discover what the fighting was all about.

Marshall eventually found them, and spent many days with both the Sudan Liberation Army (SLA) and JEM in west and north Darfur. Marshall was one of the first outsiders to see the devastation and killing there. He learned that the grievances of the SLA were very locally based. Its leaders told Marshall that they were fighting for better treatment and more political representation for Darfuris at a national level, but only within the existing political dispensation. The JEM fighters, however, seemed to be quite different. They were far better equipped and had a much sharper sense of public relations. Marshall recalled for me that they had a more national agenda, around 'Islam and regime change . . . but very slick, didn't actually say it'. As Marshall explained to me: 'It's not about Darfur [for JEM], it's how to effect some kind of political change in Khartoum. They were not looking at Darfur, they were looking at the nation.'

This probably accounts for the strength of the military offensives against JEM in the first months of the counter-insurgency campaign in 2003, and again in the first quarter of 2004. President Bashir knew that the eccentric, effervescent Turabi would always represent one of the best rallying points for opposition to his regime. To the self-regarding 'moderates' in power, the Turabi extremists were an existential threat; they not only stood to disrupt the CPA, the new government's only path back to international respectability, they also threatened to overthrow the regime itself.

Evidence for a coup by Turabi's supporters within the government apparatus was supposedly unearthed at the beginning of 2004, and in early March hundreds of mainly Darfuri officers in the army, air force, intelligence services – and even some politicians – were arrested as a result. Almost all were members of Turabi's PCP. This is a murky episode, but Salih Osman, who was also arrested for opposing the government over its offensive in Darfur, remembers that once exposed, the plotters were quite open about their intentions. He remembers them preparing their shared defence: 'They were going to try to overthrow the regime. They did not deny this. Their justification was that the government was asking them to kill their own people in Darfur and they could not do it.' In the end, although most of them were convicted and received ten- to fifteen-year jail terms, many were released early. The supposed ringleader, Turabi, was sent back to Kobar prison; his cell was just down the corridor from Salih Osman's.

Even if they were justified in seeing the Darfur 'rebellion' of 2003 as nothing less than an attempt at regime change, could the government carry out its 'surgical' strike on JEM and the other rebels in a manner that would make the whole Darfur issue go away *before* it began to threaten the peace deal over the south? The answer proved to be a resounding no.

Why did the Sudanese Armed Forces (SAF) 'mess up' so badly? I put the question to the presidential adviser Ghazi Atabani again. He paused for just a moment, smiled, examined a spot on the ceiling, and then said: 'Because we have a lousy army.' Having got that off his chest, he then launched into a long, heartfelt diatribe on the uselessness of the Sudanese military, a common rejoinder among government officials. There was an old joke doing the rounds within the government at the time, Atabani told me: 'The army took two years to do in Darfur what it took fifty years to do in the south: turn a conflict into a civil war.' Rather than being surgical, the SAF and their proxy killers quickly proved to be a blunt and bloody instrument.

TERRIBLE WEAPONS, LETHAL TACTICS: THE SAF AND THE *JANJAWEED*

To find out just how blunt an instrument that was, in 2008 I went to visit the UN base in the town of El Fasher in Darfur. Here, in two anodyne prefabs, was the UXO team of UNMIS – or rather the unexploded ordinance department of the United Nations Mission in Sudan. Their job was to clean up after the SAF. Just outside their office, against a wall, was a small trophy collection of Sudan's UXOs picked up by the unit since 2003. The man who talked me through it was Philip Rowe, a friendly, laconic Australian who had done the same job for the UN in Rwanda, Afghanistan, Sri Lanka and Iraq. He had just come back from a mission blowing up unexploded bombs in a rebel area in north Darfur and had some nasty pictures of dead and mangled SAF soldiers after their base had been overrun by SLA rebels.

He showed me his collection in order of height. First up was a huge aerial bomb, weighing 250lb and standing about five feet tall, with a suspension lug for attaching it to the aircraft bomb rack. This bomb was unusual, he said, and also extraordinarily primitive: 'I haven't seen anything as basic as this anywhere in the world.'

Then there was a 125lb bomb, about three feet long. This was the most common type used in Darfur, he explained, and didn't even have the suspension lug. The delivery mechanism consisted of simply rolling it out of the back of a plane – in this case Russian-made Antonov 26s. These bombs, and their method of delivery, were ideal for indiscriminate killing. They were dropped from no more than about 200 to 300ft, to maim, kill and terrorize people.

Then there was the standard stuff of African warfare: rocket-propelled grenades, mortar shells and small rounds. There was a Russian marking on the mortar shell, in the batch number, but that was the only clue as to where any of this might have come from. In any case, it could have been meaningless. Philip explained that these were all generic weapons, based on Russian or Chinese originals. 'The specific ones could have been made anywhere.'

In fact, they were most likely made in the GIAD factory south of Khartoum. The Chinese helped to set up the armaments part of this complex in the mid-1990s and the Iranians were involved as well. When I was in Khartoum in March 2008, the Iranian minister of defence was on a visit, promising to strengthen the two countries' military ties. Either way, the overall impression, for Philip Rowe, was that the armoury of warfare in Darfur was all 'cheap, nasty and basic stuff'. None of it was intended to be remotely 'surgical'. 'The explosives that they are producing here are shit,' he told me. That was the main reason why he was able to collect so many bombs; when they hit the soft sand, they failed to explode on impact. Often they just stayed there, perhaps to blow up days later when children gathered round to play with them.

The counter-insurgency tactics that the SAF used in Darfur were just as blunt as the weapons that they used. Mao Zedong had famously ruled that the successful guerrilla or rebel should be one who moves seamlessly through the people that he fights on behalf of – the fish in the sea, to use his overworked metaphor. So the classic counter-insurgency doctrine was to drain the sea to kill the fish – eradicate the civilian population in order to deprive the rebel fighter of his support network and resupply bases. Some would argue that it was actually the British who had invented this technique, against the Boers in South Africa. There, the regular British army, frustrated by its failure to bring the Boer guerrillas to battle, had simply rounded up their families and forced them into the world's first concentration camps. The Boers capitulated soon afterwards.

Employed in Darfur, these tactics quickly descended into what was effectively ethnic cleansing, as whole populations were cleared from their villages and concentrated into policed refugee camps. Moreover, judging by the tactics and weapons that the Sudanese government used in Darfur, it was clear that they willed this outcome from the very beginning. For the so-called counter-insurgency operation focused from the outset on the indiscriminate clearing of civilian areas, rather than on specific attacks on rebel soldiers and camps.

The relentless assaults on the Darfuri villages followed a regular pattern. First, during the night, the Antonovs swooped low over the *tukuls*, the traditional houses made of mud and reeds, and those 125lb bombs were rolled off the ramps at the back of the plane – about ten of them on one run. This started people running from the village. Next came the MI-24 (Hind) attack helicopters, flying low, strafing the people as they fled. And then, at first light, came the camel- or horse-mounted *janjaweed*, the Arab militias, often joined by regular Sudanese soldiers. Often they would arrive in 'technicals', the converted Toyota pick-up trucks that are the transport of choice for swift desert movement. The *janjaweed* would set fire to much of the village, shoot or rape anyone they could find, and make off with what was left.

Here is the testimony of one Sudanese soldier describing what it was like to participate in these assaults:

> The first village I attacked was Abu Sukeen in South Darfur in 2002. It was a big village, with perhaps 300 families living there, many of them farmers. When we attacked we did as were told and started killing elderly people, children and women. Survival depended on the strength in their legs – if the villagers were fit enough, they fled. We had fifty cars full of soldiers that day, and at least 300 Arabs on horseback and camels. We destroyed Abu Sukeen in less than three hours. Then we moved on to another village.
>
> Soldiers were ordered to shoot people whether they were armed or not. We didn't leave anyone alive and we didn't take prisoners. When we attacked villages we were ordered to destroy everything that might aid survival and existence, even pots and pans. We were given instructions to poison the wells. Soldiers would test the poisoned wells on donkeys. The donkey died and the soldiers said 'This is good, it means it's working. This way the civilians could die without us even killing them.' The intention was to drive the population away from the well and from the area.
>
> Refusing to rape during the attacks was often a death sentence. Our commander made it clear that rape was a compulsory part of our duty, especially the rape of young girls. The *janjaweed* would shout 'kill the slaves!' and 'fuck the slaves!' They raped and tortured the girls. They want the children to be different in colour, to be like them. Raping was an order. One soldier who refused was hit in the stomach with a rifle butt. He fell and was about to be stabbed with a bayonet, but because his friends were there the officers stopped and didn't kill him.
>
> In Abu Sukeen, my immediate superior forced me to rape at gunpoint. He said 'If you don't to it, I'm going to shoot you.' He forced me to do it. The girl was around eleven or twelve years old. Not older. First they forced me to rape her, and then after me another soldier raped her. The girl was crying and saying 'Why

are you doing this? I'm a young lady.' She was screaming. Screaming and screaming. When four or five men had raped the girls, we just left them lying there. Just like dead bodies.

The employment of the *janjaweed*, what this soldier calls 'the Arabs', became the most notorious aspect of these operations. Their victims coined their name, which means 'devils on horseback'. They evolved largely out of the NIF-inspired Popular Defence Forces (PDF) that had been formed in the early 1990s. As much as anything, their widespread employment in Darfur reflected the weakness of the SAF. Many of the regular army soldiers came from Darfur and the military high command feared that these men wouldn't attack villages where their own families lived.

We can trace the intimate involvement of the government in the arming of the Darfuri Arab tribes through the testimony of several former *janjaweed* fighters and commanders who later defected. Like the regular soldier quoted above, they gave long interviews to a British charity called the Aegis Trust, which collects evidence against those committing genocide and crimes against humanity. It is thus possible to describe the origins and intentions of the *janjaweed* tactics from the inside.

One senior commander says that he was summoned to a meeting to mobilize the militias only days after the initial rebel attack on the airport at El Fasher in 2003. It was clear to him that the government was not interested in a political solution in Darfur; they had decisively chosen the military option. The vice-president himself, Ali Osman Taha, travelled from Khartoum to El Fasher to brief local leaders of the PDF. In the words of the *janjaweed* commander: 'He [Taha] said to us, just bring your people, Arab people, from there, and I give you the weapons, the money, the horses the camels, the uniforms, everything. Like that.' The commander understood that he was to attack the rebels and civilians. 'He [Taha] said to us, we need only land. We don't need the people here. We need only land. That is what he said to us.'

It was therefore clear from the start that this military campaign was going to be much more than just a 'surgical' action against specific rebel targets. The non-Arab Darfuri tribes were to be forced to make way for Arab resettlement. The commander was asked by the Aegis Trust interviewers whether there was a racist intention from the Sudanese government to attack and kill people who were not Arab. He replied:

> It is a racist and tribal issue. Because we are attacking villages and areas where there are the blacks, the niggers. These people are civilians. They have no weapons. They are not with rebels. They are civilians. We are as *janjaweed*, soldiers with weapons, we are armed and attacking areas of civilians. They have no weapons. They have nothing to defend themselves, and we know very well they are not from Arab tribes. It was tribal. Primarily tribal. We knew they were from Zurga tribe [meaning 'African'] . . . we knew that they were not active members of the rebellion, and we knew that we had to exterminate them.

Thus the politics of 'Arabization' now reached a logical conclusion, as years of ethnic poisoning were exploited by the leaders in Khartoum to turn the nomadic Arab tribesman into killers. The *janjaweed* had been taught to have no respect for their victims. Their usual battle cry as they charged into the villages, as the soldier above remembered, was 'Kill the slaves! Kill the slaves! Kill the blacks! Kill the blacks!'

They were not only encouraged to kill as many people as they wanted; they were also under specific orders to make their destruction of the villages as permanent as possible. The same commander recalled:

> When we attack a village, the purpose of attacking a village was to completely eliminate any ability for people to come back. When we would cut the trees, it was to prevent them from coming back. When we would bury the sand inside the wells of whatever, it was to make sure that the people had no chance to come back . . .

189

These instructions, it is come from Khartoum. Because there is a promise to a *janjaweed*. Besides the money he gave them, he might take everything in the village. As loot. Looting everything in the village.

Judging by the testimony of *janjaweed* soldiers, money and the promises of loot were strong motivations for their participation in attacks. One recalled that he got a camel worth two million dinar, and was promised a monthly salary of 500,000 dinar (around US$2000, a large sum). All this, and the weapons, came from the government. A former army paymaster has said that money came in sacks from Khartoum and was distributed by the notorious Ahmed Harun, later indicted for war crimes, direct to the *janjaweed* commanders in the field.

As well as being given salaries and weapons, the *janjaweed* recruits were also given training of up to a month in makeshift camps in the open desert, with hundreds at a time being processed. The training seems to have been supervised by regular army officers. Every recruit picked a weapon, and was then instructed how to use it. They were divided into horse and camel riders and shown how to attack villages. Much as the young, poor, ignorant Sudanese had been brainwashed in PDF camps in the 1990s to be cannon-fodder for the *jihad* in the south, so these equally young and ignorant militia recruits in Darfur would now be deceived into believing that their killing was right and just. One defector recalled of his camp training: 'The government has misled us. They deceived us. They told us, you have to get trained to protect your livestock, yourselves, your land. And they told us, the rebel groups are against you; they are coming to get you.'

Just as the training was co-ordinated by the Sudanese army, so the attacks on the villages were co-ordinated between the *janjaweed* commanders, the army and the security and intelligence ministries in Khartoum. The *janjaweed* were trained to scout and observe the villages in order to assess how many troops might be needed for an attack. Sometimes, if a village was small and the attackers were confident that they would meet no resistance, they would attack on their own without the more usual support of the Antonov bombers and the Hind helicopter gunships. The defector *janjaweed* commander has described the command-and-control process:

> We take information from our source. We analyse this information, and we give it to the co-ordinator of the PDF in Nyala. He sends it immediately to Khartoum, to the central PDF in Khartoum. And he takes the decision. If he says 'Attack this village', OK. We have people, it's ready. We have *mujahideen*, it's ready. Just he sends us the money for the operation.

During the attacks, the camel and horse riders would be accompanied by men in cars from a distance. They would be relaying information to the helicopter gunships attacking from the air.

With the SAF and *janjaweed* in full flow by the summer of 2003, Darfur was quickly turned into a death zone. After about the first year or so, between 100,000 to 150,000 people had died as the result of the fighting, and over a million had been displaced. By the time of writing, in 2010, about 300,000 had died (by the UN's best estimate), and about three million had been forced into refugee or internally displaced person (IDP) camps, in Darfur and Chad.

However weak the army, if the Sudanese government was, as it has claimed, seriously intent on a 'surgical' strike to knock out the Darfur rebels quietly and quickly, it seems absurd that they should have again resorted to the practice of employing Arab militias. As we have seen, this tactic dated back to the mid-1980s in Kordofan and the Nuba Mountains. But the tactic had proved, again and again, to be not only barbaric but ineffective. After all, the SPLA rebellion was never quashed, and to date the Darfur rebellion has not been either.

In the Nuba Mountains, the *murahileen* had looted, raped and burned their way through the region. Now the heirs of the *murahileen*, the *janjaweed*, were to do the same in Darfur, with the same murderous results. The killing rapidly got out of hand, and again, as in the Nuba Mountains, it was to bring the furious censure of the outside world down on the heads of the Sudanese government. With the experience of the war in the south before them, it is almost impossible to believe that the people who directed these attacks would not have known what the outcome would be: mass killing, mass displacement and scorched earth.

When I met up with President Bashir's adviser Dr Ghazi Atabani, five years after the beginning of the Darfur campaign, he appeared to be in a state of complete exasperation with the army. It 'did not seem to be capable of any modernization', he complained. 'It has no capacity to accurately gauge the risks of what they are up against. In Darfur, it is open land . . . with Landcruisers moving swiftly across the desert. The army could never adapt to this style of warfare.'

He asked *me* why the army had still not developed any special forces, as the British had for counter-insurgency warfare in Malaysia. 'That is why they [SAF] are not winning the war . . . they have lots of money, but not well spent.' To which one might reasonably reply: if the Sudanese government really did want to carry out a limited, Malayan-style counter-insurgency in Darfur, why did they employ exactly the same tactics that had wreaked such havoc in the other parts of the country over the previous twenty or so years?

The fact was that the use of the Arab militia had several advantages, which came to be more and more appreciated over time. It was cheaper than using the regular army, and also allowed Khartoum to fight using what Alex de Waal has called 'deniable intermediaries', the classic advantage of mercenaries.[3] So the Sudanese were able to lapse into their Orwellian denials of state-sponsored violence in Darfur and elsewhere.

However, like all mercenaries the *janjaweed* were biddable, and their allegiance to President Bashir's regime could not be taken for granted. There is evidence that the Amirs of the Arab tribes would at times be unhappy with the course of the war in Darfur and the destruction that it caused. Particularly in 2007 and 2008, as the counter-insurgency strategy faltered and the battle lines became more confused, so *janjaweed* militias would sometimes even turn against government troops. Soon after I visited El Fasher in 2006, discontented young militiamen shot up the market, causing several deaths. It was a reminder of the fact that these Darfur Arab tribes also suffered great economic hardship, and had also suffered from the lack of development and investment in Darfur that we have discussed. They had their own reasons to resent the riverain elite – until more blood money came their way.

On one occasion, in 2005, the *janjaweed* commander interviewed by the Aegis Trust remembers that word reached Khartoum that some of the commanders wanted to 'stop the war in Darfur'. Soon afterwards, four billion Sudanese pounds, about US$2 million, arrived at the PDF headquarters in Nyala. This, apparently, encouraged the Amirs to become 'active again to regain their positions and start recruiting more people and carrying on the war'. Fortunately for the Sudanese government, money was one commodity that was never in short supply, courtesy of the oil bonanza.

UNCOVERING THE TRUTH

The all-out assault on the civilian population of Darfur was, however, happening largely out of sight of any outsiders in the autumn and winter of 2003–4. There were no journalists there and even the UN, as we have seen, had only a rudimentary reporting team in place. Anyway, this was a time when the world's attention was focused almost exclusively on the US-led invasion (and bungled occupation) of Iraq. The Anglo-American attack on Iraq began at pretty much the same time as the Darfur rebels launched their own first offensives. Iraq was to cast a baleful shadow over all the high-level politicking and diplomacy that was to ensue around Darfur, as it did over so much else.

As we have seen, the Canadian mediator Andrew Marshall brought out some of the first oral accounts as well as the first photographic images of the burning villages of Darfur. He also brought back his own first-hand experience, having been bombed himself. He slept one night in a *wadi* with the leadership of JEM, only to be awoken by the noise of an Antonov bomber circling overhead trying to locate them. Everyone leapt up and turned on their radios to alert the nearby villages. There was a loud cackle of voices in Arabic. But it soon became clear that they could hear the pilot on air, just as he could hear them. Suddenly, a voice spoke out in clear English over the radio: 'We see you fuckers', and a shrapnel bomb hit the ground just a few metres away, blowing up several houses.

Now armed with hard intelligence from Marshall about at least some of what was going on in Darfur, Mukesh Kapila, as head of the UN in Sudan, decided that it was time for him to alert his bosses in New York. He was also required by diplomatic protocol to report what he knew to the Sudanese government itself. The responses he got were to set the tone for the rest of his time in Sudan.

The government flatly denied that there was anything untoward going on in Darfur. The UN in New York listened, but did not want to get involved. The argument put to Kapila by Sir Kieran Prendergast, the former British diplomat in charge of the UN's Department of Political Affairs, was that if there were killings in Darfur they were a humanitarian problem, not a political one. This distinction was vital as it relieved UN officials of any responsibility for bringing the issue to the attention of the Security Council. Technically, only if a conflict or issue endangered regional peace and security could it be brought before the Council.[4] As the UN representative in Sudan, Kapila was thus authorised to organize humanitarian relief for the *victims* of the conflict (and the UN issued its first $139 million appeal for assistance for Darfur on 15 September), but his bosses decided that there was no case for an intervention to stop the conflict. Thus, as Kapila recalls, he was bluntly told: 'The Sudanese should fight it out among themselves.'

Kapila disagreed profoundly. So on a round of visits to Western capitals in late October 2003 on regular UN business, he also tried to drum up some interest in Darfur through direct contact with the West's politicians and diplomats. He went to London, Washington, Paris, Brussels and Oslo. But on the subject of Darfur, everywhere he went he was met with the same answer. As he paraphrases it: 'Be patient. Wait until the CPA is signed. This will solve all of Sudan's problems' – answers that struck him as both 'immoral' and disingenuous. The people of Darfur, it seemed to him, 'were going to be sacrificed on an altar of a potential peace agreement that was anyway not going to be signed anytime soon'.

The signals, especially from the Americans and the British, were clear: don't rock the boat. This attitude vexed Kapila and a few others, all the more so when they discovered that the CIA and other agencies were taking satellite photographs of Darfur that clearly showed villages before and after they had been destroyed by *janjaweed* attacks. Kapila was shown these images in Khartoum and London and they must have been the same ones that were shown to US congressman around the first quarter of 2004. To Kapila, this proved that the Western powers knew pretty much exactly what was going on in Darfur, but were anxious not to publicize it. At the same time, for instance, the new Reuters correspondent in Sudan, Opheera McDoom, observed US diplomats putting pressure on the Western aid workers who were beginning to arrive in Darfur to care for the growing number of refugees to 'keep quiet about Darfur, not to make it a big issue'. As least one aid worker she knew received a direct call from a US official warning him not to talk about anything that was happening in the region.

Thus Darfur was consumed in the wider geopolitics of the time. According to Kapila, the officials he met in London and Washington agreed that there were 'terrible things going on' in Darfur, but not only was there the CPA to consider, there were also '*global considerations*' to think about too. This was shorthand, as Kapila understood it, for the valuable intelligence co-operation that the CIA and MI6 were getting from the Sudanese. Britain and the USA did not want to jeopardize the intelligence pipeline by making trouble for the Sudanese government over Darfur when the 'War on Terror' was at its peak.

The British were, ironically, far more intransigent on this point than the Americans. It was, after all, supposed to be primarily President Bush's 'War on Terror'. Yet the US government's position on Darfur was more nuanced than Britain's because the White House and US

Congress were always subject to countervailing pressures on Sudan about human rights from the Christian right and the black caucus. No such lobbies existed in Britain, or, indeed, anywhere else.

Thus US officials could at least *appear* a bit more flexible and willing, perhaps, to consider some sort of action on Darfur. In practice, however, they deferred to the British preference for inaction. Kapila for one, was told by staffers on the White House's National Security Council that the USA would only bring the issue of Darfur to the UN Security Council with British support, and Britain had refused to do that. The Americans were reluctant to press the British on this because of the enormous political risks that Tony Blair's government had taken to support the US invasion of Iraq. Besides, the British had the better relationship with the northern Sudanese in Khartoum, from whence, as we have seen, flowed most of the vital intelligence on al-Qaeda. Above all, the Americans must have wanted to preserve this vital conduit.

In any case, who could be clear as to what was actually going on in Darfur? Charles Snyder recalled for me the mood in the State Department at this time. He acknowledged that they had a fair idea of what was happening on the ground, including the assaults on the villages and the population displacements. But the satellite images and other intelligence revealed only so much. How were they to interpret the information?

Like most diplomats Snyder, in fact, largely agreed with the Sudan government's own analysis of the situation: that it was more of a civil war than anything else. For him, JEM must have had 'inside informa-tion' on how to launch successful attacks on El Fasher airbase and other well-defended targets in April 2003. 'The riverain Arabs felt threatened . . . and struck back,' Snyder told me. To him, the Sudanese were employing the classic strategy of dividing the tribes, turning one group against another. He remembers: 'Plenty of us were saying that this was just a standard African civil war.' But not genocide, or mass killing.

Snyder also asserted that when the USA became aware of just how appallingly the Sudanese army was behaving in Darfur, some moderate pressure was put on Khartoum to rein in its attacks. Snyder says that the message to the Khartoum government was: 'This has to be ended quickly . . . this is stupid, boys.' Snyder also assumes that Khartoum thought that the USA 'would not react to the killing of Muslims [in Darfur] . . . that the US would only be interested in the Christians in the south'. If so, it was to prove a bad miscalculation. As it turned out, it was the Muslims in Khartoum (and elsewhere) who were slow to react to the killing of Muslims in Darfur – the Christians in the USA (and elsewhere) reacted immediately and very loudly.

The situation in Darfur worsened considerably over the northern hemisphere's winter months. The few UN personnel that Kapila had managed to get on the ground there by December 2003 had to be evacuated on the security advice of his officials, who warned that the thirty-odd foreign nationals and locals would get caught in the crossfire of an impending SLA attack on El Geneina in west Darfur. As it turned out, the UN team and other international NGOs would not be allowed back into the region by the Sudanese authorities until 20 February. This was probably the period of maximum slaughter. Indeed, so intense was the Sudanese army's onslaught that President Bashir felt confident enough even to declare 'victory' in Darfur on 9 February.

On arriving back in the region, the UN staff immediately began to get dozens of reports of mass refugee movements, gang rapes and mass killings. Fears as to what was really happening in Darfur were also raised by the first reports from Amnesty International and Human Rights Watch, the latter written by Julie Flint, who walked into Darfur from Chad. The International Crisis Group, based in Brussels, wrote about Darfur in December 2003. The NGO Médecins Sans Frontières, which had been in Darfur for a while, was also influential in gathering information on the worsening conflict.

The first refugee camps had to be set up. Kapila wrote a string of formal démarches to the Sudanese government, as he was technically required to do, outlining the mounting evidence of horrendous rapes, massacres and physical destruction. But, as usual, the Sudanese just denied that anything unusual was happening in Darfur; what little trouble they admitted to they blamed on 'lawless elements'.

WOULD ANYONE LISTEN?

At the UN in New York, however, the reporting from Kapila and others did evoke a strong reaction from at least one person, the top humanitarian official in the organization, Jan Egeland. A lean, restless, plain-speaking Norwegian, in 2003 he was the head of the Office for the Coordination of Humanitarian Affairs (OCHA). He quickly picked up on the information seeping out of Darfur, and held his first press conference on the subject in November of that year. Likewise, OCHA got the then Secretary-General, Kofi Annan, to say his first words on Darfur (through his spokesman) just before Human Rights Day on 10 December.

To get a vigorous response from the UN as a body, however, the matter had to be discussed at the Security Council, and this singularly failed to happen. No country's representative of the five permanent members wanted to put it on the agenda, for reasons that we have seen. Annan himself, advised by the political department, left it alone.

Egeland pestered everyone about it at the beginning of 2004, but, he told me, he 'got no reaction from anybody and no media interest either'. Egeland tried to meet with 'everybody and anybody' but got 'polite interest and no more'. The Norwegian asked for a lunch, for example, with the US permanent representative, John Negroponte, in the delegate's dining room. Egeland urged him to put Darfur on the agenda of the Security Council. Negroponte listened intently, knowing little about the subject, and asked, 'Why not?' At which point his better-briefed deputy chipped in to say that Washington did not want to upset the final stages of the Naivasha talks on the CPA. It was to become a familiar argument to UN officials, especially from the British and Americans. Oliver Ulich, the young German chief of staff to Egeland, recalled: 'Neither the UK nor the US wanted Darfur on the agenda until March [of 2004] . . . we were pressing them from December/January.'

Thus it was Britain and the USA, in fact, that shielded Sudan from the consequences of Darfur at the UN Security Council during the vital first year of the conflict, when most of the killing was done. Later on, China did the same, as to a lesser extent did Russia as well – as the USA and UK then piously pointed out. All four countries had their reasons. China wanted to protect its oil supplies. Russia supplied arms to the Sudanese government. The motives of the USA and UK, during 2003–4, were a mixture of the noble and the ignoble. Neither Western country wanted to endanger the flow of intelligence from Salah Gosh by antagonizing the Sudanese government, and both countries wanted to get the north–south peace agreement. President Bush, indeed, viewed getting the CPA as a vital part of his re-election campaign.

Even at the time, however, to those who were learning about what was happening in Darfur this approach of 'sequencing' the CPA and the Darfur conflict seemed completely wrongheaded, even immoral. As Egeland put it, it was a 'complete mistake to ignore massacres in one place in the hope that it might have helped make peace in the south'. Kapila and Egeland believed that at this time, early in 2004, the conflict might have been easily contained, or even stopped, by concerted pressure and action.

It was an analysis that the Kenyan General Sumbeiywo came to share too. 'The Americans knew about Darfur – I knew that,' he told me. 'And they did sacrifice the people of Darfur for the CPA, for a success for Bush.' He said that a 'unified front' against Sudan in 2003–4 would have stopped the killings in Darfur, but too many people already had too many agendas to achieve that. One contemporary observer and experienced aid worker, Hugo Slim, reviewing this period a short time later, reflected, 'An earlier embrace of linkage might have been far more effective than the tacit sequencing strategy which predominated in early 2004 and which involved dealing with one war after the other. A sequencing policy would get around to Darfur eventually, but it would not stop the terrible atrocities in the meantime.'

As it was, Andrew Marshall, acting as mediator, did help to negotiate an early ceasefire in Darfur in April 2004 with the help of the African Union and the Chadian government. Egeland tried to get big US and UN involvement in these talks in order to underwrite the outlines of a peace deal, but was told that both had 'too few resources to help much'. As he points out, a bigger investment at this time could have saved billions of dollars on the world's largest humanitarian operation later on. The N'Djamena ceasefire collapsed soon after it was signed, the fate of many other subsequent 'ceasefires' over the following years.

The humanitarians' camp (Kapila, Ulich, Egeland) in the UN argued that over and above everything else the organization had a duty to speak out about the serious crimes that Sudan, a member nation, was committing against its own people. The 'political officers', Prendergast and others, argued the opposite: that to use what Prendergast described to me as 'inflammatory' language about Darfur would merely force the Sudanese government into 'extreme defensive mode' and make them harder to deal with on everything else, such as the CPA. Prendergast, and later his chief political assistant, the Eritrean Haile Menkarios, deployed the argument that Snyder and the other diplomats used. Bashir's government, they said, was threatened 'by a coup by harder-line people' (in the shape of JEM), and so the task of outsiders was to 'strengthen the moderates at the expense of the extremists (like Turabi)', rather than bash the supposed moderates over the head with allegations of ethnic cleansing or genocide.

At first, those pressing for quick action on Darfur were at least prepared to listen to the Western diplomats' rationalizations for their passivity. After all, the arguments for keeping Khartoum happy to save the CPA, or to get more intelligence on al-Qaeda, were serious. But for most of them there came a tipping point, a moment when the evidence for the killings of Darfur became too overwhelming and the neat theoretical division of the Sudanese government into supposed 'moderates' and 'hard-liners' broke down in the face of what was actually taking place on the ground. For Kapila this point came when he read a report in early March 2004 by one of his officials, Daniel Christiansen, of a *janjaweed* attack on Tawila in north Darfur.

Here, two World Food Programme workers just happened to pass the town after the violence and witnessed the immediate aftermath. Other UN officials went in on 3 March to interview survivors, who gave vivid first-hand accounts of the dawn raid by 500 *janjaweed* in co-ordination with attack helicopters. Of the 14,000 residents and 9,000 refugees who were in the town beforehand, the UN officials could only find 2,000 to 3,000 left. According to the report: 'Over 100 women had been raped, six in front of their fathers who had later been killed.' In the whole of the Tawila administrative area, thirty villages had been burned to the ground, with evidence of another 200 people killed and 200 women raped. The UN officials found it all 'deeply shocking'.

This was all terrible enough. But what chilled Kapila above all was the report's conclusion:

> It should finally be noted that those we spoke to in Tawila town stated that government helicopters were providing ammunition to the *janjaweed* during the attack which if true would be a pattern reported following several other *janjaweed* attacks in the Darfur area. They also claimed that the *janjaweed* were using Landcruisers provided by the government, and in any case it is no secret that the government has armed and trained the *janjaweed* for use in the war against the SLA (even local GOS officials will admit this in private).

Here was strong evidence of the government co-ordinating the mass killing, rape and displacement of its own citizens. It elevated what was happening in Darfur from random acts of violence to something much more premeditated and sinister.

Kapila's fears were confirmed by conversations with Sudanese officials and even ministers. Despite official government denials that anything was happening in Darfur, individual officials would visit him at home to vent their anger and disgust at the actions of their own government. Some said that they wanted to change the policy on Darfur; one mid-level official hinted at a coup. On one occasion, the protocol officer who escorted Kapila from the foreign ministry to his car after yet another unproduc-tive meeting whispered in his ear: 'Thank you for saying all that you did in the meeting. Some of us in the government are very ashamed of what is going on. We are terribly upset by what our government is doing to our own people. May God bless you.'

The UN man was unsure how much credence to give to these indiscretions, but they all added to his conviction that the killings in Darfur were the direct result of a co-ordinated military policy. In other words, there was clearly 'intent', as defined under the 1948 Convention on the Prevention and Punishment of the Crime of Genocide. So in his official letter about the Tawila attack to the UN in New York, Kapila now described what was happening as 'akin to ethnic cleansing'. Indeed, he went further: 'There is concern . . . that the situation in Darfur is reminiscent of the earlier period of the crisis in Rwanda.'

What made Kapila so convinced that the gravest of human crimes was being committed in Darfur in 2003–4 when so many others were determined to play it all down? Kapila had one crucial advantage over all his contemporaries in the unfolding horror of Darfur – he had already been a witness to two genocides, so he knew exactly what the signs were. Indeed, his reading material on the flight into Khartoum on 1 April 2003 had been the official UN reports into the massacres in Srebrenica in 1993 and Rwanda in 1994, the two undisputed genocides of the previous decade. His reading was not prompted by idle curiosity. As an aid official for the British government, one of his jobs had been to 'pick up the pieces' in Kosovo and Rwanda immediately after the killings there. The images were burned onto his mind; he was, in his own words, 'steeped in all that'.

Rwanda, in particular, had left a deep impression. Kapila had arrived only a day after the six weeks of killings had ended, when about 800,000 Tutsis and their Hutu sympathizers were hacked to death by the Hutu *genocidaires*. He had then driven into the Rwandan capital Kigali. 'One could smell the bodies,' he later told me, 'lying by the side of the road.' What had confronted him in one church was particularly appalling. As Kapila recalled, it was 'piled with smashed-up bodies . . . body parts hacked off. And the [numbers of the] hymns were still on the wall, and the bibles were still open . . . a sweet, sickly smell. The patches of blood on the wall were still bright, congealing. There were machetes lying around . . . babies and little children with their limbs cut off.' Talking about it in 2008, fourteen years later, still brought back the smell for Kapila, and he had to break off his account.

In Rwanda, Kapila had promised himself that he would do everything in his power to prevent anything similar happening again 'on my patch'. At the time of that horror, Kapila had been aware that the UN, USA, France and everybody else had struggled as hard as possible *not* to get involved. They had therefore resisted any calls to label the Rwandan killings a 'genocide', as this would automatically have triggered some action. In the subsequent years, countries and individuals had apologized for their inactions at the time – but this was not going to bring 800,000 dead Rwandans back to life.

Now, exactly ten years later, in the spring of 2004, Kapila was determined not to stand idly by while another Rwanda unfolded in front of him. Increasingly, as his warnings to New York, to the Sudanese government and to Western capitals were ignored, he became ever more determined to 'call it' in Darfur as it happened. Retrospective remorse, Rwandan-style, was not enough.

The tragedy of Kapila, though, is that within the UN system the very characteristics that impelled him to speak out on Darfur also undermined the seriousness with which his reporting was taken at headquarters in New York. Impatient, passionate, unorthodox, belligerent and clever, Kapila was no respecter of the byzantine, turf-obsessed bureaucracy of the UN. A relative newcomer to the organization when he arrived to take up his post in Khartoum, he immediately embarked on a campaign to streamline the UN's presence in Sudan and reduce what he regarded as the inordinate amount of overlap and superfluous activities that characterized the UN's activities in the country (and everywhere else). A self-confessed 'change-agent', Kapila saw this as an integral part of his brief to prepare the UN in Sudan for the new era of peace that the CPA was meant to usher in.

All very laudable, perhaps. But it put him at loggerheads with the in-country heads of the various UN agencies (UNDP, UNICEF and so on), all anxious to protect their own baronies from the cost-cutting

Kapila. He was regarded by many knowledgeable and honourable people who worked with him in Khartoum as arrogant and hard to work with – and his reporting on Darfur was probably discounted as a result. The only time that his political boss, Kieran Prendergast, ever talked to him in Khartoum was to confront him with a litany of complaints from within the bureaucracy. Prendergast warned Kapila that he was likely to be fired because of his 'imperious temperament'. Indeed, in January 2004 Kapila was told that he could only stay on for the second year of his two-year contract if he accepted what would, in effect, be a demotion, from overall head of the UN in Sudan to being in charge of just the UNDP in the country. He was told that this was because he had made himself unpopular with the Sudanese government for pestering them too much on Darfur, and because he had also made himself so disliked by the UN agencies. Kapila therefore decided to leave Sudan towards the end of his twelve-month tour of duty, which was due to finish at the beginning of April 2004.

THE WHISTLE BLOWERS

The comparisons between Darfur and other cases of mass killing were also being deployed by the only other group of people interested in Darfur at this stage: those American aid bureaucrats and legislators, most of them Christian evangelicals, who had made the Sudanese government's destruction of the south in the 1990s such a high-profile issue of conscience in the USA. Sam Brownback, the senator for Kansas, says that it was Andrew Natsios, then the head of USAID, who 'hit the button on Darfur'. Natsios showed Brownback and a few others the same CIA intelligence photos that Kapila had seen: 'Shocking pictures of whole villages being wiped out.' Brownback could see it all happening 'almost in real time'. 'Here we go again,' Brownback thought, familiar by then with the Sudanese government's murderous tactics in the south. 'I was deeply disturbed, and more convinced than ever that it was the fault of the same Islamist Muslim government.'

Natsios and his colleague at USAID, Roger Winter, were crucial in mobilizing the first American assistance for the victims of Darfur. Winter had had long experience of Sudan and was later to become a key figure in the Darfur lobby in the USA. In testimony before Congress in June 2004, Winter recounted how USAID had delivered its first humanitarian assistance to Darfur as early as August 2003; Natsios led a mission to Darfur in October of that year, and Winter followed in February 2004. Even at this stage the US government was pledging $300 million to help Darfur, the beginning of a massive American emergency relief operation for the region.

The politicians of the Sudan lobby got to Darfur almost as quickly as Natsios and Winter. Brownback and Congressman Frank Wolf travelled to Darfur with the World Food Programme in early 2004 to see matters for themselves. 'It was ghastly,' Brownback recalls, 'we saw the *janjaweed* on camels circling the IDP camps there . . . that haunted me for a long time afterwards.' In particular, Wolf and Brownback heard the stories of the mass rapes and indiscriminate slaughter that were now becoming familiar.

'We started the push to call it a genocide when we came back,' says Brownback. The point, as Kapila was also arguing, was to 'call it while it happened', not later. Only then would their efforts save lives. Congressman Donald Payne, leader of the black caucus, worked closely with them to get a bill through Congress on 22 July that called the events in Darfur 'genocide' – the first time that the word was used publicly. Prendergast, watching on at the UN, thought this was 'disgraceful'.

But that is to run ahead. At the beginning of March 2004, despite the efforts of Natsios, Winter, Brownback and others, the killings in Darfur were still not well publicized and certainly not a public issue in the West. After getting no response to his own graphic reports about the killings at Tawila, Kapila embarked on a second round of visits to the major Western capitals and the UN headquarters in New York. But on the issue of Darfur he was still met with the same stonewalling. The UN, according to Kapila, insisted that it was not its business to get involved in the politics of the conflict. At the British Foreign Office in London he was told, in no uncertain terms, that he was 'being a nuisance'.

Clearly, if Darfur was going to get the attention it deserved, something would have to change. Kapila decided to speak out, as loudly and controversially as possible, over the heads of all the diplomats, UN officials and aid workers, to create the necessary storm. He knew that his days in Khartoum were numbered, but at least he could leave the country on his own terms. He asked his press secretary to arrange a live interview for him with the BBC's *Today* radio programme on 14 March.

Today was carefully chosen. It is the preferred early-morning listening for most of Britain's politicians, journalists and chattering classes. Here, an interview would have maximum impact – and it did. In a ten-minute segment, Kapila exposed the horrors of Darfur for the first time to a public audience. He not only called it the 'worst humanitarian crisis' in the world, but also the worst 'human-rights crisis'. He described the conflict as 'ethnic cleansing' and, most sensationally of all, he directly blamed the government of Sudan for all of it.

This made instant headlines all over the world. He spent the rest of the day with AFP, Reuters and every other news agency that could contact him. The effect was electrifying – never again would the problems of this remote region of Sudan be confined solely to the darker corners of official Whitehall and Washington. Kapila had made it everyone's problem.

He certainly opened the floodgates at the UN. With a public outcry over Kapila's allegations against the Sudanese government convulsing delegates, Jan Egeland was finally allowed to present his long-demanded briefing to the Security Council. Two weeks after the *Today* broadcast, on 2 April, Egeland addressed the council in the briefing room next to the main chamber. He received even more publicity than Kapila had for his BBC interview. Egeland reported on the 'widespread atrocities and other grave human-rights abuses against the civilian population'. Without specifically calling the events in Darfur a genocide, he left his audience in no doubt as to who was chiefly to blame: 'International humanitarian law and fundamental human rights are being violated systematically and in a climate of impunity. Even when government authorities have been alerted to specific ongoing atrocities, they have either failed to respond or intervened too late to prevent further deaths and violations.'

This presentation transformed the public discourse over Sudan. The country's war-torn western region went from being a place nobody had ever heard of to the West's principal news story in about a week. The UN was now fully engaged. On 25 May the international body issued its first full statement from Kofi Annan after a 'high-level mission' had been sent to Darfur at the end of April. The first full resolution calling on the Sudanese government to disarm the *janjaweed* followed on 30 July. By that time both Colin Powell, the US Secretary of State, and Annan himself had visited Khartoum and Darfur to see and hear for themselves.

Also very much on everyone's mind at the time was the tenth anniversary of the Rwandan genocide. Diplomats and politicians, like Kapila, were very conscious of their failure on that occasion and this gave them an added incentive to address Darfur in 2004. As head of the UN's Department of Peacekeeping Operations in 1994, Kofi Annan had disastrously failed to rise to the challenge of Rwanda. Now, as Secretary-General, he included a reference to Darfur in a speech he had been due to give anyway on the anniversary of the Rwandan genocide. The two events were beginning to be linked together in the public's mind.

A media circus started. Having received no attention at all, Darfur now got wall-to-wall coverage. To the uninitiated public, jaded by Iraq, Darfur seemed to be a simple story of good versus evil: shiny, virtuous rebels against evil extremist Islamists in Khartoum. The professional diplomats who had been dealing with Sudan were horrified, predicting (correctly) that a mass emotional response might cloud their delicately calibrated political calculations. But human rights and NGO activists were energized; this was a new high-profile issue that they could rally around.

More importantly, Darfur now drew in a whole new cadre of people who had never campaigned before, let alone heard of Darfur. One of those was the Hollywood actress Mia Farrow. That summer of 2004 she read an article by an academic called Samantha Power about the Rwandan genocide which also referred to Darfur. Power's book *A Problem from Hell: America and the Age of Genocide* had first come out two years earlier and was to be enormously influential in shaping the US public's response to Darfur. Power chronicled the instances when the USA's politicians, despite vowing 'never again', had, allegedly, stood by to let genocides happen in the twentieth century – in Bosnia, in Kosovo and in Rwanda. Now, the argument went, the USA was doing the same in Darfur. Power's article, like her book, was a call to arms.

It certainly sparked Farrow off. 'It was a jaw-dropping moment,' she told me in 2008. She had never campaigned on anything like this before, but she began to google the experts and resolved to go to Darfur to see for herself.

'For that first trip,' she recalls, 'I had prepared myself as responsibly as I could ... but the reality was staggering. The unacceptable, immeasurable, levels of suffering. It changed my life. I could never be the same again.' On that first trip she too listened to the stories of rape and also caught a glimpse of the *janjaweed* around an IDP camp. 'I came back to tell people,' she remembers. 'Then it was Dar-where? Now it is synonymous with suffering. It has been the largest response to Africa since apartheid.'

In that summer of 2004, Mia Farrow and others came together to found the SaveDarfurCoalition. Rather than doing diplomacy in a vacuum, politicians and diplomats now found themselves operating in a new (and unwelcome) world of activist pressure, Hollywood stunts and popular interest. But none of this, as everyone was to find out, made the conflict in Darfur any easier to resolve. Indeed, in many ways it was to push peace in Sudan even further out of reach.

LIVING WITH THE GUILT

But what of Mukesh Kapila, the man who had triggered all this in the first place by going public on the BBC? He saw out the last two weeks of his posting in Khartoum after his radio interview. He was plainly unwelcome back in the Sudanese capital, and even received death threats. His faithful Canadian security officer became so concerned that he sat up at night in Kapila's bedroom while his boss tried to sleep. Kapila left the country on 1 April 2004, a year to the day after he had arrived: the UN honoured his two-year 'Sudan contract', except that he served out his second year on secondment to the World Health Organization in Geneva.

It took him some time to recover, physically and mentally, although he did not suffer the same degree of post-traumatic stress as afflicted the unfortunate Romeo Dallaire, the Canadian soldier who had been in command of the small UN force in Rwanda in 1994. Dallaire had also had his warnings about impending massacres ignored by his bosses in New York. He was unable to prevent what was happening in front of his own eyes, and he was wracked by guilt as a result. Only a few months after the genocide in Rwanda he had a death wish, as he later recalled: 'At the end of my command, I drove around in my vehicle with no escort practically looking for ambushes. I was trying to get myself destroyed and looking to get released from the guilt.'[5] His life disintegrated thereafter. In 2000 he was found unconscious on a park bench in Quebec, drunk and alone, having tried to commit suicide.

He recovered, and later wrote of 'the anger, the rage, the hurt' that seemed to overpower him after Rwanda.[6] Mukesh Kapila later went on to work for the International Federation of Red Cross and Red Crescent Societies in Geneva. Compared to Dallaire, he lives a relatively healthy, normal life. But he still feels all the anger and rage over Darfur that Dallaire felt about Rwanda. Some congratulated him on his whistle-blowing efforts in Sudan, but Kapila felt no great sense of vindication. He knew full well that the Sudanese government had carried out most of the raping, killing and destruction that it had planned by the time that he appeared on the *Today* programme, precisely during the period when he had been the world community's chief representative in Sudan. Ultimately, in his own mind, he had failed to draw sufficient attention to the destruction of Darfur while it was actually going on. He remained convinced that that if everyone had reacted appropriately in 2003, the killings could have been stopped. But after 2004, it was too late.

Kapila was taken into the witness protection programme of the International Criminal Court, which one day hopes to try President Bashir and other Sudanese ministers for the war crimes committed in Darfur. Even if that does eventually happen, it will, at best, be retrospective justice. Better than nothing, perhaps, but the fact remains that, at the time, the killings were allowed to happen.

CHAPTER SIX

DARFUR: THE VORTEX

In October 2005, about a year and a half after Jan Egeland's briefing to the UN Security Council, I visited Darfur for the first time. I tagged along with a team accompanying the British government's newly appointed minister for Africa, David (Lord) Triesman. It was a high-profile official visit, so visas were procured in a day (rather than months or never). I felt somewhat safer amidst the protective embrace of the minister's generous allocation of armed 'close protection' officers – six in all. The two-day visit was a very visible sign of the importance that Western governments now attached to this remote region of desert and scrub in the middle of Africa. Unheard of just eighteen months before, Darfur was now very firmly on every foreign minister's must-see list.

The Sudanese government in Khartoum seemed accommodating enough, letting journalists travel with the minister to report from an area that was normally very difficult to get into. But we were kept mostly within the confines of the West Darfur capital of El Geneina, almost on the border with Chad. Nonetheless, visiting the nearest displaced peoples' camps on the fringes of town, we were able to pick up a good understanding of what had happened in Darfur since April 2003.

The sprawling Al Riyad camp, for instance, now housed about 15,000 people. The shelters were constructed out of plastic and woven sacks thrown together with bits of corrugated metal. Several refugees spoke to us of how they had fled from villages after attacks by camel- or horse-mounted *janjaweed*. One twenty-seven-year-old we met, Mahmoud, was married with two children. Both his parents had been killed in an assault on their village in December 2003.

What was most striking about the refugees was their continuing fear of attack, even in a camp that was now tended by dozens of Western aid workers and after, technically, a ceasefire had been signed the year before. Troops from the African Union (AU) had arrived to monitor the ceasefire, but, as we discovered, nobody was taking them too seriously. Mahmoud said: 'Security is really bad . . . in the evening you can't go anywhere.' Most of these refugees had fled from villages only half a day's walk away, but all the women were afraid to go back to them because of the fear of rape.

Everyone complained to us that the AU soldiers did not do anything; many alleged that the African soldiers were in fact working 'with the government'. One 'camp elder', as the village leaders are called, told us that the Sudanese government's Humanitarian Assistance Commission (HAC), the organization that had been mandated to care for them, was a 'terrorist organization'. What would the future bring for these people? This elder was probably going to flee to Chad, to join hundreds of thousands of other Darfuris in refugee camps over the border. Another elder, though, was determined to stay in Darfur, but he demanded 'white faces with blue helmets'. In other words, proper Western UN troops to protect them.

That became a mantra of the Darfuris (as well as many abroad) throughout the following years. A lot of faith had been placed in the arrival of the AU troops in 2004, but their deployment proved to be very much the beginning of the international community's problems in Darfur, not the end of them. If only a couple of thousand AU troops *had* worked! But it was on this same trip to Darfur in 2005 that we heard the news that the first AU 'peacekeeper' had been shot dead on patrol. It soon became clear that the AU force was largely ineffective; it could barely protect itself, let alone the millions of displaced persons scattered around Darfur. Already, this was the world's biggest human-itarian crisis, and the two million or so who had fled the fighting were subsisting solely on the World Food Programme's largest emergency feeding programme. What would follow was a long battle to get UN troops into Darfur to replace the AU, and to find a political solution to the crisis.

THE 'SAVEDARFURCOALITION' STARTS UP

The fact that a British government minister was in Darfur at all in 2005 was in itself remarkable enough, and mainly testimony to the power of the Darfur lobby – the activist campaign that quickly came into being after the revelations of Mukesh Kapila and Jan Egeland. The campaign to 'save' Darfur dramatically altered the international context within which Sudan's problems were handled and the way in which Western – and other politicians – engaged with the country.

As we saw in the last chapter, almost immediately after Egeland publicized what was going on in Darfur, new and often unlikely people responded to the outcry over the Sudanese government's actions against its own people. Darfur began to attract widespread attention in the US and Western media. The first journalist to give the Darfur issue consis-tent, serious attention was *New York Times* columnist Nicholas D. Kristof. From the start he was arguing, to quote from one 2004 column: 'Sudan's behaviour in the Darfur region easily meets the definition of genocide.'

Everyone I met who had been involved in activism on Darfur had read Kristof's early and urgent pleas for swift and decisive action. Like Kapila, he argued that the world was in danger of sitting by and watching another genocide unfold without doing anything about it. A mocking headline from one of his columns, written from 'along the Chad–Darfur border', was ' "Never again", again and again'. In the same piece, he wrote: 'I'm not arguing that the United States should invade Sudan. But one of the lessons of history is that very modest efforts can save large numbers of lives. Nothing is so effective in curbing ethnic cleansing as calling attention to it.'

Kristof's arguments resonated strongly with one particularly powerful US constituency: Jews. Just as the descendants of slaves had felt a deep personal responsibility to rescue the slaves of southern Sudan, so the victims of a historical genocide felt an equal responsibility to save what they saw as the victims of a contemporary genocide. Congress called Darfur a 'genocide' as early as 22 July 2004. When Colin Powell also called Darfur a genocide on 6 September of the same year, it was a very significant moment for the US Jewish community – in effect, a call to arms.

Ruth Messinger, head of the charitable US Jewish World Service, told me of the single most repeated maxim in the Torah: 'Remember you were strangers.' The moral of the phrase is to look after people who you don't even know, Messinger explained: 'You should draw from that a high level of empathy and compassion for those who are victims.' It was a Jew, Raphael Lemkin, who had coined the word 'genocide' in the wake of the Holocaust, and who had drafted the 1948 Convention on the Prevention and Punishment of the Crime of Genocide. Jews felt a particular obligation to act on his words and work. The bitter memory of the USA's failure to act in Rwanda in 1994 was another spur to action. For Messinger: 'Many of the people who leapt onto the bandwagon with us [over Darfur] are conscious of what they did not do in Rwanda.'

On 14 July 2004, Messinger and Jerry Fowler, the head of the Committee on Conscience at Washington's Holocaust Museum, hosted a meeting in New York to form the SaveDarfurCoalition. Elie Wiesel – the USA's most respected Jewish activist, Nobel Peace Prize winner and Holocaust survivor – spoke at the meeting, as did the most aggressive secular activist on Sudan, John Prendergast, who had dealt with the country during his time on Bill Clinton's National Security Council. Together with Gayle Smith he was later to found the Enough Project, a self-styled activists' genocide prevention network.

Very quickly the SaveDarfurCoalition drew in the existing activists from the Christian right and the black caucus to cover the full spectrum of US politics. Bostonian Pastor Gloria White-Hammond, a long-time campaigner against slavery in southern Sudan, joined the board, as did representatives of the Christian right. Funding would flow in from wealthy individuals such as Pierre Omidyar, the founder of eBay. In the autumn of 2004, a Swathmore college student called Mark Hanis, the grandson of four Holocaust survivors, started a young person's activist network on Darfur, the Genocide Intervention Network. Soon, utilizing the internet as a campaigning tool, it had 1,000 student chapters at middle schools, high schools and colleges.

The SaveDarfurCoalition thus became the most politically inclusive and effective foreign-policy lobby group on Africa since the anti-apartheid movement of the 1980s. The coalition's first mass rally in Washington DC in April 2006, attended by hundreds of thousands of people, was a wonderfully eclectic mix of orthodox rabbis, scruffy students, bible-belt Christians, New York intelligentsia, black activists and film stars. Some of the latter became the most visible faces of the coalition. Mia Farrow had joined early on, followed by the black actor Don Cheadle, who starred in a Hollywood movie treatment of the Rwandan genocide, *Hotel Rwanda*, also released in the summer of 2004. The real star power came later, when George Clooney gave a press conference at the UN and went on a high-profile trip in 2006 to the Chad–Darfur border with his television-anchor father, one of several visits by the actor to the Darfuri refugee camps in eastern Chad.

It is hard to argue with Ruth Messinger's argument that without the coalition: 'This issue [of Darfur] would have been invisible to the American public.' Foreign news is, at best, a minority sport in the USA. There is scant coverage of anything that does not directly concern immediate US interests, either on TV or in the newspapers (beyond the *New York Times* and *Washington Post*). The coverage that the SaveDarfurCoalition was now able to get on Sudan, by contrast, was overwhelming, with documentaries, op-ed pieces, reportage and photo-essays all spreading the word.

The principal aim of the coalition was to cure the USA – and the UN – of 'Somalitis', the reflexive fear of engaging with places where there was no clear-cut and immediate political dividend. The 'Black Hawk Down' episode in Mogadishu had given the Clinton administration a profound aversion to all but the most pressing interventions abroad. The SaveDarfurCoalition's argument, however, was that a late and half-hearted response to Darfur risked repeating all the same mistakes of Rwanda. Just as an early, robust intervention there could perhaps have prevented disaster in 1994, so it could have done in Darfur in the summer and autumn of 2004. In her book *A Problem from Hell*, Samantha Power had concluded:

> It is in the realm of domestic politics that the battle to stop genocide is lost. American political leaders interpret society-wide silence as an indicator of public indifference. They reason that they will incur no costs if the United States remains uninvolved but will face steep risks if they engage. Potential sources of influence – lawmakers on Capitol Hill, editorial boards, non-governmental groups, and ordinary constituents – do not generate political pressure sufficient to change the calculus of America's leaders.[1]

The Darfur activists set out to change this by creating a grassroots movement that would make as much noise as possible.

They succeeded, even if not quite to the extent they would have wished. From the summer of 2004, they made Sudan a public issue rather than a bureaucratic one. At the UN in New York, for instance, Jack Christofides, an official in the political department, noted an immediate change. As he told me later: 'When we were in Khartoum, after reading a Nicholas Kristof article in the *New York Times* we could set our stopwatches to see how long it would take New York to do something.'

Likewise, the congressmen and senators who had been toiling away on Sudan for years in relative obscurity now found a much more receptive audience on Capitol Hill. They started to look at more ways by which a receptive legislature could pressurize the Sudanese government over Darfur. This would lead to the passing of disinvestment legislation, for instance, and unqualified support for White House demands for more sanctions against Sudan.

All this, again, was carried on with broad cross-party support. Indeed, so successful was the Darfur coalition in the USA in drawing together people from all points of the political compass that Darfur was the only issue about which Barack Obama and John McCain publicly agreed not to disagree at the start of their presidential contest in 2008.

In George W. Bush's White House, of course, the coalition was pushing at an open door. As the coalition was composed of two core constituencies of the Republican Party, Christian evangelicals and Jews (the latter group smaller in number but also important), it could hardly have been otherwise. Already concerned by the persecution of Christians in the south, Bush seems to have been equally motivated by the plight of Muslims in Darfur. On the eve of the SaveDarfurCoalition march on Washington in April 2006, for example, its leaders were received at the White House by a sympathetic president. Andrew Natsios, the Republican appointee to head USAID, watched as Bush, responding to the political pressure building up around him, telephoned President Bashir no fewer than twelve times to try to persuade him, in Natsios's words, to 'stop the atrocities in Darfur'.

The immediate effects of the SaveDarfurCoalition campaigning were thus largely positive. Having ignored Darfur absolutely while the killings were taking place in 2003–4, from summer 2004 onwards the West swamped Darfur with almost too much attention. It is probably not a coincidence that the rate of killing there declined from then on, just after the Sudanese government's counter-insurgency campaign began to attract all this unwanted scrutiny. Khartoum was as sensitive as any other government to charges of mass murder and genocide, especially when those charges came mainly from a country with which it was trying to repair tattered diplomatic relations.

Furthermore, the huge publicity given to Darfur was an extraordinarily useful campaigning tool in the hands of the UN and other NGOs. It helped to persuade donors to fulfil their financial pledges to the various humanitarian organizations operating in Darfur and elsewhere. Jack Christofides of the UN told me that after the campaign started, extra money began to flow into the World Food Programme, the UN refugee agency and others helping in Darfur. It is often forgotten that most of these agencies have to raise their own funds from donor governments – they do not receive funds automatically from within the UN system. The publicity over Darfur meant that the UN and other agencies could sustain an extensive humanitarian relief operation there from 2003 onwards. In fact, that relief operation quickly became the largest and probably most successful example of its kind in the world, undoubtedly saving thousands of lives. The full UN peacekeeping missions that were eventually inserted into both southern Sudan and later Darfur cost about US$2.5 billion a year between them to fund. That the money was made available to do this remains a remarkable tribute to the energy and vision of the Darfur activists.

BUT WAS IT REALLY A GENOCIDE?

However, for those who had been engaged for years in negotiations with the Sudanese government about the south, terrorism and other issues, the unrelenting public focus on Darfur from the autumn of 2004 onwards was less welcome. Many of them felt that too much of the new media attention was uncritical and over-simplified.

Thus began a dangerous split between, on the one hand, the attitudes and interests of the professional diplomats – those who had to deal with the Sudanese government on a day-to-day basis – and, on the other hand, the activists. The former lived in a world of negotiations, deals, incremental progress and the fine grain of local politics. The latter breathed the purer air of universal principles and moral absolutes. The problem was that there was very little communication between the two, let alone much respect for the other's point of view. The diplomats readily conceded that the Darfur coalition had raised the profile of Darfur and Sudan as an issue. But this was, for many of them, a matter for regret rather than celebration.

In particular, the diplomats worried about the instant designation of events in Darfur as a 'genocide', and how this would frame the often shrill public debate over Sudan. The US Congress used the term, as we have seen, partly based on the experience of dealing with southern Sudan. The designation of genocide given by the State Department in 2004 was based on limited interviews in the refugee camps in Chad. But how true, or authoritative, were these descriptions? Many had their doubts. To what extent, for instance, were these descriptions coloured by past events – in Rwanda or southern Sudan – rather than being based on the real evidence of what was happening on the ground in Darfur?

In fact, the rush to designate Darfur as a 'genocide' split the Western approach to the crisis. No other country apart from the USA officially used the term, and neither did the UN. In October 2004 the UN consented to a US-led request to investigate the killings. But, in contrast to the State Department, the consequent UN commission of enquiry, published in January 2005, did not call Darfur a genocide. The commission acknowledged that there had been dreadful attacks on the civilian population, and that: 'The use of military force was manifestly disproportionate to any threat posed by the rebels.' But the commission nonetheless concluded: 'The crucial element of genocidal intent appears to be missing . . . It would seem that those who planned and organised attacks on villages pursued the intent to drive the victims from their homes, primarily for the purposes of counter-insurgency warfare.'

For the record, this is a conclusion with which I would agree. Article 2 of the 1948 Convention on the Prevention and Punishment of the Crime of Genocide argues that the crime is only committed if there exists 'intent to destroy, in whole or in part, a national, ethnical, racial or religious group . . .'. Although the consequences of the government's actions in Darfur in 2003–4 did amount to a partial destruction of some of the ethnic groups there, I do not believe that this was ever the government's initial intent, unlike the cases of Rwanda or Nazi Germany. Darfur was a bungled counter-insurgency operation that got wildly out of hand and ended up as ethnic cleansing. Furthermore, almost all of the mass killing took place in the first year; by the time the genocide activist campaign really got going after 2004, Darfur was much more of a low-intensity guerrilla war than an arena for genocide.

Some thought that the exact designation of the killings did not really matter; dreadful atrocities had taken place, and that was enough. But it mattered a great deal in campaigning terms. The cry of 'genocide' recruited people to a cause, and mobilized the influential Jewish community in the USA. However, it also, unfortunately, opened up a gulf of non-understanding between these activists and the rest of the world, particularly Asia.[2]

'Genocide diplomacy' also left little room for subtleties. The narrative of genocide demanded a relatively simple good/evil calculus to interpret events in Darfur, whereas in fact, as we have seen, the causes of the conflict were varied and complex. As Stephen Morrison, who had worked on Sudan under Clinton, later told me, the 'genocide fixation . . . locked' US policy on Sudan. 'The campaigners only have one gear and have a lock over Congress. It left our diplomacy helpless, left the US without the ability to put much on the table with Khartoum.' Because of the public pressure to treat Darfur as a genocide, politicians and other officials felt obliged to swap insults with Khartoum to appease a very vocal domestic constituency regardless of whether this might have helped or hindered the actual resolution of the conflict.

For the US diplomats trying to finish the tricky negotiations on the Comprehensive Peace Agreement (CPA), for example, the public name-calling made their jobs harder. Charles Snyder, the chief diplomat who had to deal with the Sudanese government on a daily basis, told me later that when the politicians got involved on emotive, political issues 'all the day-to-day glue goes'. This was the glue that had allowed the US–Sudanese relationship to develop from a Clintonite 'cold war' to sharing intelligence and fixing a north–south peace deal. 'The small boys are the keys to these peace deals,' Snyder explained. 'As the big politicians take over, with the big megaphone politics, the UN etc. . . . that is what changes and why it falls to bits.'

This was the downside of celebrity activism. Ultimately, the diplomats argued, however terrible the killings in Darfur, the conflict still required a political solution within the existing Sudanese constitutional framework. The Darfuris, unlike the southerners, were never secessionists; so any deal between the rebels and Khartoum would require all the usual compromises and horse-trading that inevitably accompanies such negotiated solutions. For many, however, branding Darfur a genocide somehow transformed it into a completely different category of conflict where the normal, rather pedestrian laws of diplomacy need not apply.

Every time I went to Khartoum after 2005 I would hear a rant from US diplomats there about the latest foolishness over Darfur from US activists and the politicians in Washington who felt obliged to pander to them. In autumn 2008, one official whom I had seen regularly on my trips unburdened himself completely. He complained of all the 'posturing involved on Sudan', of the people advocating war against Sudan over Darfur to advance their political careers and make political points: 'They are loons in Washington,' he fumed. 'It's celebrity diplomacy. All these celebs want the glory of posing on Darfur, but not the hardship of actually living here. These Darfur activists say things that make absolutely no sense at all.' Speaking in a torrent, the diplomat spotted a newspaper article on the table: Mia Farrow had just advocated sending in guards from Blackwater, a particularly notorious American private security company, to protect the internally displaced persons (IDPs) in Darfur. 'It's insane,' he expostulated. 'These guys are the American *janjaweed*. I saw them in Iraq and Afghanistan. I know this.'

Some of the aid workers in Darfur from 2003 onwards also despaired of the simplifications and distortions that seemed to accompany much of the Western campaigning. Caroline Nursey, the east Africa regional director of the major British aid agency Oxfam between 2003 and 2005, and programme director in Sudan in 2006–7, spoke for many aid workers when she told me later: 'At times I felt that the SaveDarfurCoalition was responsible for much of the harm going on there.' In her view, their message was 'so simplistic it made it very difficult for the government to back down'. It became impossible to 'persuade people that the rebels are not just the good guys'; this stopped anyone from putting any pressure on the rebels to be reasonable in their negotiations with the government (of which more later).

Nursey, like most aid workers in Darfur, refused to term the situation a genocide. Such a description of the conflict was, in her view, 'untrue, unhelpful, so emotive and drove the government into a corner . . . there were war crimes, but no genocide'. She continued, 'Everyone thought it was a repeat of Rwanda . . . That triggered the genocide comparison, which did not help. It's too quick trying to grab easy answers.' Altogether, the experience of following the propaganda of the SaveDarfurCoalition from Darfur itself, where Nursey could actually see what was going on, forced an experienced humanitarian worker like herself to reassess her whole career: 'It's made me question myself when I have gone out and waved banners without really understanding things. Was I really right to do that?'

If the aid workers worried about the loss of detail, texture and even truth in the megaphone activism blasting from the USA, like the diplomats they also tired of the constant stream of special envoys, foreign politicians, aspiring politicos, film stars, elder statesmen and even journalists who popped into Darfur (often for the inside of a day) to pledge support – or to boost their own profiles and careers. The 'disaster tourism' of Darfur, as one diplomat described it to me, provided excellent photo-opportunities, but it was seldom evident to the local staff who had to facilitate these visits that they were of any benefit to the Darfuris themselves.

By 2008, five years after the start of the war, many people on the ground had become truly exasperated by the circus. I met a UN spokesperson in Khartoum with whom I was supposed to discuss the usual facts and figures of Darfur. However, within a few minutes she had got on to what was obviously her current obsession – celebrities. Of the George Clooneys, Mia Farrows, Don Cheadles and others who had passed in and out, she expostulated:

They have done a lot of damage in Darfur. They don't fully understand the conflict. They're not reflecting Darfurian feeling. They
paint it as a 'good' and a 'bad', but miss the complexity. They get
their facts wrong – they scream about starvation in Darfur when it
is just not the case. They become bigger than the people on the
ground, and it takes a lot of our time to organize these trips and
organize security etc. It does not help a practical solution.[3]

The activists in the USA seemed to make little attempt to synchronize
their activities or campaigns with the wide range of international staff
in Darfur, such as the NGOs who actually worked on the ground. The
aid workers were seldom consulted on how the SaveDarfurCoalition's
message might 'help' (or hinder) their work. Many humanitarian staff
in the region were particularly irritated by the fact that Darfur
continued to be described as a 'humanitarian disaster' by the activists
in order to raise awareness (and money). It certainly was a disaster
in 2003–4. However, in subsequent years a well-funded and well-
organized relief operation, run by thousands of dedicated people,
successfully reduced the incidences of death and starvation in Darfur
to relatively low levels despite a lack of co-operation, hostility even,
from the Sudanese government. Indeed, after a few years Darfuris
were eating rather better than some of their compatriots in other,
more peaceful parts of Sudan. By 2008 Darfur no longer even counted
as an 'emergency' situation in aid-agency terms, let alone a disaster,
even though low-level fighting continued throughout the region.[4]

THE LIMITS OF WESTERN POWER: 'THOSE GUYS ALWAYS BLINK FIRST'

Despite the emerging differences over Darfur, the long hoped-for
Comprehensive Peace Agreement was finally signed on 9 January
2005, theoretically at least bringing the fifty-year war with the south to
a close. This was not only a diplomatic triumph in its own right. To a
degree, it also now absolved the British and Americans from the

obligation, as they had seen it, to go soft on the Sudanese government over the killings in Darfur.

This new freedom allowed the White House, in particular, more leeway to heed the call of the activists' campaign for punitive measures against the Sudanese government for its actions in the region. Having themselves shielded the Sudanese government from any embarrassing questions or resolutions at the UN from April 2003 to April 2004, the Americans and the British now became the most vociferous critics of the Sudanese government at the Security Council, demanding 'action' on Darfur.

However, this did the Darfuris little good. Stepping into the shoes of the British and Americans, the Chinese, with their own interests in Sudan to consider, thereafter became the Sudanese government's main protectors at the UN Security Council, closely followed by the Russians. In September 2004, China abstained from voting on the very first Security Council resolution concerning Darfur, which set up the commission of enquiry into the alleged crimes in the region. China also promised to veto any further resolutions that proposed sanctions against the Sudanese government for its actions in Darfur. This established a pattern for the following three years or so. From the autumn of 2004 to October 2007, the Security Council drafted and voted on fourteen resolutions of varying importance relating to Darfur. China insisted on removing language that was too tough on the Sudanese at least nine times, and abstained from voting on the resolutions five times.[5]

The effectiveness of the Chinese support for Sudan, based on decades of friendship and a good deal of mutual self-interest (as we saw in Chapter 1), betrayed a harsh truth; by the time that President George W. Bush had largely committed himself to the Darfur activists' camp, he found that his ability to change dramatically the situation on the ground in Darfur had all but drained away. Western politicians, generally, found themselves strangely impotent in the face of a wily Sudanese government and a new set of realities, increasingly common to the whole of Africa, which they had scarcely appreciated before. As a result, the promises of effective, practical action gave way to moral grandstanding and empty threats, which merely emboldened the Sudanese regime to transgress further. And all the while, the demographic transformation of Darfur against the wishes of its people continued apace, while the tough work of *implementing* the peace agreement with the south was quietly forgotten about.

Michael Gerson, Bush's speechwriter in his first term of office and a presidential adviser on developing-world issues in his second term, saw the US government's frustrations over Sudan at first hand. He first went to Khartoum as a presidential emissary in November 2005 with Robert Zoellick, then the deputy secretary of state at the State Department dealing with Africa. The two Americans met several times with President Bashir and Foreign Minister Ali Osman Taha, mainly to discuss Darfur; these meetings showed how both sides, having spent several years in close agreement with each other, were now going to spend the next few years talking past one another.

Gerson and Zoellick largely articulated the prevailing views of the Darfur activists, repeating the number of those killed and displaced – to which the Sudanese replied that Darfur was merely a counter-insurgency operation. Zoellick said that in signing the CPA Sudan had made a 'strategic decision' to be more engaged with the West, yet the Sudanese government was now making a series of tactical errors that worked against this, mainly over Darfur. In other words, they had to stop the assault in Darfur before they could be truly 'engaged' with the West.

For their part, Bashir and Taha responded that they had done exactly what the USA had asked of them – signing the CPA – and so they now expected the existing sanctions against Sudan to be lifted. 'They did not seem even to acknowledge that anything was going on in Darfur,' recalls Gerson. Clearly, the Sudanese thought that they had nothing to be ashamed of, or to make amends for. To Gerson, they looked like people 'that seemed to be under no pressure at all . . . They were the opposite of being defensive; they were on the offensive.' He had some sympathy with the Khartoum government on how the crisis had started, but none with how they were trying to resolve it: 'You can't expect a government not to respond to rebel attacks, but the response was so extreme that it amounted to genocide.'

Gerson took several impressions away from the visit. Altogether, these were to shape much of the Bush administration's policy on Sudan. First, he had 'deep doubts' that Khartoum really had made a long-term decision to co-operate with the West after signing the CPA, as they claimed. Secondly, Khartoum felt under little pressure concerning what its army and security services were doing in Darfur because they were 'protected by a series of shields': China, Russia, the Arab League and the Egyptians. Finally, Gerson concluded that the 7,000-strong African Union force that had been inserted to monitor a non-existent ceasefire at the end of 2004 was wholly inadequate. He concluded: 'A bigger UN force would be the only thing to change the dynamic on the ground.'

On his return to Washington DC, Gerson had lunch with President Bush. They agreed that 'the Darfur policy was a shambles'. Bush was appalled by Gerson's accounts of what he had found; he proved open to Gerson's idea of pushing for greater UN intervention. The other question at this point, however, was how far the USA itself should get directly involved in Darfur. At the time it was bogged down in Iraq and Afghanistan, with the former conflict going particularly badly.

To explore the matter further, Gerson told me, a series of meetings was arranged with the second-in-commands at the various government departments, such as State and Defence. Stephen Hadley, Bush's National Security Adviser, led the charge for maximum US pressure, while Zoellick, from State, argued that by getting heavily involved in Darfur, Bush would be investing himself politically in a situation with no good outcomes. Hadley's advocacy, however, won the day, and so the USA now pressed ahead with a new dual-track strategy. First, the USA would fight to get a UN Security Council resolution authorizing the dispatch of a large peacekeeping force to Darfur. Secondly, the USA's own national-security apparatus would look at ways of putting pressure on the Khartoum government

Throughout all this, his staff noted, Bush was morally and emotionally engaged on Darfur to an unusual degree. Within the Washington bureaucracy, this gave a much-needed sense of urgency to US policy. It also made the president correspondingly sensitive to domestic criticism from the SaveDarfurCoalition that he was still not doing enough on the issue. This was the power of the lobby: to cajole, remind and irritate. To move things along faster, Gerson used to send Bush press clippings full of complaints about the administration's supposedly lacklustre approach to Sudan. These articles did not go down well in the Oval Office. On one occasion, Bush called Gerson in to complain that he was 'angry and upset' and felt that 'many of the articles were unfair'. He was 'going to do something about this . . .'

This 'something' eventually turned out to be a 'Principals' Meeting' on Darfur: a gathering of the full national-security team, including the Secretary of Defense (Donald Rumsfeld), called by Bush to discuss what military pressure the USA could exert on Sudan. However, despite Bush's resolve it quickly became apparent that Rumsfeld and the Department of Defense (DoD) were reluctant to devote any time and energy even to planning action on Sudan, for fear, as Gerson told me, 'that they would actually have to do something'. The USA was already overstretched in Iraq and Afghanistan and the DoD did not want to undertake peacekeeping operations of the kind that might have been necessary in Darfur. Even the less intrusive operations in Sudan that might have yielded results, such as a blockade of Sudan's oil exports, or enforcing a no-fly zone over Darfur, were considered to be impossible. Yet it is useful to remember in this context that only four years before, the CIA and the DoD had threatened the Sudanese regime with the destruction of its oil industry (and economic lifeline) in an afternoon in order to extract all the intelligence that they wanted on al-Qaeda. That threat had worked pretty well.

So, within the Washington bureaucracy, unilateral military action was ruled out. Unfortunately, however, Bush had already spoken publicly about the prospect of enforcing a no-fly zone over Darfur in order to prevent the Sudanese Air Force's deadly Hind helicopters from operating there. Other politicians in Europe, such as Britain's prime minister Tony Blair, were also raising it as a possible option.

They wanted to convey the impression that they were serious about doing something bold on Darfur. But this merely started a fatal divergence between what the politicians, responding to pressure from the Darfur lobby, publicly threatened the Sudanese government with, and what they could actually deliver.

In Britain, for instance, those who advocated firmer action against the Sudanese government were caught in a similar bind to Gerson and President Bush. The Foreign Office minister with responsibility for Africa, David Triesman, also asked for military assets to enforce a no-fly zone over Darfur. But he too was told by the Ministry of Defence that Britain was already fully committed in Afghanistan and Iraq. President Bush talked to the NATO secretary-general on this, and to the French president, Jacques Chirac. The French, it was hoped, might have taken a lead because they actually already had some airforce jets in neighbouring Chad, where they propped up President Déby's wobbly regime. But, as Triesman told me: 'In the end nobody would actually bite the bullet.'

A stricter arms embargo, restrictions on travel for the senior members of the regime in Khartoum and naval blockades were also discussed in public in 2006 and 2007, but nothing ever happened. There was even some loose talk of sending a couple of thousand British Royal Marines to Darfur. In the United States, two Republican senators, John McCain and Robert Dole, both presidential candidates at different times, joined together to call for the UN to force its way into Darfur unilaterally if needs be. Reflecting on the whole Darfur saga in 2008, after he had left government to run the English Football Association, Triesman told me:

> The international community has substantially failed. There has been an unwillingness, when we get to the tough stuff, to do the things that would convince the [Sudanese] government and the rebel groups that things would end badly for them . . . We have gone to the brink so often, and then not done it. The biggest source of comfort they [the Sudanese] have is that they can think – those guys always blink first.

The Sudanese regime judged this Western posturing on Darfur all too accurately. With the USA and Britain mired in Iraq after the summer of 2003, the Sudanese knew that however much the West's politicians got worked up about Darfur the two most militarily capable countries would not be able to afford, politically or financially, a simultaneous military action in another Muslim country. In essence, an intervention that might well have been justified in Darfur on humanitarian grounds was ruled out due to an illegal and largely spurious military adventure in Iraq.

If hope of US, or British, military action against Sudan fizzled out as 'empty threats', the UN route went little better. In January 2006, after Gerson's briefing to Bush, the US push to get a big UN force into Darfur began in earnest. However, this ran into immediate difficulties on two accounts. Despite some enthusiasm for the idea in Kofi Annan's entourage, others within the UN system were considerably less keen, particularly in the Department of Peacekeeping Operations (DPKO), the body that would actually have to get the troops into Darfur. For there was no 'peace' to 'keep'; there was not even a working ceasefire agreement in place. The host Sudanese government definitely did not want foreign troops in the region and, in any case, the logistical problems of supplying a force that might amount to 25,000 troops and police in the middle of a desert would be horrendous.

As well as a sceptical DPKO, the campaign for a UN force ran into the brick wall of Chinese resistance. Khartoum, of course, wanted the battlefield of Darfur to itself – the Sudanese army did not want thousands of foreign troops interrupting its 'counter-insurgency' war there, or sniffing around for evidence of war crimes. The Sudanese thus derided any plans to insert foreign and/or UN troops into Darfur as Western neo-colonialism, and the Chinese, by and large, agreed with them, as did other formerly colonized Muslim countries that were temporary Security Council members. Pakistan and Algeria, for example, abstained on key votes against Sudan over Darfur. On 31 August the UN Security Council passed Resolution 1706 which authorized the deployment of a UN force in Darfur of up to 21,000 troops and police – but the Chinese again abstained on the vote. They argued that the consent of the Sudanese had to be obtained for such a deployment, and the Sudanese adamantly refused to give it.

Thus began a novel campaign of Western diplomatic pressure on the Chinese to change their minds, alongside a more high-profile activists' campaign against China as well. They had some leverage. China, anxious about its status as an emerging world power, did not want to be isolated on such a high-profile issue as Darfur. This must partly explain China's acceptance of the UN Security Council's resolution 1593 in 2005, which referred the killings in Darfur to the newly formed International Criminal Court (ICC). To the surprise of some, China did not block this but merely abstained from voting, although the country did its best to shield Sudan from prying investigations in other forums, such as the UN's Commission on Human Rights in Geneva.

China had staked an enormous amount of prestige and goodwill on a successful Olympic Games in Beijing in 2008 and this was cleverly turned into the country's Achilles heel over Darfur. The linkage of the Beijing Olympic to China's stance on Darfur was very wounding – the tag of the 'Genocide Olympics' was a clever and effective campaigning tool used by Mia Farrow and other activists. Nicholas Kristof was one of the first to publicize the connection, writing in the *New York Times* in April 2006 that China, through its economic, military and diplomatic support of Khartoum, was 'underwriting its second genocide in three decades' (after Cambodia). As has been well chronicled, China began to abandon its much-lauded policy of 'non-interference' in Sudan's affairs in response to this pressure. Slowly, it started to persuade the Sudanese government to relent over letting UN troops in, despite considerable stalling over the winter of 2006–7.

However, the Chinese shift of position was only limited. Although the Sudanese were pushed by the Chinese into abandoning their outright objection to allowing UN blue helmets into Darfur, Chinese support remained sufficient for the Sudanese to win unprecedented control over the make-up of the force and its command-and-control structure. So, for instance, the Sudanese were able to insist that the troops for the putative combined UN/AU mission could only come from Africa or, at a pinch, Asia. The UN effort would, in theory, be a 'hybrid' operation, with the existing AU soldiers rolled into it. This meant that, in practice, most of the troops would be left-overs from the previous ineffectual African force.

Even after the new United Nations and African Mission in Darfur (UNAMID) started deploying at the beginning of 2008, the Sudanese still kept tight control over its ability to operate on the ground. The Sudanese authorities were as obstructive as possible about letting the UN bring any equipment in; there were long delays getting anything from Port Sudan to Darfur. The Sudanese government also made the most of the small print governing the predominantly 'African character' of the force. Thus they hounded any new, non-African personnel in UNAMID with dogged determination.

When I visited the blue helmets in March 2008 just after UNAMID had begun operations, Khartoum's bête noire of the moment was a sandy-haired British brigadier bearing an uncanny resemblance to Peter O'Toole in the film *Lawrence of Arabia*. The British and Americans had quietly managed to insert him as the chief of staff and third-in-command of the operation. He was bringing some much-needed zest and new ideas to UNAMID – and thus making himself correspondingly unpopular with the worried Sudanese authorities. Desperate to get him 'PNGed' (declared *persona non grata* and thrown out), the Sudan authorities questioned the British officer's status relentlessly, until after just a few months the brigadier left and was subsequently not allowed back in. Scandinavian engineering platoons were unwelcome, as were any Americans. As this sort of mix of skills and nationalities normally provided the backbone to the most effective peacekeeping operations, UNAMID, bound by the fine print of its mandate, was hamstrung from the beginning.

In short, although the UN could at least congratulate itself on having got a force into Darfur after years of pressure, the Chinese provided the Sudanese with enough cover to ensure that UNAMID's role would be strictly limited. Indeed, in the years immediately after the mission began, Sudanese government military operations continued much as before. UNAMID, even with about 20,000 policemen and soldiers at its disposal by 2010, rarely proved able to act as a deterrent against any armed groups in Darfur, whether government or rebel.

All along, Khartoum had played a clever game at the UN, exploiting the divisions on the Security Council to the full. Yet the fissures at the UN were, at the same time, also real and deep, reflecting the fact that the issue of Darfur, like the invasion of Iraq, helped to define new attitudes in a world order in which 'third world' states expressed increasing solidarity with Sudan against the perceived bullying of the West, regardless of what was really going on in Darfur. Muslim countries in particular contributed little to the initial relief efforts in Darfur – partly because they felt the need to be seen standing shoulder to shoulder with another Muslim government at a time when the whole of the Muslim world felt under threat from George W. Bush's administration.

China, Russia, South Africa, Congo, Indonesia, Qatar and Libya all rejected, at one time or another, criticisms of the Khartoum government and its human-rights record. Arab and African states usually backed Sudan, and most strongly on 'justice and accountability issues'; most obviously when the ICC announced, on 14 July 2008, that it would investigate President Bashir for war crimes in Darfur. African and Arab members of the UN asked for a suspension of the ICC proceedings, something the Security Council has the power to order, backed by Russia and China as well as temporary members Indonesia and Vietnam.[6]

THE ART OF GESTURE POLITICS

But the reasons for UNAMID's lack of effectiveness went beyond the shortcomings of the UN system, Sudanese obstructionism and the quality of the African soldiers. Just as importantly, none of the military forces inserted into Darfur was ever fully funded or supported; none of the commanders ever had anywhere near all the equipment – the helicopters, the armoured transport vehicles – that they needed. Foreign countries had pushed a theoretical UN peacekeeping force into the region, but they subsequently failed to match fine words with real money or troops.

This pattern started with the original AU force that began to deploy in Darfur in 2004, called the African Mission in Sudan (AMIS). Anxious to be seen to be applying 'African solutions to African problems', as the mantra of the day had it, the AU sent soldiers of its own into Darfur. Nigeria, Senegal, Rwanda and others all contributed varying amounts of troops to what would be Africa's first large-scale 'peacekeeping' exercise. However, the national troops arrived in the expectation that other countries, from Africa and beyond, would pay for the operation, given how concerned everyone seemed to be about the situation. But the funding that they had hoped for never arrived.

Cage Banseka, a Cameroonian-born Briton with a higher degree from Germany, arrived to take up a job as a political officer with AMIS in 2006. He saw all its disappointments at first hand. The African Union raised the troops, but for some countries giving troops to the AU mission seemed to be little more than a way of claiming more money for them than they would have been paid in their own countries. The Arab League, for its part, Banseka remembers, 'made a lot of promises and pledges but never made good on them'. It had seemed at first only natural that the Muslim world should do the most to help fellow Muslims in Darfur. Banseka went to meetings with the Arab League representatives where they pledged $150 million, but only a fraction of that sum ever arrived. When he told them, as he often did, that he was still waiting for any sign of the promised money, he was always reassured that 'it was in the pipeline'. But it never emerged out of the pipeline. Banseka concluded that they were just 'playing games'.

As result, what little money was available for AMIS mainly came from the West. But, even so, the AU troops were left in a desperate state, often unpaid for months and lacking the most basic equipment. Not surprisingly, morale among the soldiers plummeted, and their mood was not improved when they started to get shot at over the summer of 2005. Bandits, rebels and others realized that the AU troops were almost sitting ducks, and began to ambush them for their radios, cars and weapons. Inevitably, AU soldiers started to get killed. It was clear that they could barely protect themselves, let alone the millions of internally displaced persons who continued to be harassed in their camps or while gathering firewood outside.

The insertion of a full UN force into Darfur was supposed to overcome the failure of the AU. Yet having spent all those thousands of diplomat hours getting the troops in, the world again refused to match its political commitments with boots and cash. UNAMID took over the existing 8,000 or so AMIS troops in January 2008, and was supposed to scale up to 19,000 troops and 7,000 police by the end of that year. In fact, the complement was up to barely 10,000 by the start of 2009 – and most of these were still left over from the old AMIS force. The Nigerian general in command of UNAMID complained long and hard about his lack of 'force multipliers' – choppers – to get his men around the vast region. By the late summer of 2009, when General Agwai retired from his post, he claimed that he had still not received one military helicopter. By the beginning of 2010, two years after the start of its deployment, UNAMID was still some 6,000 soldiers and policemen short of its mandated manpower.

The Arab League contribution was, again, desultory. But it was the West that was expected to contribute sophisticated kit, such as helicopters. Yet almost nothing arrived, certainly not at the start. Western politicians took a great deal of credit for getting the UN resolution on UNAMID, but a show of hands in New York did not actually require them to dig into their pockets. To fund these operations properly would have required sacrifices from other budgets, maybe even domestic budgets, but politicians were not prepared to make the tough arguments to voters at home that would have allowed them the political space to make those sorts of choices. The Sudanese, of course, understood the dynamics of gesture politics very well. After 2004, they happily discounted any threats or menaces that Western politicians made, safe in the knowledge that there would be little follow through. Much more could have been made of UNAMID when it started, but the political will was not there. As one disillusioned UNAMID political officer confided to me in Darfur in 2009: 'We are just here. And the Sudanese have managed to make us irrelevant.'

The Sudanese government, for its part, was resistant to any peace in Darfur as long as it thought it could win a counter-insurgency campaign by military means. The result was that the regime oscillated between belligerence and diplomacy according to the demands of the moment and the military circumstances on the ground. Generally, the warmongers in the army, security and intelligence apparatus had the upper hand, although the so-called moderates sometimes exerted a countervailing pressure. On the whole, though, so tightly did Khartoum play its cards that it was usually impossible for Western governments and analysts to detect exactly where the centre of gravity lay between the two factions at any one time.

RAISING EXPECTATIONS – ACTIVISM AND THE DARFUR REBELS

Apart from the ineffectiveness of a divided UN and the equivocations of the Sudanese government, the rebels too played their own part in pushing peace out of reach. And here again there were some perverse incentives at work. The two main rebel groups, the Sudan Liberation Army (SLA) and the Justice and Equality Movement (JEM), were lauded as the heroes of the war by the Darfur lobby in the USA. The rebels were fortified by this support, but they were also encouraged to overestimate what they could reasonably expect to get out of the Sudanese government in negotiations.

In essence, as we have seen, Darfur was a political problem. All the rebels conceded that their differences with Khartoum would have to be solved within the borders of Sudan; there was rarely mention of Darfur breaking away from the country like the south. Yet often the rebels showed little willingness to negotiate in good faith with Khartoum. There were good reasons for this reluctance, of course – the government was rarely to be trusted. But there were bad reasons too. Often, the rebels would mistake the moral outrage of individual Americans on their behalf for real political and military commitments to topple President Bashir's regime. The rebels were often left with the impression that a settlement of the conflict in their favour would be imposed on Sudan by force, from outside.

These expectations were raised early on in the conflict. When Andrew Marshall, the mediator sent to Darfur by Mukesh Kapila, first met some of the rebel leaders towards the end of 2003 they were already reluctant to negotiate with the government because they seemed to be convinced that the USA was going to help them bomb their way to Khartoum, after which the government of Sudan would be handed to them on a plate. It is clear that they were encouraged to believe this by some activists, as well as sympathetic US officials.

One correspondent who was in Khartoum at the time saw all this going on at first hand, in not very great secrecy, in cafes and private houses. The journalist recalled for me: 'I've heard conversations between low-level guys in the [American] embassy and rebel leaders, advising rebel leaders on tactics. Some rebel leaders were under the impression that they would get material assistance from America, uniforms, other equipment.' Charlie Snyder, in Washington, obviously with the benefit of inside knowledge, told me that somebody must have 'encouraged them to think this'. Sometimes, activists publicly argued for the arming of rebel groups, so as to level the playing field with the Sudanese army.

In fact, all this turned out to be fantasy, and in the long run it was very damaging to the cause of the rebels. Most of their field commanders in 2003–4 were young men, in their mid-twenties, or early thirties at the most. They were ill-educated and certainly did not understand the inner workings of the US government or the UN. They did not know, and did not care to learn, about the differences between some lowly US embassy wallah, a senior diplomat, a smooth-talking activist and the head of a UN department. All these people were taken equally seriously, especially if they had a message that the rebels wanted to hear. Some fighters would thus assume that outspoken activists like Eric Reeves, or John Prendergast, *were* the US government. In fact, of course, for all their words, most of these people had almost no power to affect the military situation in Darfur. Too often the rebels were led to expect things that were never going to happen.

To one African diplomat who was called in to try to help resolve the conflict for the UN, this sort of foreign meddling (and the money that came with it) fatally undermined the customary way that a Darfur-type African conflict would have been resolved. He argued, 'The ideology of the SaveDarfurCoalition penetrated the rebel elites; they assumed the conflict would be resolved by others. They were waiting for NATO, or the Americans, or UNAMID . . . [They were] to be saved by an external agency, just like Kosovo. This mentality really distorts their responsibility about what they should do.' Thus all the discussions over sending UN troops could easily be misconstrued as well. Alex de Waal was an adviser to the AU at a long drawn-out round of Darfur peace talks in the Nigerian capital Abuja in 2006 and saw at first hand how 'the prospect of being "saved" by UN troops raised the hopes of the Darfurians and made them consider any political compromises . . . an unacceptable second best'.[7] Partly as a result, most of the rebel commanders refused to sign a partial 'Darfur Peace Agreement' that the Khartoum government signed in Abuja with only one leader, Minni Winawi of the SLA. He was rewarded by being appointed a special adviser to President Bashir. At the time of writing, the Abuja talks remain the only Darfur peace discussions that came anywhere remotely near a successful conclusion, though more recent negotiations have been led by Qatar in Doha.

Moreover, the rebel 'armies' failed to evolve into coherent political groups, with clear structures or chains of commands. As a result, the coherence of their negotiating positions quickly collapsed after the failure of the Abuja talks. The two main groups, the SLA and JEM, fractured into dozens of rival factions and sub-groups. Again, this process was partly driven by the dynamics of the foreign interest in

Darfur, and in particular by the often fawning and uncritical attention that the fighters enjoyed from Western activists and the media.

As Banseka, who had to negotiate with many of them, observed, they 'fractured not on ideological grounds but on personal grounds'. Basically, too many were vying for the position of top dog. Mostly young men, they 'all wanted to have a seat at the negotiating tables with Britain and the US and stay at four-star hotels'. During the Abuja peace talks Banseka noted that at the hotel where the rebels were staying there were no less than 8,000 entries in the guest book for prostitutes. Surprised by the amount of nocturnal activity, he had specifically asked the hotel to add up the numbers. 'It was like coming out of prison for the Darfuris,' Banseka commented.

The lesson of the CPA for the Darfuris seemed to be that only violence won you a place at the negotiating table. Offers of money from the West to 'rebuild' Darfur or to 'encourage the Darfur peace process' merely encouraged young, desperate Darfuris to take up arms so that they could appropriate some of the new money on offer for themselves. One mediator told me: 'In order to force themselves on the international community, they will burn down a village to establish their credentials as a new rebel force.'

And sometimes there were, indeed, rich pickings on offer for a credible rebel. Unusually, for example, rebels were paid $4,970 a month – a huge sum in Sudan – to sit on a 'ceasefire commission' in El Fasher that was meant to monitor the largely fictitious ceasefire. Not surprisingly, this produced a scramble to represent a 'rebel group' – any rebel group – on the commission. When I attended a sitting of the commission in March 2008 I counted at least seven groups there. The entire morning-long discussion revolved around exactly how much, and by what method, everyone would be paid – to the obvious disgust of the Rwandan UN peacekeeping officer chairing the meeting. A former guerrilla fighter himself, he occasionally appealed to the higher ideals for which the Darfuris were meant to be fighting. His efforts were cordially ignored.

To Cage Banseka and others these sorts of payments were an obvious mistake: 'People will pursue the attendant resources of being associated with the insurgency.' The proliferation of rebel groups after 2006 made it impossible for them to forge any sort of common nego-tiating position against the Khartoum government. This made outside attempts to bring the 'two sides' together all but impossible – one 'side' did not exist in any meaningful sense of the word. The resulting confu-sion of purpose and the cacophony of rebel voices claiming to speak on behalf of the people of Darfur also discredited the fighters even with those who had originally looked to them for leadership and protection.

This also led to a serious disjuncture between the accounts of the Darfur conflict that continued to be circulated in the USA and the reality of what was happening on the ground, especially after 2005. Despite everything, many activists still continued to maintain their Manichean division of 'good' rebels and 'bad' government long after the situation no longer remotely justified such distinctions. Some of the rebels themselves had become involved in violence against humanitarian workers and AU troops in Darfur as early as 2005, often for nothing more noble than personal gain. Three leaders, for instance, were indicted for war crimes by the ICC for a ruthless attack on AU troops at a village called Haskanita in 2007, which left twelve of them dead. However, more often than not, the rebels' responsibility for the contin-uing violence in Darfur went virtually unreported in the Western press.

Readers and viewers thus gained an increasingly distorted version of events in Darfur as the violence morphed from a genuine uprising, with clear-cut distinctions between the two main insurgent groups and government forces, into a messy, confusing, more generalized conflict where allegiances shifted and motivations changed. These media distortions mattered. For far too long foreign politicians and negotia-tors were reluctant to challenge the prevailing activists' view of the rebels, with the result that little pressure was put on them to be real-istic in any negotiations with the Sudanese government. As far as I am aware it was Andrew Natsios, the US special envoy, who finally broke the taboo against publicly criticizing the rebels in his speech to the last unsuccessful Darfur peace conference to date, at Sirte in Libya. But that was not until early November 2007, by which time any chances of a 'peace process' had evaporated. So bad were the splits among the rebels at that point that almost none of them turned up in Sirte, dooming the event to failure before it had even begun.

The most mercenary and recalcitrant of the rebel leaders proved to be Abdul Wahid al-Nur of the SLA. He eventually settled himself in some comfort in Paris after initially fleeing to Eritrea soon after the conflict began. Despite his distance from the battlefield in the years after 2003, however, he seemed to exert an almost mesmeric influence over his Fur kinsmen in Darfur. In particular the elusive al-Nur always commanded enormous support in the IDP camps where, as I would often hear, the refugees regarded him as their undisputed champion. This was mainly because he had astutely promised these IDPs $1,000 each, if he succeeded in negotiating a very favourable peace deal on their behalf. As a result, of course, they wanted to stick by their man until they got their money.

Despite the eternal hopes of UN mediators, Wahid al-Nur steadfastly refused to be drawn into any peace deals or negotiating process, always preferring to go his own way. In particular, his refusal to sign the Darfur Peace Agreement in Abuja in 2006 condemned it to fail. Sarah Panutliano, the researcher and expert on Arab pastoralists in Sudan, remembers confronting al-Nur in the Eritrean capital Asmara in the autumn of 2006. Sitting in front of a big TV in his house with CNN playing continuously, he talked about his refusal to sign in Abuja. Darfur would sometimes come up on the news behind him, at which point he would gesture towards the screen and exclaim: 'Why should I sign a deal with these people [the government in Khartoum] when the whole world is behind us? The world is with my people.' His sense of self-worth inflated by his (temporary) status as a world celebrity, he was confident that he could hold out for much more than just a grubby political compromise with Khartoum.

Eventually, even the insurgents' most steadfast supporters tired of the moral and political posturing of the 'movements'. By 2008, one such, Julie Flint, was warning:

Darfur's rebel movements initially gave many Darfuris great hope, despite their initial error of failing to embrace Darfuri Arabs, who feel equally abused by the regime in Khartoum. The movements must now make gestures of their own to 'save Darfur'. If they do not, the international community must break the mould. In any future peace talks, once the immediate danger of conflagration is past, Darfur must be represented by a wide range of its sons and daughters – not just by unelected men with guns who have forgotten their dream.

A LITTLE LOCAL DIFFICULTY – THE SUDANESE GOVERNMENT AND DARFUR

So much for the international community, the UN, the activists and the rebels. What about the Sudanese government, which had provoked the war in its western region in the first place?

As we have seen, when the Sudanese government signed the CPA in Kenya on 9 January 2005, it was fully expecting the quid pro quo of being removed from the State Department's list of state sponsors of terror. It was also expecting to be reintegrated into the international community more generally – the ruling National Congress Party (NCP) felt that it had conceded more than enough in the CPA to claim all this in return. After all, the northern Sudanese would probably lose the whole of southern Sudan and its oilfields in a referendum in 2011. And they were certainly going to have to share power with John Garang and other Sudan People's Liberation Movement (SPLM) politicians in a so-called 'government of national unity'.

Sudanese officials were so confident of their position at the start of the Darfur imbroglio that they would talk quite openly about the rebellion in the west, and even discuss their tactics for putting it down. It seems almost astonishing in retrospect, but in October 2004 the government's security chief, Salah Gosh, revealed almost everything about the government's strategy in Darfur in an interview with Opheera McDoom of Reuters. Yes, Salah Gosh admitted, the government was bombing villages: 'It will attack those villages because the villages were attacking them.' Yes, the government had armed and trained the Arab tribes in response to the rebellion, although most of these militias, he argued, had been absorbed into regular units of the army. He acknowledged that there had been human-rights violations, and vowed that those responsible would be brought to justice.

He even admitted, tacitly, how the counter-insurgency strategy in Darfur had gone awry by referring to the situation in the east, where the Beja had taken up arms: 'We have the lesson from Darfur, we have learned a lesson and we have not used the tribes in the war in the east. We are going to recruit people inside the army.' You couldn't get much franker than that.[8]

However, as we have seen the Sudanese government's reward for making peace with the south never came, as the Bush administration blanched at the prospect of making 'concessions' to Khartoum in the face of the new Darfur lobby. With no reward for what they saw as giving away so much on the CPA, the Sudanese government retreated into a bunker mentality. The Sudanese virtually broke off any reasonable co-operation with the West over the south, Darfur or anywhere else. Instead, they cultivated a sense of betrayal and suspicion. Within the regime in Khartoum, those who had negotiated the CPA were now, to a degree, discredited and sidelined. After all, they had promised their colleagues renewed relations with the USA, only to be rebuffed. The stars of the moderates in the regime, Ghazi Atabani and Ali Osman Taha, waned. Instead, the hardliners from the security and intelligence apparatus, men like Salah Gosh and Nafie Ali Nafie, were in the ascendancy. They would prove much tougher over the war in Darfur, and indeed over everything else.

With their hopes of a transformation in Sudan's relations with the world dashed, the NCP settled into a more limited strategy of containment. The NCP no longer had a strong Islamist agenda to advance – that had all gone with Turabi and the grotesque abuses of the Islamic revolution. Neither did they have a diplomatic agenda to advance – that had, in their view, been snatched from them by the betrayal of the

USA over the CPA. Instead, they opted for a policy of merely hanging onto power, enjoying the oil revenues and toughing out the Western hostility over Darfur.

From being relatively open about Darfur, policy instead turned to one of denial. Rather than investigate any of the killings in Darfur, as Salah Gosh had suggested to Opheera McDoom, or rein in the militias, the Sudanese government instead chose to deny any direct responsibility for the fighting in Darfur and to minimize the extent of the violence as well.

Most egregiously, this took the form of denying any links to the *janjaweed* killers, despite all the evidence to the contrary. It also involved a game of numbers. Much of the debate over what happened in Darfur turned on the number of people who had died as a result of the fighting. Relatively early on the SaveDarfurCoalition plumped for the very high number of 400,000; given that the population of Darfur in 2002 was probably only about 6 million, that level of deaths would indeed suggest a catastrophe, possibly even a genocide. In 2007 their use of this figure in publicity materials was successfully challenged by a pro-Sudanese lobby organization; the British advertising watchdog ruled that the coalition could quote this number only as an opinion, not a fact.

The Sudanese government, on the other hand, consistently claimed that no more than 9,000–10,000 had been killed in the whole of Darfur since 2003, although they admitted that more might have died from disease and other causes as a result of the conflict.[9] In reality, because of the difficulties of reporting from Darfur, nobody has been able to compile exact figures, so the best estimates are based on extrapolations. The UN's position at the time of writing, based on the most authoritative sources available, is that approaching 300,000 Darfuris have died as a result of the conflict since 2003.

Either way, almost everyone's estimates were far higher than the Sudanese government's. Sudanese officials stubbornly insisted on attributing the strange, very large discrepancy in estimates to the nefarious machinations of the 'Western media'. Indeed, as by the Sudanese account very few had actually died in Darfur, officials claimed that the conflict in the region was therefore largely fictitious, part of what the Sudanese politician Osman Mudawi told me was 'an unparalleled Western media campaign'.

Mudawi is an NCP stalwart. In his late seventies when I met up with him in early 2009, a fluent and engaging English speaker with a house and family in north London, he joined the Sudanese Islamist Movement in Khartoum in 1951, just after it was founded. Sitting down with me in London, his explanation of the Darfur conflict can serve as the standard regime template for the events in Darfur. It was an account I heard dozens of times from the ministers and officials of Sudan's government.

First, the story goes, there was very little going on in Darfur anyway. Mudawi suggested that even Khartoum's figure of 9,000 deaths in Darfur was probably exaggerated. In any case, what deaths there had been were attributable only to 'armed robbers', who were endemic to the region; during the wars with Chad the Libyans had poured arms into the Darfur area, thus increasing the levels of violence. This was, in part, true. Also true was his assertion that Darfur, far from being horribly deprived and poor in comparison with the rest of the country, was a relatively rich area. Thus, in his view, the Darfuris had less reason to revolt than most.

In 2003, Mudawi argued, 'the whole of Sudan was on the verge of a great transformation' with the signing of the CPA – but this hope was dashed by the armed insurgency of the Justice and Equality Movement which had to be met by force. 'If they do represent the people as they claim,' argued Mudawi, 'why did they opt to come to power with the gun?' JEM, he continued, was the armed wing of Hassan al-Turabi's extreme Islamist movement, dedicated to a coup. Mudawi also attributed the success and endurance of the Darfur rebel groups to the financial and military support that they got from outside sources. Mudawi fingered the French as arming the rebels – otherwise, he asked: 'Where would they [JEM] have got the weapons from?' He claimed that one JEM operation, an attack on Omdurman in the spring of 2008, aimed at overthrowing the government by force, must have cost about $500 million.

That figure is vastly over-inflated. But, nonetheless, JEM did get outside help for its operations, mainly from Chad; and the Chadian government of Idriss Déby was propped up by the French, the country's former colonial masters. Indeed, Déby survived several coup attempts solely because of French government support. Thus, like much else of Mudawi's case, there were enough grains of truth in it to construct a persuasive narrative about the Darfur conflict that convinced most northern Sudanese, many fellow Africans and much of the Arab world. JEM did have close links to Turabi, and he was indeed responsible for the coup of 1989 and much of the violence and destruction that followed. The figure of 9,000 deaths in Darfur was absurdly low – but the figure of 400,000 that was bandied around in the West at the time was not credible either. That exaggeration made people more willing to listen to Mudawi's lower figure.

In Mudawi's estimation there was so little going on in Darfur that anything that did happen there should have remained a strictly internal Sudanese affair. He thus attributed only malevolent intentions to those outsiders who tried to intervene in Darfur. On this logic, it stood to reason that the only possible Western interest must have been an Iraq-style invasion of the region in order to impose Western values on Muslim Sudan – as part of a new neo-imperialist crusade led by George W. Bush, Tony Blair and their successors. Of course these were not the real motives driving the vast majority of those scores of thousands of aid workers, UN peacekeepers and activists who came to the help of the victims of the conflict in Darfur. But because President Clinton fired cruise missiles into Khartoum and the Sudanese regime was, as we have seen, more or less threatened with economic decapitation by the Bush administration, Mudawi's arguments were still just plausible enough to convince many.

Moreover, these distortions flourished in an atmosphere of domestic ignorance about Darfur. After the war broke out there in 2003, the government did its best to keep its own people as unenlightened as possible about the conflict. The most important aspect of this informa-tion battle was the concerted attempt to curb the flow of reporting coming out of Darfur. Most threatening to Khartoum, in this regard, were the thousands of aid workers, many of them Western, who flooded the region after 2004. After some initial attempts at obstruction, the Sudanese were obliged to accept this influx of eager, articulate and highly committed volunteers to run the burgeoning number of refugee camps that were set up to provide 'temporary' shelter for those fleeing the *janjaweed* attacks.

By as early as 2005, the number of these IDPs had risen to probably two million, and as the Sudanese government itself showed almost no inclination to help these people, about 50,000 aid workers did the job instead. Many of them were local Sudanese. Their numbers were divided among the main UN agencies, such as the World Food Programme (WFP) and the big NGOs, such as Mercy Corps, Oxfam, Médecins Sans Frontières (MSF) and World Vision, as well as scores of smaller ones. It rapidly became the biggest single humanitarian operation in the world, and remained so at the time of writing in 2010. Or, put another way, the world now started paying hundreds of millions of dollars to keep alive the victims of a military campaign orchestrated by a comparatively rich government which pretended nothing was happening (of which more in the next chapter).

With so many Westerners now running around Darfur, the Sudanese government was naturally alarmed that they would catalogue and publicize what was really going on in the region. So the Sudanese sought to prevent them from seeing the *janjaweed* attacks or gaining access to the areas where these attacks were occurring. Moreover, UN agencies and the NGOs were forced to strike a Faustian pact with the Sudanese authorities: in return for access to Darfur, aid workers and NGOs were obliged to desist from giving out or publishing any information about the region that was deemed by the Sudanese authorities to be 'political' rather than strictly 'humanitarian' – as defined, of course, by the government. The Sudanese censors in Khartoum would comb through all press releases and bulletins to ensure that this rule was respected. No comment or information was allowed out other than on topics such as the numbers requiring food aid or the number of wells sunk.

The weapon that the Sudanese government wielded to enforce this ban was the visa. Quite simply, if an NGO worker or agency infringed the rules, then they were denied a visa to enter and work in the country, and all visas were short term. So rather than people being 'expelled' or 'deported', which would have attracted a great deal of adverse publicity, aid workers would simply not be allowed back into the country once their visas had expired. That sort of incident could be made to look more like bureaucratic fastidiousness rather than anything more sinister.

In effect, the aid agencies were forced to collude with the Sudanese government in keeping a lid on much of what was happening in Darfur. It was a price that aid agencies accepted that they had to pay in order to save lives. One senior British aid worker, who did not want to be identified in this book, arrived in the early days of the emergency in the autumn of 2004. He told me four years later: 'It was always self-censorship.' He continued: 'We made the assumption that we would be kicked out. Overt reporting of human-rights abuses, we just didn't do. We would be kicked out because the government doesn't care. So we had no leverage . . . And it has always been the case in Darfur.' For him and many others: 'The humanitarian imperative takes precedence here.'

On the ground, NGOs and UN workers had their movements tightly controlled by an agency that George Orwell would have appreciated: the Humanitarian Affairs Council (HAC). This was the official Sudanese body charged with the relief of Darfur. In fact, the job of the HAC, largely staffed by security personnel, was to make the operations of the NGOs as difficult as possible, and to ensure that NGO workers never strayed far from their prescribed areas of operation. Permits and paperwork were the HAC's weapons of choice. Hard-nosed officials would allow no deviation from closely worded instructions. In the words of the British aid worker, working in Darfur 'was a war of attrition between the ex-pats [from the NGOs] and the HAC'.

Because all the NGOs were obliged (and wanted) to recruit locally, the assumption was that many of these new employees would, in reality, be spies – undercover HAC officials or even internal security agents. They would monitor the comings and goings of the ex-pats, bug them, follow them and try to break into computer files. None of this contributed to the atmosphere of collegiality, trust and transparency that NGOs traditionally try to foster in their workplaces. It could sometimes hamper their work.

Of all the information they were trying to control, the Sudanese authorities wanted above all to stop any details about rape from getting out of Darfur. Mass rape was a widely used weapon of war in the 'counter-insurgency' campaign. Yet it was also, of course, demeaning and deeply embarrassing to Muslims in a Muslim country. This, more than anything, was the dirty secret of Darfur. The authorities would go to any lengths to stop this being reported.

Mass rapes took place as villages were attacked. Also, women in IDP camps would be raped while walking a few miles from the camps to collect firewood. As they then returned to the camps and told aid workers their stories, the news should have got straight to the outside world. Yet, here again, NGOs and the UN preferred to keep quiet. The aid worker I spoke to recalls that he discussed it with MSF, but they 'did not make a stand against not being allowed to report rape'. Organizations like Amnesty International did report on rape, and he argues that this was Amnesty's line of work rather than his. But from the Sudanese government's point of view, Amnesty was also easier to dismiss as a biased and hostile Western pressure group.

So the small amount of reporting that did come out of Darfur was distinctly patchy. Accounts were often exaggerated, uncritical and ill-informed from the Western side, erroneous and complacent from the Sudanese side. And when too much of what was going on did emerge, as in 2004–5, it quickly became clear anyway that Khartoum had allies, the Chinese, Russians and others who preferred to believe the government's version of events rather than that of the West. Importantly, the Sudanese government's Darfur narrative was just plausible enough to be believable for those who wanted to take Khartoum's side anyway.

Thus the world's response to the Darfur crisis was distinctly mixed. The unprecedented Western activism saved thousands of lives, but at the same time Western engagement with the rebels probably made a political solution less, rather than more, likely. The UN eventually pushed thousands of blue-hatted soldiers into Darfur, but the world body's response to the crisis was in fact so divided that such a force would make little difference on the ground. Partly, these divisions stemmed from the initial failure to agree on what had actually happened in Darfur, the price paid for some people rushing in so quickly to call it a genocide.

Sudan's Islamist regime might have tottered somewhat in the wake of the al-Qaeda terrorist attacks of 2001 and the outrage over Darfur in 2003–5, but these international divisions ensured that, remarkably in many ways, it survived and even prospered. Instead, as the 2000s progressed, it was the newly semi-autonomous state of southern Sudan that ran into the most difficulties, while President Bashir's government found new sources of political, economic and diplomatic resources on which to draw.

CHAPTER SEVEN

SURVIVING IN THE NORTH, FAILING IN THE SOUTH, 2005–10

Darfur was only one part of Sudan, of course. But the incessant concentration on the region after 2004, particularly by the West, meant that the problems there overshadowed everything else that was happening in the country. In particular, many people seemed to forget about the peace agreement signed between the north and the south on 9 January 2005. Signing the peace deal was one thing, but the success of the Comprehensive Peace Agreement (CPA) depended on much more than just a few signatures. Both sides had committed themselves to a complex series of joint projects and actions that had to be executed according to a fairly tight schedule over the following years for the CPA to fulfil its objectives.

Unfortunately, however, most of the political energy needed to keep the CPA on track was consumed by the international wrangling over Darfur, despite the fact that negotiating the CPA had dominated diplomacy on Sudan for so many years. The slow or even non-existent implementation of the CPA contributed to mounting instability and renewed fighting in the south, particularly after 2008. Similarly, much of the money pledged to Sudan by the international community as a reward to its politicians for signing the CPA – about $4 billion in all – was either never delivered or diverted away from the south to much-needed emergency funding in Darfur. As southern Sudan neared its referendum on independence in 2011 the CPA was looking more and more in danger of collapsing altogether.

One of the major weaknesses of the CPA was that it was an extraordinarily complex document. In order for it to work, the north and south had to set up a bewildering variety of joint commissions and committees, about forty in all, shepherded along by the international troika of Britain, the USA and Norway. How the SPLM, fresh from a twenty-two-year bush war, was supposed to staff all these often highly technical bodies was not clear. These joint institutions were meant to implement the various confidence- and nation-building policies contained within the agreement and encourage the two sides to work together, to make 'unity more attractive', as the agreement put it. Although the south was given the right to break away if it wanted to in 2011, keeping Sudan as one country was much the preferred option for all the foreign countries involved in the negotiations; allowing Sudan to break up would set a dangerous precedent for other fragile states.

However, due to all the diplomatic and political force exerted on the Sudanese government over its actions in Darfur, there was little international energy left to persuade it to honour its many and detailed commitments in the CPA. This was a curious reversal of the previous situation, in 2003–4, when Western governments had been loath to put any pressure on Khartoum over Darfur to 'save' the CPA. The problems were compounded by the fact that the northern government was never really minded to fulfil its side of the CPA anyway, since it felt betrayed by the USA because of the broken promises caused by the Darfur conflict. Thus, in the years that I travelled to southern Sudan after the CPA was signed, diplomats were mainly dealing with what was politely described as 'slippage'. The joint committees and commissions either never started to function or did so much later than they were supposed to, and then only half-heartedly.

The north was often to blame for this. Take military integration, for example. The two sides were allowed to retain their own forces, but they were also required to form new joint units (21,000-strong in total) that might form the basis of a truly national army. But by the autumn of 2008, over three years after the CPA had been signed, there was only one fully functioning Joint Integrated Unit (JIU) – to give the official term – in the whole of the south. Those JIUs that were formed later were usually 'joint' in name only. The north proved deeply reluctant to commit any jeeps or trucks to them, as would have been necessary to make them at all effective. Sometimes fighting would actually break out between the Sudanese army and SPLA components of a JIU, as happened in the town of Malakal, for instance, in February 2009, resulting in the death of more than thirty-three civilians.

Likewise, the obligation in the CPA to have national elections by the summer of July 2009 throughout the country, originally viewed by Western donors as the best way of leveraging Bashir's government out of power, was taken very lightly: elections were postponed, and postponed again. The census, on which voter registration had to be based, took an age for the northern government to complete, and when the results were finally published in May 2009 they were immediately seen as flawed. In particular, the government-controlled body that did the census under-counted the two areas of greatest opposition to Khartoum, namely Darfur and the south. This consequently led many opposition politicians and activists to dispute the veracity of the subsequent voter register. By the time that the polls did eventually take place, in April 2010, most people had lost faith in them as a legitimate means of bringing about change in Sudan. With their minds on Darfur, foreign donors seemed to sleep-walk through this calamity. The money that they had pledged to make these elections workable, or even credible, either never appeared or arrived far too late. A country that had had no national elections since 1986 was woefully unprepared for the polls of 2010.

However, apart from the elections, the north had good reason to be dilatory or even just downright unco-operative over the CPA. As we have seen, the agreement obliged the north to make 'unity more attractive' in the hope that the country would stay together. Yet there was little or no incentive for the north to spend money on setting up JIUs, for example, if the south was just going to split off into a separate country after six years. And since it was clear from the very beginning that opinion in the south favoured independence, the north, never keen on building a national consciousness in the first place, saw spending money on fancy things like JIUs as money down the drain.

A PRE-FAILED STATE?

So much for the government in Khartoum and the CPA. Equally, however, the diversion of political and diplomatic energy to Darfur also let the former guerrilla leaders of the SPLM off the hook. They now ran the largely autonomous Government of Southern Sudan (GOSS) and for several years after 2005 they were allowed to carry on pretty much as they pleased, despite the mounting evidence that they were doing a poor job of running the putative new state. As Darfur burned, the failure of the south to rebuild was largely overlooked, despite the fact that by 2011, just six years after signing the CPA, the new country of 'Southern Sudan' was supposed to be ready to stand on its own feet. In fact, by 2010, southern Sudan looked extremely under-prepared for such an eventuality. Indeed, it remained one of the least developed places on earth.

For too long John Garang and his lieutenants had been able to bask in the almost unconditional adulation of the West. They had blamed anything that went wrong in the south on the *jihadists* in Khartoum and usually, of course, they were right. This continued to be the case even after the CPA was signed. Take oil, for instance. Under the terms of the agreement the north had agreed to split the revenue from the south's oilfields equally with the southern government, and by 2009 GOSS had duly received about US$6 billion worth of revenues from this source. Nonetheless, Khartoum's NCP officials remained firmly in charge of calculating the total revenue from oil and almost certainly used that power to under-report the amount, maybe by as much as 20 per cent, so as to reduce the southern share.[1] Thus the GOSS received less money from its own oil than it was entitled to.

However, as time went on it also became clear that blaming the north for everything was also a convenient way for the GOSS to avoid its own share of responsibility for the failure to rebuild southern Sudan. The GOSS's supporters demanded a period of grace, a 'honeymoon period', during which it was to be indulged and forgiven all its shortcomings, given the awful recent history of the Sudan. But this period seemed to stretch on for far too long.

When I first visited Juba in the late summer of 2005, eight months after the CPA had been signed, the newly designated capital of southern Sudan was only just starting to show a few signs of life after decades of war. Much of the town had been razed by shelling and bombing. There were only two small hotels left, both now occupied by the Sudan People's Liberation Army (SPLA), so the hundreds of UN personnel and NGO workers who had arrived to help to rebuild the south were forced to pay an emperor's ransom to stay in tented camps on the banks of the Nile. Little else appeared to be functioning.

All this was to be expected. However, what was most noticeable over the following years was how little actually changed. Of course, the SPLM had an extremely difficult task: to build a functioning state almost from scratch. But it also had a lot in its favour too. As well as substantial oil revenues, the south also got hundreds of millions of dollars in aid from the West and any amount of goodwill and support from the USA. But in truth, after four years or so of rule from Juba, GOSS had little but nice offices, new weapons and salaried soldiers to show for that $6 billion or so of oil revenues.

GOSS was quite open about the fact that it spent most of its precious oil money, its only direct source of revenue, on the army. Southern ministers, usually former guerrilla fighters themselves, would tell me that up to 70 per cent of the budget went on army pay and pensions, as well as new tanks, helicopters and other hardware. This was their insurance policy, they argued, in case the north tried to dispute their right to break off after the referendum in 2011.

However, spending this proportion of the budget on arms meant that virtually every other demand for funds in one of the poorest and most devastated places on earth was ignored. The government made barely any attempt to rebuild the region's battered infrastructure. I sat down with one UN development expert in May 2009 to sort through what the southern government had achieved in this respect over the previous four years. He reckoned that in 2005, Juba had had seven miles of good bitumen road at the signing of the peace agreement – the only paved road left in the whole of the region after decades of war. By the end of 2008, he estimated that Juba had just over seven miles of good bitumen road – and that was it. A report that came out at the beginning of 2010 was a little more generous, suggesting that there were now about 11 miles of road in Juba – but only 30 miles of tarmac road in the whole of southern Sudan.

It was the same depressing story in health and education. Peace was supposed to bring a 'dividend', but for most southerners this simply never materialized; rather the opposite, in fact. By the end of 2009 some of the health indicators were actually slipping into reverse. Malaria, cholera and HIV/AIDS had always been killers in the south. But now polio, leprosy and measles were making a comeback. In April 2010 the World Food Programme reckoned that the rate of malnutrition had risen again, up to 47 per cent, and one in seven children died before their fifth birthday. In terms of education, female illiteracy remained extremely high (at about 90 per cent) and the number of children in primary-school classes that I observed often numbered seventy or more. Little teaching was done; classes were more a matter of crowd control.

Dispiritingly, the southern government seemed blindly determined to repeat all the mistakes of the northern government in Khartoum. As well as spending the lion's share of the oil money on weapons and the army, GOSS ran a highly centralized administration, spending most of what cash was left over from military spending on itself in Juba. After more than five years of peace, by 2010 the only really shiny new bit of town was the government quarter. Several new ministries had been built here, complete with street lamps and even car-parking spaces, marked out by neat little white lines. It all looked very impressive. But these seemed to be the only significant construction works that the new government had undertaken 'for the people', loosely defined.

Ordinary people in Juba struggled to get by as prices shot up, caused mainly by the sudden influx of thousands of well-heeled foreign UN and NGO workers. The few miles of roads were clogged by the ubiquitous white Landcruisers of the aid community, which paid very good wages to a lucky few who got jobs as drivers and guards. As southern Sudan produced nothing of its own, everything had to be imported from Kenya or Uganda, which only added to the spiralling inflation. Bizarrely, for a while Juba was reckoned to be the most expensive town in Africa.

Outside Juba, in the rest of the south, the new government's performance was even more abject. Elias Taban, the bishop in Yei, reflected ruefully when I visited him in the autumn of 2008 that he could not name one project or programme that *his* government had started and finished in the area since coming to power. Any new health projects, clinics, schools, roads or stores were still being provided by the churches or foreign donors, as they had always been. In the rainy season the dirt tracks still turned to mud, making it virtually impossible to drive from Juba to Yei. Rather than developing the country 'broadly', spending money on micro-finance and other schemes to spread as much benefit as possible at the bottom, GOSS spent almost everything on itself in Juba. Would the south, I wondered, also turn into a one-city state?

The counterpoint to the money and attention lavished on the centre of Juba was an almost complete lack of thought or money devoted to the building up of strong, or just adequate, local administrations in the ten southern states. One serious consequence of this was that, just as in the north, the peripheries of the south became increasingly anarchic. By the beginning of 2009, there were hundreds of people being killed in inter-tribal violence in southern Sudan, an ominous throwback to the divisions within the SPLA in the early 1990s when the Nuer leader Riek Machar had split from the Dinka John Garang. In 2009 as a whole about 2,500 southerners were killed and 350,000 displaced by violence, a worse death toll for that year than in Darfur.

Some of these killings took place along the frontier with the north, as usual, but others happened in more worrying places like Nasir, near the Ethiopian border. Here different groups of Nuer clashed over food and aid supplies, killing hundreds, including women and children who were murdered where they slept. Some of this violence was probably stoked by the north, sticking to its old tactic of supplying some ethnic groups with weapons to attack others, but the SPLA seemed powerless to prevent it. Already, the writ of the Juba government did not seem to extend very far. Worryingly, southern Sudan was beginning to resemble a new African phenomenon, a pre-failed state – prostrate and enfeebled even before it was born.

Corruption seeped into the system at an early stage too, particularly at the mid-level of administration. In its defence, the government claimed that at least people were regularly sacked for corruption; this was supposed to demonstrate that at least the GOSS was being honest and transparent about the problem. Officials from the army, the finance ministry and other parts of the bureaucracy were indeed dismissed, but this did not seem to deter anyone. The money going into the finance ministry from the oil revenues was sometimes tight, especially when the oil price dropped dramatically in 2008–9. But even when the finance ministry claimed it was paying out to the various ministries, employees of those ministries would sometimes not be paid for months at a stretch. Teachers, and even SPLA soldiers, were going on strike regularly by the end of 2008 in protest against not being paid.

The 'donor community' scarcely distinguished itself on the question of finance either. In 2005 foreign governments, aid ministries and international institutions like the World Bank pooled money into an account called a Multi-Donor Trust Fund (MDTF). This money was meant to be used to build up the GOSS's administrative systems and help with infrastructure and basic services. It was trumpeted as a pioneering model of how foreign donors could disburse money to fragile states in the most cost-effective and bureaucratically simple way. From 2005 onwards, therefore, foreign agencies sank $524 million into the MDTF (and the southern Sudanese put in a further

$179 million in counterpart funding). Yet the mechanisms required to access any of this money proved so cumbersome and complicated that by the end of 2009 $350 million was still sitting in the MDTF; it had never been disbursed. Foreign NGOs argued that this was a catastrophe for the region. They were supposed to be the main beneficiaries of these funds, as they still provided a full 85 per cent of the primary healthcare in the south. Yet their work was severely hindered by the lack of steady long-term funding that the MDTF should have provided. Eventually new funding mechanisms were set up to try to bypass the MDTF bottleneck, but this came very late in the day.

The donors, however, preferred to deflect blame for the lack of progress back onto the southern Sudanese government. By 2009 corruption was perceived to have become so bad that foreign governments were no longer willing to put money directly into the government's coffers for fear that it would just be leached off by crooked officials and politicians. The donors had a point. The GOSS ministers rushed around Juba in long motorcades of blacked-out SUVs, shuttling between their big houses and gleaming new ministries, often jetting off to the Kenyan capital Nairobi for a little shopping or even to the glamorous new destination of Dubai. Meanwhile little else of a more serious nature seemed to get done.

The evident corruption was a source of disillusion and disappointment for many of the SPLM's erstwhile supporters, both in Sudan and abroad. And with the corruption came cronyism. Among southerners, the SPLM had to start defending itself against charges that too many of the new jobs and opportunities in this desperately poor country went to the dominant Dinka and Nuer groups, who formed the majority of the ruling southern coalition. Plum diplomatic jobs representing the GOSS in Western capitals began to go to relations of SPLM ministers.

Such ethnic favouritism was very much at odds with the ideology of the 'New Sudan' vision championed by John Garang. Indeed, the substance of that vision seemed to have died with him when his helicopter crashed in appalling weather over south Sudan in July 2005. His untimely death was a big blow to the south; his leadership was badly missed. Moreover, he was the only figure in either the north or the south who could have made the appeal to unity in the CPA really work; he believed to the end that all the oppressed peoples of Sudan could unite on the issue of economic marginalization to trump the ethnic and sectarian politics of Bashir and the Islamist regime in Khartoum.

After Garang's death his successor, Salva Kiir, and the remaining leaders of the SPLM paid lip service to the 'New Sudan' vision, but no more. Instead, Kiir and others like Riek Machar turned inwards to concentrate on the politics of the south, rather than those of Sudan. Machar, in particular, now the deputy leader of the SPLM, had never been interested in working for the country as a whole. It had been just about possible to imagine Garang uniting the diverse peoples of Sudan – the Fur in the West, the Dinka in the south and the Beja in the east – into a bloc that could have challenged the NCP's hegemony in Khartoum at a national general election. Garang, after all, was probably more popular in some parts of the north for opposing the NCP than he was in the south. But it became increasingly impossible to imagine Salva Kiir, a relatively uncharismatic, low-key former bush fighter, or any of the other southern politicians achieving such a feat. Indeed, the SPLM did not even put up Kiir against Bashir to contest the national presidency at the general election of 2010. Instead, the leader of the SPLM stood only for the presidency of southern Sudan, thus endorsing the status quo. Yassir Arman, a relatively unknown secular Muslim member of the SPLM leadership ran against Bashir in place of Kiir, and he pulled out of the contest anyway a week before polling as part of as SPLM protest against vote rigging.

Not surprisingly, as anxiety deepened in the south over the perform-ance of the SPLM in government so opposition groups and leaders began to emerge to challenge the old guerrilla movement's political hegemony, as they had done in the early 1990s. These opposition leaders were derided by the SPLM as stooges of the north, or worse. A few of them might have been, but they also expressed a genuine sense of grievance against the Juba regime. One of these opposition leaders was the old warrior Bona Malwal, who had been one of the few southern ministers in President Numeiri's government back in the 1970s before being incarcerated for his pains. He founded the South Sudan Democratic Forum to articulate an alternative to the SPLM, and argued in 2009 that the SPLM 'does not want the election [of 2010] to take place because they cannot defend their utter failure before the people of South Sudan in an election campaign . . . They have failed to deliver any peace dividend to the people of South Sudan.' His words were an early sign of an indigenous revolt against the failures of the presumptive government of the new southern Sudan.

BUSINESS AS USUAL IN KHARTOUM

While the south struggled, President Bashir's regime in the north not only survived but positively prospered, despite all the sanctions and international opprobrium directed against it. As the dream of a modern caliphate administered from Khartoum rapidly faded after the departure of Hassan al-Turabi, Bashir's men aspired merely to hold on to power. Despite all the forces ranged against them, they managed brilliantly to do this. It was a virtuoso, if tragic, performance.

Technically, the Comprehensive Peace Agreement was supposed to have ushered in a new era for the government in Khartoum. Under the terms of the agreement the 'Government of National Unity', as it was called, was sworn in as the new government for the whole of Sudan. It was composed of the NCP in a ruling coalition with the SPLM. The leaders of the former guerrilla movement, first John Garang until his death and then Salva Kiir, became not only presidents of southern Sudan but also vice-presidents of the whole of Sudan in the Government of National Unity. Technically, they were second in rank only to President Bashir. The SPLM also got a share (about one-third or so) of the ministerial posts in the cabinet of the Government of National Unity. The two parties were supposed to rule together on behalf of all the Sudanese until 2011 – and perhaps beyond that time.

In name only: the 'unity' government of Salva Kiir, President Bashir and
Ali Osman Taha

The reality, however, was very different. In fact, the NCP retained
all the power and nearly all the money for itself. SPLM ministers
might formally run ministries, but their remit was often just notional.
They seldom had access to the flow of information in their own
ministries (mainly staffed by northerners) and would find their
decisions bypassed by other NCP-run ministries.

Even more importantly, the SPLM was kept well away from
exerting any control over the vital National Intelligence and Security
Services (NISS) despite, nominally, having a junior minister in it. Run
for a long time largely by Salah Gosh out of a vast, ramshackle site in
downtown Khartoum, the NISS provided the units and agencies that
ran the war in Darfur, controlled access to the oilfields in the south,
and much else. These agencies, together with the Sudanese Armed
Forces (SAF), consumed most of the national budget, which neither

the SPLM nor any other opposition party had any say in. One Sudanese economist who kept a close eye on Sudan's finances in the 2000s told me that about 74 per cent of all the oil money coming into Khartoum's coffers was spent on internal security, the army and weapons. Essentially, the NCP ran a warfare state (directed, some-times, against its notional partners in government). Even if the 'part-ners' of the NCP in the Government of National Unity had wanted to do something more constructive with their new powers in Khartoum, there was little money left over in the budget for them to do so. Basically, the NCP maintained rigid control; most of the government's income went straight to ministries and agencies controlled by the party's most hard-line ministers and supporters.

At the heart of the NCP's hold on government was always the same little clique that had risen to power after the 1989 revolution, and that controlled the security apparatus of Sudan. Salah Gosh was of prime importance, only retiring from the NISS in 2009, perhaps because of health problems. Equally prominent was Nafie Ali Nafie, himself a former head of the security services. Imposing and forceful, Nafie Ali Nafie led the government's negotiations over Darfur for several years before taking charge of fixing the 2010 elections for the NCP. He often led delegations abroad as well. Vice-president Ali Osman Taha, who had been at school with President Bashir, was never far away from the centre of power either. Together with Bashir, this inner circle often acted inde-pendently of the rest of the government, not to mention their supposed partners in the SPLM. A good example of this came in 2009 when thirteen international aid agencies were expelled from Sudan in retalia-tion for the International Criminal Court issuing a warrant to arrest President Bashir. It was clear that almost no other part of the bureaucracy outside of the security agencies had been apprised of this decision; Sudanese diplomats were left floundering as to how to explain this vindic-tive act to foreigners. For all its plethora of agencies, special advisers and ministries, the Sudanese government remained highly centralized.

In legal terms, the National Security Forces Act of 1999 gave these men at the head of the internal security agencies almost carte blanche to operate as they wanted. The act codified the arbitrary powers wielded by the NCP in the 1990s. Security officials could arrest and detain suspects for long periods without judicial review, and often did so. The act also gave them sweeping powers over the media, allowing the NISS to carry out regular pre-print censorship of newspapers that wanted to publish articles on sensitive issues such as Darfur, human rights or political opposition. As a Human Rights Watch report summarized: 'Security officers have used powers under this law to arbitrarily arrest and detain journalists and human-rights defenders and to suspend and otherwise penalize newspapers.'[2] For all the slight loosening of social control in the mid-2000s, the regime continued to keep the space for political opposition and dissent as restricted as possible. The 'presidential elections' that were held in 1996 and 2000, in order to give the regime a veneer of legitimacy, were tightly controlled affairs, with a limited electorate. In 2000, after an opposition boycott, Bashir's only opponent proved to be the ageing and discredited former president Jafar Numeiri; Bashir won 86.5 per cent of the vote, apparently.

The 'warfare state' continued even after Khartoum had formally concluded peace in two of the country's three rebellious regions. Despite the upsurge of violence in Darfur after 2003, the CPA was signed in 2005 and in October of the following year Khartoum consented to the 'East Sudan Peace Agreement' as well. Signed in the Eritrean capital Asmara, this brought an end to ten years of hostilities in the east and ended the long-running conflict with the Beja, who had lately formed the rebel alliance known as the Eastern Front. The northern leaders felt that they never gained sufficient credit from the West for settling these two long-running insurgencies.

These two peace agreements should have at last allowed the Sudanese government to release some money for purposes other than fighting its own people. Sudan might even have been hailed as a promising example of a post-conflict country working to transform itself, especially in the years of the oil boom. In fact, however, peace in the east and the south seemed to make little difference to the country's sorry lack of development. Why?

The answer is that by the 2000s the warfare state had ossified into a vast patronage network, designed to keep the NCP in power. This network was to prove its real worth when President Bashir came to face the greatest challenge to his rule during the Arab Spring. The finances of the Sudanese state were usually too obscure to allow any close examination. But I got a small glimpse of what lay beneath the surface when I visited the three eastern states of Gedaref, Kassala and Red Sea in 2009. Less well known than the regions of Darfur or the south, these three states also saw their own share of fighting between 1995 and 2006. Despite the formal cessation of hostilities in that year, resentment and bitterness against Khartoum remained because of the fundamental perception of unfairness in the east's relationship with the capital.

DEVELOPMENT PLEASE – BUT ON OUR OWN TERMS

Like Darfur, the east is not necessarily 'poor'. The problem is that most of its wealth has flowed directly into the central coffers in Khartoum, entirely bypassing the local people who might otherwise have benefited from it. The large-scale agricultural schemes of Gedaref state and the commercial activities of Port Sudan in Red Sea state are both major sources of revenue; yet the people of those states, principally the Beja pastoralists, remain, by most measures, among the poorest and least healthy in the whole of Sudan. In 2004, Red Sea state recorded an income per head of just $93 per year. In 2003, the World Bank argued that neonatal, postnatal and infant mortality in Red Sea state were the highest in the country. According to the UN, in 2006 malnutrition rates were running at 25 per cent in east Sudan, and even exceeding 30 per cent in some places. It is a sobering thought that when the conflict in Darfur was at its height, one of the government's arguments in its own defence was that even despite the devastation there, Darfur was still better off than the east.[3]

To find out exactly how so much money could do so little for so many, I went to see the minister of finance for Red Sea state in Port Sudan. An elderly Beja member of the ruling NCP, he was engagingly honest about how it all worked. Yes, the revenues from the port operations were huge, collected through two major institutions: the seaport corporation and customs. But 'all' the money from these two went straight to the central government in Khartoum. The state government was left to raise about $24m a year itself in local taxes, levied on cars and the like.

Of this figure, over half went on the salaries of state employees. Some were worthwhile beneficiaries, such as teachers. But most were unelected bureaucrats, local councillors, state politicians and so on, supported by fleets of Landcruisers, drivers and flunkeys. One accountant who had had the rare privilege of looking at the books was astonished to find that the state was paying over 60,000 such people to look after a population of just over a million, most of whom were nomads scratching a living from the parched deserts of the interior.

In effect, Red Sea state was operating a vast patronage system, guaranteed by the NCP-appointed state governor, or *wali*. His job included making sure that the money in the system trickled down to a very local level. Just to the south of Port Sudan I visited desperately poor Suakin, a port that had once been Sudan's most important gateway to the outside world, but now a picturesque ruin. Here there were 350 'civil servants' on the payroll for a population of about 100,000. These 350 public-minded individuals consumed fully 60 per cent of the locality's meagre revenues – lucky them.

Naturally, the local and state expenditure on salaries left very little over to spend on what UN types like to call the development of 'human capital', or even 'capacity building'. In the very opaque world of Sudanese government finance, the government is supposed to transfer money back to the states for capital projects, such as building hospitals and roads. But the minister of finance for Red Sea state, warming to his theme, confessed that he did not really know how much money he was likely to get from Khartoum in 2009 – maybe 25 per cent of what he had been promised, or perhaps 30 per cent. He wasn't sure. This made any long-term planning impossible, and thus development erratic. 'The services I provide are limited,' confessed the minister. Yes, he often argued with Khartoum for more resources – but this was how the system worked.

What little development there had been in Port Sudan was to be found almost entirely in the centre of the city. Here there were broad new pavements, with drains and street lights. Like Khartoum, however, the fringes of the city were crowded with shanty towns, inhabited by victims of the region's various conflicts or by local pastoralists who had come to look for a job in the port. Beyond that, outside Port Sudan, there are almost no federally or locally funded projects. Instead, the UN and other foreign aid agencies have been grudgingly allowed to work on local projects that the state government has no money to fund. Unfortunately, this willingness by aid agencies to step into the breach has merely encouraged what one Sudanese researcher has described as 'a government tendency to abdicate its responsibility and leave the welfare of vulnerable citizens to NGOs'.[4]

Yet allowing NGOs access to feed people did not mean surrendering any political control over those people. The *wali*'s underlings decided exactly who worked on these NGO projects, and for how long. The *wali* also scrutinized all access to these projects, even by their own national workers. The message was plain: we are happy to take your money, but don't expect this to change how we operate. The NGOs and UN agencies were often called 'partners' in the 'development' jargon; but in fact any development took place entirely on the terms of the Sudanese government.

In this sense, Red Sea state was a microcosm of how the whole of the country had come to operate by the mid- to late 2000s. Foreign governments, the UN and NGOs spent billions of dollars on providing basic services for the wretched peoples of Sudan, while the Sudanese government itself spent most of its considerable resources on weapons and feathering its own nest. The foreign-aid machine provided just enough relief to the people of Sudan to ensure that the system ticked along without any major ruptures. In the name of 'humanitarianism', or 'capacity building', it thus colluded in the survival of a government that provoked most of the violence, poverty and disease in the first place.

All this worked very well for the National Congress Party, but perpetuated Sudan's dangerously self-destructive loop. Wealth was drained from the regions in the form of oil, customs and taxes to pay for the central government in Khartoum, leaving the Sudanese people angry and resentful towards their own government. This enfeebled the regions, making them easier prey for predatory neighbours (Libya in the west, for instance, or Eritrea in the east). So central government then had to spend more and more money on weapons to quell the consequent uprisings and fend off the neighbours. This left no money over for the essential grassroots regional development that might have endeared Khartoum to local people and strengthened the peripheries – the sort of policies that might have forestalled many problems before they became so intractable and deadly.

THE ELECTIONS OF 2010: COUNTER-INSURGENCY BY ANOTHER NAME

As I travelled around Sudan between 2005 and 2010, it seemed to me that most of its citizens were indifferent or hostile to the regime, but that through the patronage system the government did just enough to keep the people it needed onside. My anecdotal impressions were borne out by a secret poll that the government itself commissioned in 2008 to test its popularity ahead of the national elections mandated by the CPA. Out of a big nationwide sample of 22,517 people, only about 29 per cent told the pollsters that they would be likely to vote for Bashir and the NCP, while 57 per cent said that they were undecided as to whom to vote for. The only comfort for the NCP was that the northern opposition parties, many of them moribund after twenty or so years of harassment, expulsions and property sequestrations, fared much worse.

When circumstances arose, the government lost no opportunity to nurture that 29 per cent, to 'mobilize the base', as Karl Rove might have put it. On these occasions, buses of Islamist supporters would be produced in Sudan's main cities – Khartoum, El Fasher, Port Sudan – to show fervent and vocal support for the regime. When a British teacher named a teddy bear 'Mohammed' in her class in 2007, or when the International Criminal Court (ICC) indicted President Bashir two years later, to give just two examples from the ridiculous to the sublime, within hours (or even minutes) thousands of cheering supporters would appear in front of the presidential palace, or in main squares across the country, to denounce the imperialists and apostates. Bashir would revel in this, orchestrating and leading the crowd in its chants and protests. He used any threat to Sudan's 'sovereignty', as he framed it, to great effect. Many of those acclaiming the president would also have benefited the most from the new dams, roads and electricity supplies that the government had built in the riverain centre as a consequence of the oil boom.

Nonetheless, given what the regime's own polling indicated about its relatively narrow base of support, Bashir and his ministers knew that the elections of 2010 posed a real threat to their survival. The polls were originally intended to bring about the 'democratic transformation' of the country as part of the CPA. If the opposition parties could connect with the 57 per cent of undecided voters, and campaign openly to win their votes in a fair election, then the government might be overthrown at the ballot box. And unlike the complete shams of 1996 and 2000, the 2010 elections were an integral part of the CPA, guaranteed by foreign countries and the SPLM – so they would have to at least appear more rigorous and transparent than previous contests. They would certainly be heavily scrutinised by hundreds of foreign observers.

Under pressure, the government thus treated the elections more as a national security problem than as an exercise in democracy. Certainly, their intention was to minimise the risk for the regime from the outset, by fair means or foul. Nafie Ali Nafie, from the heart of the security and intelligence apparatus of the state, was put in charge of the operation. As he later boasted, he started preparing the ground for Bashir's victory as early as 2007, long before any of the opposition parties, or foreign diplomats transfixed by Darfur, had even started thinking about the elections.

As we have seen, rigging started from the very beginning of the 'electoral process' with the census, carried out in 2008. NCP-dominated areas of Sudan were found to have more people living in them than many estimated; areas where the NCP were weakest, such as the south, were under-counted. The bias was most obvious in Darfur, where the government had good reason to feel most threatened by the voters. Here, the number of pro-Arab groups and nomads seemed to have grown exponentially since the last authoritative census in 1993. In North Darfur, for instance, the census claimed that 38 per cent of the total population were now Arabs, compared to just 12 per cent in 1993. Conversely, the majority of African-Darfuri households around the three big towns of Darfur were not counted at all – the state census takers claimed that these areas were just too dangerous to visit. In what was presumed to be another hotbed of anti-government feeling, the black belt around Khartoum, one survey found that only 5 per cent of people had been counted.

Moreover, the government-appointed National Election Commission (NEC) manipulated the constituency boundaries to suit the NCP. Again, the gerrymandering was most obvious in Darfur. West Darfur, where the NCP was weakest, was allocated only fifteen seats in the national assembly whereas North Darfur, presumed to be the most 'Arab', gained twenty-four. The rebel stronghold of Jebel Marra in South Darfur disappeared altogether as a political entity. With a population of 35,000, according to the 2008 census, it wasn't allocated any seats at all; in 1993, by contrast, Jebel Marra had had about half a million inhabitants, and in the 1986 elections had four directly elected single-candidate constituencies.[5]

In the two or three months leading up to the voting itself, political campaigning was also tightly controlled in favour of the NCP. In a small nod towards freedom of expression, pre-press censorship of newspapers was lifted a few weeks before polling, allowing a rare outpouring of criticisms of President Bashir. However, newspapers have a very small circulation in Sudan; opposition politicians were kept well away from the radio, the medium through which most impoverished Sudanese get their news. Airtime on TV for opposition leaders was also strictly rationed, and they often appeared late at night long after most Sudanese had gone to sleep. Opposition politicians were also apt to have their broadcasts pulled at the last minute if they wanted to stray onto controversial ground, as happened to Sadiq al-Mahdi when he tried to discuss Darfur and the ICC.

Whereas President Bashir was free to hold well-advertised rallies of his supporters, opposition parties had to apply for permission to hold public meetings seventy-two hours in advance, and this was not always granted. Under these conditions, the Umma party, DUP, the Communist Party and everybody else had few opportunities to reach out to new voters, let alone their erstwhile supporters. A few days before polling was due to begin, most of these opposition parties (except the DUP) pulled out of the race, citing numerous 'irregularities'.

Still, on the polling days themselves, 11 to 15 April 2010, the NCP left nothing to chance in north Sudan. The already very blurred lines between the ruling party, the 'independent' institutions of state power, big business and national security dissolved altogether in a devastatingly well-organized and well-funded blitz on the polling stations. The full resources of the state – aided by its copious oil revenues – were deployed to ferry people to polling centres in NCP buses. Here, in large and well-staffed NCP tents, they would be marshalled and fed by NCP officials and then directed to the polling booths – 'free' to cast their vote for whomever they chose. Nafie Ali Nafie proudly boasted that many of the country's leading businessmen had poured 'millions of Sudanese pounds' into the NCP's campaign; that was now the price of doing business in Sudan. Opposition parties, struggling to organize themselves after decades of forced inactivity, could not compete, especially as the government purposefully set no upward limit on campaign spending. The Umma party, for instance, managed to cobble together just $500,000 or so to fund its entire national effort.

The supposedly 'independent' NEC, in fact staffed by a few former NCP officials, helped with some clever subliminal polling literature. It printed the symbol of the NCP, a tree, at the top of the very long and complicated ballot papers. And by the same token, on all the posters explaining how to vote outside the polling stations there were jolly little drawings showing people patiently queuing – under a tree. A range of national 'observer' NGOs were generously funded by the government to report on events – favourably to the NPC. These 'front' NGOs were dubbed government NGOs, or GONGOS, by the truly independent observers. Likewise, several fake versions of the traditional parties were also funded by the government to confuse the largely illiterate voters.

The smoke and mirrors continued at the local level. A major weapon in the hands of the government were the 'Popular Committees', bodies that had traditionally been elected by local people to sort out issues of water supply, refuse collection and so on. Now appointed by the NCP, the heads of these committees (sometimes former government or armed-forces officials) often acted as the principal verifier of people coming to the polling stations to vote; as most people had no ID, a visual identification by the popular committee was supposed to be the next best thing. They would 'recognize' people whom they knew would be voting NCP and stop others.

In particular, they were under orders to accept the NCP cadres who were bussed from polling station to station to vote for the NCP on the dodgy registers – dubbed the 'flying regiments' by the Sudanese. Occasionally a brave and independent-minded polling station official would turn away scores of these young NCPers, none of whom could produce a local address. I witnessed one occasion when an official did just that, only for the disgruntled NCP party agent to head off with the boss of the local popular committee to find the local NEC boss, the poor official's immediate superior, who then instructed the official to reverse his decision.

There was much, much more of the same. All the above methods – the GONGOs, the 'front' organizations and parties, the 'popular committees' – should be instantly familiar to any student of eastern Europe or the Soviet Union under communism. The election was another vivid reminder that the NCP leaders were still living off the lessons they had learned from their communist foes at the University of Khartoum in the 1960s and '70s. In the end, President Bashir won the national presidency with 68 per cent of the vote, and the NCP won a vast majority of the seats in the national assembly and secured all the vital governorships in the north, even in

Darfur. The SPLM won handsomely in the south, with Salva Kiir elected to the presidency of the Government of Southern Sudan. But for the country as a whole it was five more years (at least) for President Bashir.

OUR FRIENDS IN THE EAST

This manipulation and rigging was on such a scale, and often so egregious, that the independent Western observers couldn't help but notice it. The EU missions normally bend over backwards to be complimentary to their host governments, but on this occasion they had to admit that the elections didn't meet 'international standards'. Much of this was attributed to the understandable 'logistical challenges' of holding a complex election in a poor country for the first time in twenty-four years, especially in the south where polling stations opened very late and ballot papers were sometimes not delivered. However, the EU made clear that those international standards included the freedom of opposition parties to campaign fairly and for their supporters to vote freely. Former American president Jimmy Carter, heading up his own centre's large team of monitors, said much the same thing.

This might have been a blow to President Bashir; these verdicts certainly undermined the credibility of his victory internationally. However, it mattered very little at home, as the government had fortunately invited along more friendly observers who delivered very different judgments. The Arab League, for instance, considered the elections to be 'a model for transparency and honesty', and an example to the Arab world. The African Union was even more effusive; the Egyptians were also extremely impressed. Their enthusiastic verdicts were reported prominently in the government-run papers and on the radio. The EU, by contrast, was barely mentioned.

More intriguingly, there were also observer missions from Russia and China. Indeed, it was reputed to be China's first such mission anywhere in the world; the Chinese also helped to fund the NEC. The representative of the Chinese mission stated that there were 'no violations or any sort of problems' in any of the polling stations that he had visited in Khartoum, and this was also reported prominently in the local press. The Malaysians, rather more slyly, chose to fund a British-manned 'independent' observer outfit.

This was just another example of the myriad ways in which the regime had come to lean very heavily on the support of those Asian investors, mainly the Chinese, who kept the oil flowing. Many Sudanese appreciated the Asian bounty, especially those who remembered the dark days of the mid-1990s when the country's economy was buckling in the face of economic isolation and imprudent domestic policies. Indeed, it was striking that during the election of 2010 the president chose to campaign on precisely the economic and development benefits that had been bestowed on Sudan by the Chinese in return for oil – the new electricity coming from the Merowe dam, the Khartoum oil refinery and the Chinese-built roads.

After all, what might have happened if the Chinese, the Malaysians and the Indians had not come in? Several Sudanese told me that in retrospect the US sanctions of the mid-1990s looked like a blessing in disguise. Ironically, by trying to punish Sudan, the USA drove the country into the arms of the people whom they now regarded as their principal benefactors and protectors.

In common with other African leaders, northern Sudanese politicians argue that China has provided them with a fast track to development. Indeed, the speed and extent of China's scaling up in Sudan, and in Africa as a whole, has been astonishing. Despite considerable haziness surrounding the figures, it is certain that Chinese investment in Sudan during the 2000s was huge. Aside from building Sudan's oil production infrastructure, such as the 930-mile pipeline from the southern oilfields to Port Sudan, China also invested about $20 billion in non-oil projects, such as roads, agriculture projects and power stations. To put that figure into perspective, Britain's aid development budget in 2006 *to the whole world* was about $8 billion. In 2004, as we have seen, Chinese contractors won their biggest ever international contract: to build the $650m Merowe dam, employing about 1,700

Chinese workers and engineers. A Chinese bank had already provided Khartoum with a $530m loan for the overall project, including the accompanying roads and bridges, which could have cost a grand total of $2 billion by completion. In 2007, China cancelled Sudanese debts worth $80m and also promised to build a new presidential palace worth $12m.[6]

This was all very sweet for the Sudanese government. And with the cash came the diplomatic cover at the UN too, so vital over Darfur. But what did the Chinese, Malaysians and Indians in Sudan feel about propping up President Bashir's much-criticized regime? Tellingly, despite the numbers of their oilmen, diplomats and labourers in the country, they were universally unwilling to talk about their work in Sudan.

After months of trying, to no avail, to contact Chinese and Indian oil workers in Sudan, in 2008 I eventually managed to talk with a young manager from Petronas, the Malaysian oil major. He, fortunately, turned out to be a fan of *The Economist*, the newspaper for which I work. He explained to me how the Asians viewed Sudan, and he was probably as open and revealing as an Asian oil executive was going to get with a Westerner in Africa – though he still did not want to be named. I will call him Taha.

I met him in the Grand Holiday Villa hotel. This occupies a prime site on the banks of the Nile, just up from the government ministries and round the corner from Ghadaffi's Egg. The hotel was bought by a Malaysian hotel chain in the mid-1990s and Petronas used to house its headquarters in an annexe here, before moving into a swanky new office block further down the Nile. Appropriately enough, marking the transfer of power from West to East, the hotel was originally built by the British, in low-rise colonial style.

Taha was proud of the fact that Petronas had been involved in oil exploration and extraction in Sudan since the mid-1990s as an early partner with China. Petronas had a share in oil concession blocks throughout the country, mostly as joint ventures with the Chinese. Unlike China, however, Malaysia took almost no oil from Sudan; Petronas was there 'just for business', Taha told me. Petronas was originally just a small company from an obscure Asian country that had won its independence from Britain even later than Sudan, in 1960. With so much of the world's oil reserves already cornered by the Western majors, Sudan offered a rare opportunity for a small but ambitious company to grow into a global concern.

Thus the two former colonies, Sudan and Malaysia, sharing similar post-colonial aspirations, helped each other to develop. Petronas exploited Sudan's oil reserves to grow into a global company, to rival the Western majors, while Sudan used the oil revenues provided by the expertise of the Malaysians to transform itself from a dirt-poor desert into a less poor country (by African standards).

Sudan has served Petronas very well. Taha estimated that on the 150,000 or so barrels that Petronas was exporting per day, it was getting about $3.8 billion of revenue a year (at March 2008 prices). But what of the controversy over the 'genocide' in Darfur? Taha acknowledged that Sudan had a 'bad public image', but he told me that personally he had 'no problems working there'. He argued that 'the West has exaggerated things a lot' in Darfur and that the solution to the conflict should be through gradual development, not through 'coercing' the Sudanese government into doing things against its will. This was a view, according to Taha, 'shared by Asians and the East', who viewed the Darfur problem as a 'tribal conflict' rather than a genocide. Taha added that the West and the East looked at a problem like Darfur, of a region battling against a central government, in very different ways: 'Asians believe in people working together. So when one group tries to get out of the main group, and you get into trouble, it serves you right. There is less concept of individual rights.' There was almost no awareness of the Darfur issue in Malaysia, he told me. Anyway, what would the West have the Chinese and Malaysians do? If they were not in Sudan pumping out the oil, then the Sudanese government would have no money even to *try* to develop a region like Darfur, regardless of whether it was bullied into doing so or not.

The week that I met Taha, the Chinese special envoy to Darfur was in the region on one of his regular day-long sweeps through the area.

As if echoing Taha's ideas about solving Darfur's problems through economic growth, he publicly promised yet more money for 'development' in the region. Like the Malaysians, this was how the Chinese framed the problems in Darfur. It was also very much the line given to me by a Chinese official, when, after many weeks of calling, I was finally invited to the Chinese embassy for a talk.

In east Khartoum near the Blue Nile, several miles from the centre, the new Chinese embassy occupies a suitably large site, as befits China's status in the country. Inside, all is calm, the silence disturbed only by the soft hum of air conditioning. The official who had summoned me was Yu Chunhua, the political director of the embassy. Young, probably no more than thirty-five, he had been in Sudan for about two years and dutifully testified to the 'friendliness and warmth' of the Sudanese people. He accepted that theirs was now principally a 'commercial' relationship, but added: 'China and Africa are developing countries and we need each other.' In this context he emphasized that Darfur was 'a problem of development' (that phrase again), not one of politics. In this regard, China was thus doing its bit in Darfur with countless water projects and a major road-building scheme. Were any Western countries doing these sorts of big development projects, Yu Chunhua asked pointedly?

He also emphasized that the classic policy of 'non-interference' still continued. 'We always just advise Sudan, we don't interfere.' So, given what they regarded as their munificent support for Sudan over a long period, it was not surprising that the Chinese were bewildered and irritated by Western attacks on their record in Sudan. In particular, they bridled at the accusation that they had been the main paymasters of a regime that suppresses its own people.

The Chinese also think that they have been unfairly singled out. India and Malaysia have been just as involved as China in producing Sudan's oil, but have seldom been subject to criticism. Japan has been a big purchaser of Sudan's oil; it has refineries which can take the particular Sudanese Dar blend. Yet Japan has barely been criticized at all for its involvement. Only China has attracted the world's opprobrium. Furthermore, due to the way that the Greater Nile Petroleum Operating Company was set up, it is also true that China probably exerts less leverage over Sudan than Western critics will allow. On the principle of 'divide and rule', it was more than likely that the Sudanese distributed the shares in its oil consortium the way it did precisely so that no single country – even friendly China – could ever hold Khartoum to ransom. Just as the Sudanese government proved to be adept at playing different Western interests off against each other, so by diversifying the oil sector they weakened the Asian influence as well.

ESSENTIAL, BUT UNLOVED

However, despite my Chinese official's protestations, critics of China's role in Sudan have argued that China should indeed be singled out – because there has been much more to its involvement in Sudan than just oil. There is, crucially, the question of guns. The crux of the argument against China is twofold. First, that it has generated most of the Sudanese government's revenue through oil exports, thus enabling Khartoum to buy weapons to use against its own people. Secondly, China is also frequently accused of having built two (or maybe even three) small-arms factories in Khartoum that supply the government with weapons. It is thus directly involved in the arms trade in Sudan. One US lobby group claims that Chinese arms sales rose twenty-five-fold between 2002 and 2005, the years of the most intense fighting in Darfur. Chinese weapons were used in Darfur, in direct contradiction of a UN arms embargo.

In my interview at the Chinese embassy, Yu just repeated the party line. China sold some weapons to Sudan, but 'only on the understanding that they are not used in Darfur'. As almost the only use that the Sudanese army could have made of these weapons in 2008 was against its own citizens in Darfur, this was disingenuous at the very least.

But Yu's other point on the subject was much more germane. By the end of the 2000s the Sudanese did not really need the Chinese in this particular field, as Sudan was now Africa's third-largest weapons manufacturer in its own right, after Egypt and South Africa. The Chinese did help the Sudanese to set up the military-industrial complex at GIAD, south of Khartoum, in the mid-1990s, but by the mid-2000s GIAD was probably self-sustaining. The Iranians invested in it originally too and have maintained close military ties to Sudan, a relationship of which both countries remain extremely proud. Sudan probably enjoys closer military co-operation with Russia and Iran than with China, conjuring up nightmare visions for the Western military of technology transfers from the current theocratic regime in the Islamic Republic. The Israelis bombed a convoy of trucks north of Port Sudan that was supposed to have been carrying Iranian-made missiles and other arms to the Hamas Palestinian militia during the Israeli assault on the Gaza Strip at the beginning of 2009.

Whatever the exact extent of the military relationship, there is no doubt that the Chinese and Sudanese governments have enjoyed a mutually supportive partnership. But, more importantly for the future, do the Sudanese people themselves necessarily glow with warmth and friendliness towards the Chinese, as Yu claimed? Many Sudanese appreciate the economics of the relationship, but the Sudanese I met who knew anything more about the Chinese presence in their country than just the official version were positively hostile.

Mudawi Ibrahim Adam, surrounded by the wreckage of Sudan's industrial past in his metal workshop in Khartoum North, gave me the most comprehensive list of grudges and complaints against the Chinese, although it's a list that can be heard repeated pretty much everywhere else in Sudan. The biggest criticism was that the Chinese companies usually brought all their own workers with them, 'even down to the cleaners', as Mudawi told me, thereby creating little employment and few opportunities for the Sudanese. Furthermore, the Chinese do most of their own engineering and technical work. Mudawi complained that it was almost impossible to get work on Chinese projects, like those at the Khartoum oil refinery, a joint Sudanese–Chinese venture a few hours' north of the capital, because all the tenders were closed. This was particularly bad for a small engineering company like Mudawi's: 'We only get the smallest contracts ... And when we do get jobs, we have to get security clearance to go there.'

The Chinese, he continued, did not spend any money in the country either, because they all lived in their own compounds (like the Sudan Hotel), hermetically isolated from the rest of the country. Mudawi was exaggerating, but not by much. The conclusion that the Sudanese draw is that the Chinese are reluctant to mix with them. This is one of the most vexing aspects of the Chinese presence, the lack of interaction between the supposed benefactors and the gregarious, intensely sociable Sudanese. One joke is that back in China all these workers were in fact prisoners, brought to Sudan to serve out their term.

Mudawi reached his crescendo on the issue of human rights: '[The Chinese] don't care for the environment, they don't care for social welfare, for human rights, for anything. They don't care even for their own people.' Mudawi had worked for the Canadian company Talisman, and he had seen how it provided some healthcare and education for its employees. Western companies, he argued, were 'very sensitive to public opinion', and so would respond to criticisms. This made them, to a degree, accountable to the people among whom they worked. The Chinese just did not care, shielded as they were from the Sudanese people by the diktat of the authoritarian Bashir government. Mudawi deeply regretted that Chevron and Talisman had been forced to pull out; the consequences had been 'really damaging for the economy, for the people'.

Where the Chinese attitude towards human rights has mattered most is out in Sudan's oilfields. Here, exploration and extraction has been aggressive and often brutal, involving the mass displacement and killing of civilians who got in the way. Sudan's oil industry is anything but the benign force for good that the Chinese version of events suggests. One Sudanese official who worked in the south told me that the Chinese were hated in the oilfields. His view was bleaker than most. As he put it, they were isolated there, spent no money, abused local communities and 'eat whatever they find, dogs, donkeys and cats'. This last comment bordered on the racist, but it points to the darker side of the Chinese–Sudanese relationship.

In November 2006 I flew over the oil-rich *sudd* marshes in Upper Nile state in southern Sudan to visit a remote village called Longuchuk, near the border with Ethiopia. Here I could see for myself how oil exploration was conducted in Sudan. Villagers told of the day two years before when Chinese oil workers had arrived. They were escorted by armed men in T-shirts, whom locals later identified as Sudanese soldiers. They stayed for six months, sank four wells and cleared the land for four access roads (allegedly destroying 100 houses in the process), all without consulting the villagers.

A pool of slimy water beside one of the capped wells showed where surplus oil was dumped. A hundred cows, their livelihood, the villagers said, died from drinking the polluted water. When the oilmen – and their soldier escorts – returned, the locals, furious that they had got neither jobs nor compensation for the damage to their livestock and land, refused to let them in. One of the village chiefs said: 'Nowadays, we fear people who we don't know who come here. People who hold resources give us nothing.'

Diane de Guzman, a specialist in oil for the UN and a long-time resident in Sudan, argued that what she referred to as the 'rape of Longuchuk' repeated a pattern across the oil zones of south Sudan as the Chinese, protected and aided by the Khartoum government, searched ever more aggressively for oil. Amnesty International and Human Rights Watch have both recorded the dreadful mass clearances of villages in the Kordofan area in 2002, partly to allow for oil exploration. Indeed, as we have seen, the counter-insurgency tactics used in Darfur were honed in the Sudanese army's offensives against people living in the oilfields. An Amnesty International document from 2006 reported that the exploitation of oil in Unity and Heglig oilfields in southern Sudan was: 'accompanied by mass forced displacement and killings of the civilian population living there. Sudanese planes bombed villages and southern militias, supported by Sudanese armed forces, attacked villages, killing people and destroying homes until the area was depopulated, in an apparent aim to clear the area of people for oil exploration and extraction.'

As in Longuchuk, the Chinese worked hand-in-hand with the Sudanese armed forces in clearing the oilfields in Abyei and Korforan, though they were careful not to be directly involved. Nonetheless, Chinese oil workers, for the first time, have consequently become targets themselves in these areas. The Darfur rebel groups have understood all too well the extent of China's support for President Bashir's government and the importance of the oil revenues. So, since 2005, armed Sudanese have been attacking Chinese oil workers, for much the same reasons as the Chevron workers were attacked in the mid-1980s by the SPLA.

This has been a new experience for the Chinese, long accustomed to an easy ride in Sudan. The most significant incident at the time of writing came in the autumn of 2008, when at least three Chinese workers were killed and several kidnapped in an assault on an oil installation in South Kordofan. A rebel group claimed responsibility, and the Sudanese government was deeply embarrassed. In the oil areas, the Chinese have often been the main beneficiaries of the state-sponsored violence visited upon the Dinka and other tribes. Now, the people have learned to fight back.

GOOD INTENTIONS, NEVER MIND THE DETAIL

With the diplomatic support of the Chinese; the economic support of the Malaysians and Indians; the military support of the Iranians and Russians; and the unwitting help of the UN, the Bashir regime thus survived the 2000s, despite Darfur, the threat of regime change and tighter Western sanctions. The less ideological, post-Turabi government of the 2000s sometimes gave the impression of wanting to do the right thing as well. In contrast to the period of National Islamic Front rule in the 1990s, the government did make peace in the south and east and occasionally it seemed to be genuine in its desire to find a peaceful solution in Darfur. However, good intentions only went so far. Too often, President Bashir's commitments went unfulfilled, his occasionally hopeful rhetoric unmatched by deeds.

Take the peace agreement signed in the east in 2006, for example. A key provision of this was the setting up of the Eastern Sudan Reconstruction and Development Fund (ESRDF). The Sudanese government pledged to fund this as a way of distributing money to the marginalized areas of the east. Put another way, it was the price that the government was willing to pay to the Beja for peace. The government promised to put the Sudanese equivalent of $100 million into the ESRDF as seed money in 2007, followed by $125 million a year up to 2011. Yet by 2009, almost none of the money had been paid. As a funding agency for development, it was already moribund. This allowed the resentments that had fuelled the insurgency in the east in the first place to fester.

Another good example of the government's double-edged domestic politics was its HIV/AIDS policies. Remarkably, for a very conservative and pious Islamic country, Sudan not only acknowledged that it had a big AIDS problem but put in place a government-led response to the epidemic.

Reliable figures on any subject are hard to come by in Sudan, let alone one as sensitive as this. Nonetheless, enough research has been done to confirm some of the worst fears about the spread of HIV/AIDS in Sudan. The last big study in 2003 revealed a prevalence rate of 1.6 per cent. By 2009, that had probably risen to about 3 per cent. Anything over 1 per cent is considered by the World Health Organisation to be an epidemic.

Sudan has a much lower rate than several other countries in Africa. But northern Sudan, at least, compares itself to the rest of the Arab world rather than to Africa. In this context, the story is much worse. The prevalence rate in neighbouring Egypt, by contrast, is just 0.1 per cent. According to the UN, which includes Sudan in the 'Arab region' for its statistics on HIV/AIDS, 31,600 people died of AIDS in the Arab region in 2007, and of those 80 per cent died in Sudan.

Ironically, the sharp rise in the number of HIV/AIDS cases in Sudan in the 2000s might partly be a by-product of the gradual normalization of Sudanese life, and the restoration of commercial and social contact between Sudan and the rest of the region. Sudan already had a high rate of sexually transmitted diseases due to poverty and the widespread internal displacement caused by the country's various civil wars. But peace in the south and the east after 2005 meant that the transshipment points between Sudan and, say, Eritrea on the route up to Port Sudan became areas where AIDS flourished. Truck drivers are serviced by women euphemistically called 'tea-sellers' on the side of the roads. The more relaxed moral code under President Bashir's regime also probably helped the spread of HIV/AIDS, especially when mixed with a deep ignorance about the whole subject.

This lack of awareness, more than anything else, contributed to the spread of AIDS, and researchers have done some pioneering work to demonstrate just how profound the ignorance about AIDS is. In a study carried out among policemen in Khartoum state in 2005, for instance, only 1.9 per cent of those interviewed were aware that a condom could protect them against AIDS. At an AIDS training workshop for imams that I attended in 2009, one confessed that before the course he had assumed that there were just one or two cases of the disease in the whole of Sudan and that it was never fatal.

To its credit, despite a widespread desire to ignore or downplay the epidemic, the Islamist government of President Bashir committed itself to a nationwide anti-AIDS campaign, setting up the Sudan National Aids Control Programme. This has offices in every state, and allows for HIV/AIDS clinics to be set up in the main hospitals and even for mobile clinics to go out into the rural areas. The idea was to educate people about the disease, and thus remove the considerable stigma and shame that attaches to it.

In 2009 I met one remarkable person at the forefront of this campaign, Nagjun Eldin Mohammed Ahmed. He had been living with AIDS for six years, after having originally contracted the disease through a blood transfusion. Almost uniquely, he has been willing to talk openly about his status. Not only that, he also corralled forty-two fellow sufferers into forming one of the country's most active AIDS-support groups in Port Sudan. It was an impressive achievement. But the courageous Mr Ahmed willingly conceded that this number represented only a tiny fraction of those who were HIV-positive in a city of almost half a million people.

However, despite the apparent leadership of the Sudan National Aids Programme the government barely devoted any money to the project, thus leaving it as something of an empty shell. Instead, as so often, foreign agencies such as UNDP and the Global Fund stepped into the breach. Together, they have done some very innovative work in the Muslim north of the country. They enlisted the help of the imams and also, unusually for a Muslim country, the female religious leaders, who

A female preacher talks about AIDS in east Sudan

lead women in discussion about the Koran as the men attend Friday prayers. I met one such female preacher, Alawiya Libeb Othman, in the town of Kassala, capital of a state with one of the highest rates of AIDS in the country. She conceded that AIDS carries a huge stigma in Sudan, but also argued that it was her job to 'get people to accept that people with AIDS should not be ostracized and that AIDS sufferers have equal rights'. Dressed in the full black *hejab*, her hands gloved, with a *khimar* over her face hiding everything but her lively, darting eyes, she calmly talked about the problems of prostitution, of how the 'tea-sellers' were being forced into sex by poverty.

Similarly, some imams had begun addressing the subject of HIV/AIDS in their Friday prayers. Again, most of the religious leaders who I met in northern Sudan attributed this willingness to talk about AIDS, and often taboo subjects such as homosexuality and prostitution, to the tradition of compassion in Sudanese Sufism. 'Islam is a religion of how you treat people,' Alawiya Othman told me very firmly. 'It's a religion of tolerance and forgiveness.' Given the existing levels of ignorance about AIDS, it will probably take more than a generation for people to learn enough about it to change their behaviour accordingly. But at least Sudan has been willing to start being open about the problem, in contrast to much of the rest of the Arab region, where HIV has been spreading faster than in any other part of the world. If the government put more money into its own campaigns against AIDS, undoubtedly more could be accomplished. The rates of HIV/AIDS are even higher in southern Sudan than they are in north; the sad fact remains that AIDS will remain one of the country's most potent killers for many years to come.

A LAST AVENUE OF ATTACK? THE THREAT OF THE INTERNATIONAL CRIMINAL COURT

Having fended off almost everything that the UN and Western countries could throw at him over Darfur, whether threats, diplomatic pressure or blue helmets, President Bashir faced one last avenue of attack – through the International Criminal Court.

As part of a general move towards more effective prosecution of international justice in the later 1990s, the high noon for new thinking about liberal interventionism, 108 countries signed up to the Rome Statute. This set up a permanent International Criminal Court (ICC) that would investigate the worst offences – crimes against humanity, war crimes and genocide – and bring prosecutions against the perpetrators.

Other courts and tribunals, mixing elements of local and international justice in a so-called 'hybrid' manner, were set up throughout the first decade of this century to deal with war crimes in specific post-conflict situations. The Special Court of Sierra Leone was a good example of the hybrid, constituted to try those who had ordered or carried out the killings and amputations during the country's horrific civil war of 1991–2002. The ICC, based in The Hague, had a broader remit, to roam anywhere it was asked to by the UN, which set the court up. It began its work in 2002. The ICC was led by an Argentinian prosecutor, Luis Moreno Ocampo, who had been schooled in the nasty world of Latin American state crimes.

As we have seen, in 2005 the UN asked the Court to investigate Darfur. Thus, at the same time as the debates on whether or not to send a big UN force into Darfur, supposedly to bring 'peace', raged at the Security Council, so the same body also started down another track, that of pursuing 'justice'. Even the Chinese did not block this, although Sudan was not a signatory to the Rome Statute and did not recognize the Court's jurisdiction.

In the following years the ICC indicted several people for war crimes in Darfur. These included, in 2007, Ahmad Harun, who in 2003–4 had allegedly co-ordinated the army and *janjaweed* attacks, and the *janjaweed* leader Ali Muhammed Ali Abd-al-Rahman. A year later three rebel leaders were indicted for the attack on African Union peacekeepers at Haskanita in 2007 (see page 239). Finally, on 4 March 2009, the court issued an arrest warrant for President Bashir himself for war crimes and crimes against humanity, although not for genocide, as the chief prosecutor wished.

However, it was soon clear that the two tracks of peace and justice were at least as contradictory as they were supposed to be complementary. Once Darfur became a 'crime scene', as the chief prosecutor melodramatically declared, so this made the Sudanese government even less inclined to engage with the UN and the outside world than it had been previously. Sudanese officials already found the idea of UN troops, or any foreign presence, bad enough; if they were going to be deployed to arrest Sudanese ministers and politicians on war-crimes charges, as the Sudanese feared, the reaction was even stronger. The presence of dozens of international aid agencies in Darfur aroused similar suspicions. The Sudanese government thought that they would be engaged in handing over information gathered from their work with refugees in Darfur to the ICC. Sure enough, when President Bashir was issued with his arrest warrant in March 2009, the first people to bear the brunt of the president's vengeance were aid workers. Within hours of the announcement, thirteen international aid agencies, including Oxfam, Médecins Sans Frontières and Care, were unceremoniously expelled from Sudan.

The threat of legal proceedings hanging over the Darfur crisis thus came to complicate further the chances of finding a political solution. The ICC, so one argument ran, gave Sudanese politicians fewer incentives to negotiate in good faith with the international community. After all, Sudanese government officials could well assume that however reasonable they were with the West or the UN over finding a political solution to Darfur, they still ran the risk of being whisked off to The Hague regardless. Better, surely, to circle the wagons in Khartoum.

Crucially, the ICC has no police force to impose its edicts, so President Bashir and other indicted officials knew that to avoid arrest all they had to do was stay in Sudan or travel to countries that were not members of the ICC. The wily President Bashir made the most of this by making a great show of travelling to other Arab and African states that were also non-signatories of the Rome Statute, flaunting his support among other Muslim states. He further mocked the ICC's impotence by appointing Harun to a variety of important positions, including that of Minister of State for Humanitarian Affairs.

Unfortunately, most Arab and African countries agreed with Bashir's assessment of the ICC. Up to 2009 the ICC's prosecutions were directed solely against African rulers and warlords, so African and Arab leaders concluded that the court was just another expression of Western imperialism. Where, they demanded, were the indictments over the invasion of Iraq or the Israeli occupation of the West Bank? As a result, few countries in the region supported the prosecutions over Darfur. If anything the indictment of Bashir rallied support for him in the Muslim world.

Thus, like the UN before it, international justice foundered on the divisions of opinion over Darfur. The Arab League and African Union states demanded that the court's proceedings against Bashir be 'deferred' by the UN Security Council, as indeed they can be under Article 16 of the Rome Statute. Although deferrals are technically supposed to be for one year only, by extending the deferral year by year an accused person can, in theory, be exempted from prosecution altogether. Only time will tell whether President Bashir manages to sabotage the West's attempts at a universal jurisdiction for war crimes and genocide, just as he undermined the unity of the UN.

Almost every Darfuri I met in my visit to the camps wanted the prosecutions against President Bashir and his henchmen in Khartoum to go ahead. The prospect of seeing the president on trial for war crimes gave them some comfort amid the ruins of what had once been their home and sanctuary. However, at the time of writing the ICC is no nearer arresting Bashir. Indeed, over the past years he seems to have enjoyed flouting the ICC at every opportunity, travelling freely to as many countries as he can to prove that he is beyond the court's reach. At best, the ICC has been a mixed success, but as far as President Bashir is concerned, it has been an abject failure.

CHAPTER EIGHT

NEW NATIONS, OLD WAYS

On 9 July 2011, the world's newest country came into existence. In Juba, amidst scenes of unbridled joy, South Sudan, as it was to be called, declared its independence. In front of a small army of visiting heads of state and politicians (including Zimbabwe's Robert Mugabe, who arrived with an enormous entourage in a large jet), diplomats, activists and assorted other well-wishers, Salva Kiir was sworn in as the first president. Even President Bashir turned up, bowing to the inevitable after a full 98.3 per cent of southerners had voted for secession in the referendum held the previous January. It was a pivotal moment in Sudan's, and Africa's, history. After a half-century of civil war that had cost about 2.5 million lives, the continent's largest country had split in two. African leaders, who generally resist secessionist movements to the death, had been forced to acknowledge that in this case, undoubtedly, it was for the best.

The new country was born on a tide of international good will – and an awful lot of aid money. America, which had invested so heavily, both politically and financially, in the defence of south Sudanese interests, was the midwife. Already by the time of independence America had set up a large embassy compound in Juba; nowhere was independence greeted

Salva Kiir waves to supporters prior to declaring the independence of South Sudan in Juba, 9 July 2011

with more delight than in Washington. The Chinese, too, promised to be helpful, just as they had been in the north; rather late in the day, they had come to appreciate that the oil was mostly in the south anyway. But the most hopeful sign was the presence of President Bashir at the independence celebrations. Rather than sulking over the division of his country, he gave what was under the circumstances a remarkably gracious speech, looking forward to the two Sudans working together in the future.

I, and many others, had predicted that the new country would struggle to survive at all; that the nation-in-waiting had been too poor, too weak, too corrupt and too riven by internal conflict to succeed. But for a few moments, it was possible, acceptable even, to suspend belief and embrace the dream of a prosperous, peaceful and democratic South Sudan, the antithesis of the northern neighbour that had tormented it for so long.

That dream, however, lasted as long as it took President Bashir to fly back to Khartoum. In order to get to the point at which the old Sudan could break up at all, many of the outstanding issues between the north and south, the subject of years of internationally mediated negotiations since the CPA of 2005, had simply been deferred. This was a deliberate ploy in order to achieve separation at all, and it came at a heavy price. But there were too many of the prickly old problems left, particularly regarding the status and ownership of the border territories and the oilfields around Abyei, for each side to simply let the other be.

Indeed, within six months of independence the two old adversaries were back at each other's throats. By January 2012 negotiators had reached an impasse over how much money the south should pay the north to use its pipelines and facilities to export its crude oil overseas – the north's oil infrastructure remained the only means for the south to monetize its reserves. In frustration, South Sudan consequently shut down its 350,000-barrels-per-day oil output, thus depriving both the northern and southern governments of significant portions of their incomes. That was bad for the north, now called simply Sudan, but was positively suicidal for the south, a country that relied on the oil revenues for about 98 per cent of its national income.

SOUTH SUDAN'S DESCENT INTO HELL

An emergency budget was produced in March 2012 by the South Sudanese government predicated on a more than 50 per cent cut in government spending. A poor people were thus further pauperized. The South Sudanese government spokespeople talked of an 'austerity drive', as if the long-suffering south Sudanese people – among the poorest on earth – could afford the luxury of choosing to be austere in the first place. Furthermore, the government officials who were asking the people to make these sacrifices seemed to be happily exempt from their own strictures. Soon afterwards, in May, President Kiir wrote to seventy-five former and serving senior government officials accusing them of having defrauded the state of about $4 billion between them and asking for the money back. As Sudan expert Jeremy Astill-Brown has put it, this spoke to a 'culture of reckless entitlement' among those who, in their own view, had valiantly led the new nation to victory and independence.[1] I guess they must have regarded this money as their own peace dividend. As far as anyone knows, up to the time of writing little or none of the money has been returned, and neither, apparently, has any of the seventy-five been prosecuted for embezzlement or fraud.

The callousness with which the South Sudanese government treated its own people during the oil shutdown, the scale of the corruption revealed by President's Kiir's letter and the escalating dispute with the north quickly dispelled any notion that South Sudan was somehow going to overcome its own deep-seated pathologies. If anything, the state quickly became more dysfunctional, especially when a full-scale civil war broke out in December 2013.

There were some immediate causes of this conflict, but unfortunately they fed into a long narrative of rivalry and suspicion within the SPLM. In July 2013 President Salva Kiir dissolved his government, arguing that a fresh start was needed in the governance of the country, especially given the corruption and maladministration that had been revealed. Fair enough. But in reshuffling his cabinet the president also seemed to wilfully shatter that careful ethnic and political balancing act that had held the ruling SPLM together at independence. Most importantly, Riek Machar was sacked as vice-president. The vainglorious Machar may have been a quarrelsome and occasionally insubordinate cabinet colleague, but he was also the leader of the Nuer, the second largest ethnic group in the country. He was thus the indispensable linchpin that held the SPLM together, at least along ethnic lines.

Of course, those rivalries between Dinka and Nuer, and others, had been simmering all along as their leaders struggled for the bounty that was on offer after 2011 to rebuild the country. But the events of summer 2013 cleaved open all the old divisions again in the most dangerous way, harking back to the early 1990s when Machar and others had openly rebelled against the leadership of the Dinka John Garang, plunging the SPLM of the time into internecine warfare. Thus Kiir's actions seemed particularly reckless – intentionally designed, almost, to return South Sudan to those desperate days. Furthermore, they fed into a growing perception, shared by Machar and some of those other ministers who had been sacked in July, that Kiir was becoming increasingly high-handed and dictatorial in his rule. There were allegations that he was beginning to act unconstitutionally – for example, by sacking two elected state governors. He also began to crack down on internal dissent within the SPLM. Worse, his government sponsored two pieces of legislation that would have severely restricted criticism of his government. One was a media bill, proposing that government officials should monitor all media content. The other was a bill restricting the right of NGOs to advocate, which particularly inflamed South Sudan's frustrated foreign backers. For many, it looked as if the South was following a familiar and dispiriting African pattern of increasing authoritarianism, while as its people became ever poorer.

In December 2013 these tensions and divisions boiled over into vicious and bloody warfare. It barely mattered which side was directly responsible for starting the violence on 15 December; the more salient point is that both sides were ready and willing to fight, and were also armed to the teeth. The tone of what was to come was set on the 16th, when at least 300 Nuer men, and possibly as many as 450, were killed in Juba in a compound that had previously been used for joint military and police exercises. The Machar-led SPLM-In Opposition (SPLM-IO) was now pitted against government forces throughout most of the country, with fighting particularly fierce around Malakal, which changed hands six times between December 2013 and April 2014. The fighting destroyed at least a quarter of the city.

Both sides were accused of widespread war crimes, rape, torture and other sundry human-rights violations over the next year and a half or so. It was as if years of pent-up hatred and bitterness suddenly exploded, now that the two sides could turn against each other rather than focus on their mutual enemy in north Sudan. To give just a few instances: in April 2014 hundreds of civilians were massacred in Bentiu, including more than 200 killed in a mosque; in May 2015

UNICEF reported that government forces and militias had killed at least 129 children over a three-week period, with tales of girls as young as eight being gang-raped and others being thrown into burning buildings; and, in February 2015, a government militia abducted more than a thousand people near Malakal, including eighty-nine boys who were preparing to take their exams.

Overall, the effect of the conflict on the population was devastating. It is estimated that over 50,000 people lost their lives. Two million people, about one-fifth of the population, have been forced to flee their homes. In a terrible repeat of the earlier north–south conflict, hundreds of thousands poured over the border to seek refuge in third countries such as Uganda, while about 1.5 million became internally displaced persons (IDPs) in South Sudan. More than 100,000 of those were put up in crowded conditions in emergency UN bases. Agricultural production and harvests were severely disrupted, crops were destroyed and thousands of cattle were killed. Consequently, almost every year now, famine alerts would go out to warn donors of impending disaster. By late December 2015, more than one-third of South Sudan's population were classified as 'severely food and nutrition insecure,' an 80 per cent increase compared to 2014, according to the official Integrated Food Security Phase Classification (IPC) report. The International Committee of the Red Cross warned that hundreds of thousands faced a 'critical food shortage'. Of the 3.9 million people classified by the IPC as 'severely insecure', 3.1 million were in 'crisis', 800,000 in 'emergency' and 40,000 were facing 'catastrophe', also known technically as Classification Phase 5, the same severity as famine.

The full trauma of successive conflicts in the country, including the post-2013 violence, was captured by a survey conducted by the UNDP in conjunction with the South Sudan Law Society from October 2014 to April 2015.[2] Researchers interviewed about 1,500 people across eleven locations in six of the ten states of South Sudan. A full 63 per cent of respondents reported the killing of a close family member, and over half the destruction of their house or other property. In certain locations, the violence was almost unbearably concentrated: in Bor, 95 per cent of respondents said that a close family member of theirs had been killed, and 23 per cent reported witnessing rape at some point in their lives. During the north–south wars, the south's leaders had good cause to blame the Islamists of the north for provoking this humanitarian catastrophe. From 2013, however, they only had themselves to blame, which made the toll all the more shameful and inexcusable.

A FEW VAIN MEN

With South Sudan's politicians at each other's throats, and the country firmly set on the road to self-immolation, it was left to the neighbours, and to the international community, to try to reconcile the warring factions and to bring some small relief to the besieged population. In 2014, Uganda, Ethiopia and Kenya principally initiated a process to bring the two sides to the negotiating table under the auspices of the African Union, acting on its mantra 'African solutions to African problems', together with the Intergovernmental Authority on Development (IGAD), a regional bloc. After torturous negotiations in Addis Ababa and elsewhere, IGAD eventually secured a 'Protocol on Agreed Principles on Transitional Arrangements Towards Resolution of the Crisis'. This proposed a new transitional unity government (including Machar and others) that would rule until fresh elections could be held. It also provided for a Commission for Truth, Reconciliation and Healing and a hybrid court for South Sudan, both of which, it was hoped, would meet the demands for local justice after the frenzy of bloodletting since 2013. This protocol formed the basis for the formal peace agreement signed in July 2015.

However, to no one's great surprise, this proved almost impossible to implement, with both sides endlessly jibbing at the demands of the agreement and delaying co-operation. Deadline after deadline was missed to form the much hoped-for unity government, despite the fact that the peace agreement was also strongly supported by the UN, desperate to avoid the world's newest country descending into a complete shambles. The UN's role, strongly supported by the US on this occasion, included threatening the leaders of both sides in the conflict with sanctions unless they toed the line, and to punish them for war crimes and other abuses. The UN was acting out of a very valid concern that the war in South Sudan constituted a 'threat to international peace and security in the region'. Finally running out of patience with the warring politicians, in July 2015 travel bans and asset freezes were placed on South Sudanese leaders, three from either side in the conflict. They included the commander of Salva Kiir's special guard, Major-General Marial Chanuong Yol Mangok, and on the rebel side Major-General Simon Gatwech Dual, chief of general staff for the opposition forces and a key ally of Riek Machar. These sanctions were rolled over in 2016. After evidence emerged that both Machar and Kiir could be directly implicated in some of the worst war crimes, there were also calls for a tough arms embargo and further sanctions, but these efforts were blocked by Russia on the Security Council.

Given what has happened over the last years, if a unity government is eventually formed in Juba it will be unified in name only. Trust, the vital ingredient of any such arrangement, has all but run out. As if to strike this truth home, in December 2015 Salva Kiir suddenly announced that he was going to create twenty-eight states in South Sudan, up from the current ten. Most people would have supported further steps towards devolution of power in the country at some time, and it was indeed one of the long-term plans of the government. But coming at this particular moment, and without consulting Machar and the opposition, the move was seen as extremely provocative, even incendiary, as the whole peace deal had been predicated on a ten-state country.

As Kiir got to appoint all the new governors himself as well, it could also have been seen a power grab for his administration before he had to share power with his rivals. The new states were roughly delineated along ethnic lines, and as many as possible of them, according to one close observer, had Dinka majorities. This would entrench Kiir's authority along the country's dangerous ethnic fault lines. It certainly did not seem like the act of a statesman committed to a fresh future of peace and co-existence with his former opponents and immediately sparked off further rounds of bitter argument and name-calling between the two sides. Machar himself was quick to denounce the decision, arguing that it sent out a 'clear message to the world that President Kiir is not committed to peace'. The implementation of the peace agreement was further delayed, amidst more sharp divisions between the two sides.

But beyond the often deadly political squabbles in Juba, there is a deeper question confronting South Sudan as to whether it can ever evolve into a civilian state which might eventually allow a democracy to function properly at all. For now, however, as Jeremy Astill-Brown has argued, South Sudan is 'not a country with a military. Rather, it is a military with a country.'[3] And as long as South Sudan remains that way, there can be little hope of progress.

'A military with a country' means that South Sudan is totally dominated by the needs of a heavily militarized ruling party, the SPLM, with little left over for anything or anyone else. In this respect, the south is now even more a military state than the north ever was. In the words of one recent independent evaluation of South Sudan's economy, 'the military has essentially taken over the budget, leaving development priorities almost exclusively in the hands of foreign donor agencies'. Thus, while numbers on the military's payroll have expanded exponentially, from about 40,000 soldiers in 2004 to 240,000 in 2011, topped up by another 94,000 in a strong paramilitary reserve of policemen, prison warders and wildlife guards, so the donors have been expected to fork out increasingly for schools and medicine.[4]

In recent years, for instance, foreign donors have been funding about three-quarters of the country's health system. The difference between what the government spends on itself and what it allocates to its normal responsibilities is almost grotesque in its magnitude. The Office of the President's national security budget in 2014, which was about 6 per cent of the total security budget, was more than South Sudan's entire infrastructure budget, in a country with wretchedly few decent paved roads. During the height of the recent fighting between the government and Riek Machar's opposition forces, South

Sudan contributed only 0.5 per cent of the cost of the humanitarian operation needed to save hundreds of thousands of refugees from starving, and worse.[5]

The object, of course, of lavishing such an overwhelming amount of money on the 'security sector' is to cultivate an enormous patronage network that has become the bedrock of the regime's popular support. GOSS can still, to a certain degree, draw on the goodwill that it enjoyed in 2012 as the victor of the liberation struggle, but increasingly it has come to rely more on simply buying consent, especially from key commanders and administrators. The government was paying for no fewer than 745 generals in 2011, each with their own individual patronage networks to manage. Between 2008 and 2013 an average of 40 per cent of South Sudan's entire budget went just on payroll, of which almost three-quarters was security and veterans' spending. With little effective oversight, the scope for corruption is virtually limitless. One favourite ploy has been the creation of 'ghost soldiers', infantrymen who exist only on payroll, whose salaries have been siphoned off to the big men of the SPLA. The army's own internal audit is supposed to have discovered 40,000 ghost soldiers in 2013.[6]

So ingrained is the habit of buying consent that it has become the default position whenever the government gets into trouble, as it all too often does. Rather than attempting any serious reforms to improve the economy, reduce corruption or anything else that might compromise its own interests or make itself temporarily unpopular, it will buy more consent from those on whom it relies the most, the people who run the corrupt patronage networks in the army, police and the rest of the 'security' apparatus. Thus, for example, as inflation hit 110 per cent in early 2016 due to the chronic mismanagement of the economy, so the government increased the salaries of public servants by 300 per cent, paid for by the central bank printing money. It wasn't clear how everybody else was supposed to cope with the rapid erosion of their purchasing power.[7] It is another example of the selfishness of South Sudan's political class, whereby the SPLM's leaders have lamentably failed to put the wider public good above their own narrow interests of power and money. In this sense, as Jeremy Astill-Brown has argued, South Sudan's rapid decline has been the fault, above all, of 'a few vain men'.

SURVIVING THE ARAB SPRING

Unfortunately, the rapid implosion of South Sudan came as no great surprise to most commentators. At the time of writing, in August 2016, the country continues to limp along with no end to the old elite's political squabbles and the general deterioration of living conditions for most in sight.

Much more surprising, however, was the survival of President Bashir's regime in the north, and in particular Bashir himself. The hardliners in the regime, and many ordinary Sudanese, squarely blamed Bashir for the loss of half of the country, and with it about three-quarters of the oil production. Although the Nilotic Arab tribes of the north had invested almost nothing in persuading southerners to stay united in one Sudan in the years between 2005 and 2011, remarkably it was still assumed by most of them that the south Sudanese couldn't possibly vote to go their own way. The loss of the south therefore came as a shock to many, and consequently the government lost a good deal of credibility amongst its erstwhile supporters. As well as losing half the country, the president was also by this time, of course, wanted by the International Criminal Court on war crimes charges arising from the killings in Darfur. This counted for much less to ordinary Sudanese, most of whom considered the ICC to be merely an arm of Western imperialism, but it did seem to limit Bashir's options for alliance-building and support from abroad.

So when the Arab Spring kicked off in Tunisia in December 2010 after the self-immolation of Mohamed Bouazizi, and quickly spread along the North African littoral and into the rest of the Middle East, it looked as if Bashir would be acutely vulnerable. After all, his record in power was just as despotic as any of the tyrants to fall in Tunisia, Egypt and elsewhere, and on top of that he had just overseen the loss of half of his country. Furthermore, Sudan's economic situation deteriorated rapidly with the loss of South Sudan's oil. The budget deficit soared, together with inflation, and the currency was devalued. All this helped to stoke unrest on the streets as the price of basic commodities started to rise. The removal of fuel subsidies to reduce the deficit hurt people the most. Construction and other projects were shelved with the subsequent loss of jobs. Twice before, as we have seen, in 1964 and 1985, Sudan's presidents had been swept away by mass protests of the kind that engulfed Tunisia, Cairo, Tripoli and elsewhere during 2011 and 2012. Yet, remarkably, Bashir, unlike his predecessors, survived. How?

To begin with, in 2011, the Arab uprisings seemed to pass Khartoum by, but by the next year there were sporadic protests in the capital and elsewhere. These were all well contained by the security forces. In September 2013, however, matters came to a head with the biggest protests seen in Khartoum and other cities for decades, sparked directly by Bashir's announcement on 22 September on the reduction of fuel subsidies. Days later, 5,000 people were demonstrating on the streets of the capital, in Omdurman and a handful of other cities, motivated by the same toxic mix of resentments that had fuelled protests elsewhere. 'This is Sudan's Arab Spring – delayed only until anger finally overcame fear, as it is now clearly has done', declared Eric Reeves, the seasoned American Sudan-watcher. There were unconfirmed reports that government officials were fleeing the country with their families – the rats leaving the sinking ship.

Yet, at this moment of gravest peril, Bashir scarcely flinched, dealing with the situation in the way he knew best: with the ruthless application of force. It is estimated that over 200 people were shot dead by the security forces to quell the protest. Hundreds more were injured; most of the victims were young men and women, in their late teens and twenties, according to an authoritative Human Rights Watch (HRW) report on the shootings.[8]

This is a first-hand account of the shooting of one particular demonstrator in Khartoum North gathered by the HRW researchers. The protestors were marching on a complex of law courts at the time of the shooting:

> The national security officials armed with Kalashnikov rifles and wearing camouflage, riding in four-wheel Toyota Land Cruisers, blocked our way. They threw tear gas at us and told us to disperse . . . They started to beat us with sticks. We turned back toward the courts and stayed on the main road. While we were there we heard a gunshot and I saw Osama who was standing in front of me in the middle of the road fall down. He was shot in the head above his left eyebrow. At that time, there were national security agents in plainclothes and police standing in front of the courts. I am not sure who exactly shot him, but the gunshot came from them.

As well as the dead and injured, probably about a thousand others were detained by the dreaded NISS. Many of the detainees were released within days, but some were not so fortunate. They were locked up for months, beaten and tortured, and were seldom allowed to see their families or even legal representatives. To this day, as far as is known, no one has been held accountable for the killings. Amongst those doing the shooting was a relatively new and particularly barbaric unit called the Special Reaction Force, formed especially to operate in Darfur, as we shall see (and later, also called Rapid Support Forces).

On other similar occasions during the Arab Spring, when the security forces confronted thousands of protestors at critical moments, regimes often wilted, leading to a (usually temporary) victory for the protestors. Often, this was because the regimes themselves were not united about the appropriate course of action to take, with the hardliners increasingly in a minority (although not, for instance, in the case of Syria). In Sudan, however, Bashir managed to keep his regime together almost intact; there were, in reality, very few defections from the regime, or more dovish elements going over to the opposition, fearful of massacring hundreds of people in the streets. There were heated discussions within the upper echelons of the NCP on how to proceed, but by and large these were kept in-house.

The only prominent member of the government and NCP to resign at this point was the more liberal-minded Ghazi Atabani, one of the architects of the CPA. He had been trying to exert pressure within the regime for reform over the previous few years. He and a few others now formed the Reform Now Movement (RNM) as a sort of former insiders' popular front opposition to the government. There was an expectation that Atabani's new party would grow into a serious contender for power in Khartoum, but these hopes fizzled out during the course of 2014. He came to London in early 2015 to talk about his expectations for political change in Sudan, but sounded less than convinced that he would be able to exert any influence on the future course of events. No firebrand he. Indeed, Atabani sounded more like a man more concerned with not burning his bridges with the government than with overthrowing it.

The regime's survival, and the lack of defections and dissent within the ranks, was testimony, in part, to how assiduously Bashir had culti-vated the government's patronage system over the previous twenty-six years. At this critical moment, enough NCP officials of all ranks calcu-lated that they still had more to gain from the current regime than abandoning it for an uncertain future. Bashir's patronage system has worked all too well. According to one diagnosis, rather than spending money on schools and hospitals, most of the government's money went on paying the (relatively good) wages of state-level bureaucrats, to keep them onside.[9] It was this salariat that stayed steadfastly loyal in 2013.

Transfers from the centre (Khartoum) to the peripheries went not to the poorest states, as one might expect, but mainly to the areas of the regime's most vital support, Khartoum and Gezira state. Remarkably, after the secession of South Sudan, and despite all the consequent economic traumas (the huge dip in oil revenues for instance), central government transfers to the states increased by 8 per cent in 2012 and 2013. The IMF, for one, advised the government to cut its transfers to the states to save money and stabilize the economy, but it did no such thing – ensuring that when Bashir needed it most, the troops remained loyal. As Edward Thomas, a Sudan expert, writes: 'Some way or another, transfers to states had become part of the government's mysterious repertoire of economic and social policies that has allowed it to maintain the country's longest incumbency.'[10]

Whereas the regime stood firmly together, of one purpose, during its hour of greatest peril, the opposition, by contrast, remained hopelessly divided. Opposition parties never agreed amongst themselves as to how best to exploit Bashir's manifest political and economic difficulties; worse, they were often divided internally as to how to respond. In particular, Sadiq al-Mahdi, head of the Umma party and former president, was relentlessly indecisive as to how to react to the 2013 protests. Fearful of inflaming the situation and thereby perhaps causing more deaths, he largely sat tight at the end of September. Even if this was a justifiably humanitarian reaction to the shootings in the streets, his real failure lay in not preparing the ground for a wider uprising in the months or years before, as the Arab Spring toppled regimes elsewhere. As one foreign diplomat who was in Sudan at the time observes, 'if the opposition had been more organised, and given a clearer lead, it could have turned out differently'. The other opposition groupings, such as the Communist Party, equally failed to give a clear lead.

Sowing yet more confusion among opposition ranks, in the months after the crackdown, partly as a sop to the international community and partly to appease his domestic critics, Bashir launched a 'national dialogue'. This was advertised by the regime as a genuine attempt to reconcile the government and its critics, to heal the wounds of the September 2013 shootings and to find some way forward out of the political impasse. The initiative was supported by the African Union and its long-suffering point man on Sudan, the former South African president Thabo Mbeki. It was supposed to be an 'inclusive' dialogue, yet many opposition groups boycotted the process, denouncing it as a sham, whilst others, such as Turabi's Islamist party, the PCP, supported it. Again, the dithering and splits within the opposition over the national dialogue suggested that it was not the dialogue that lacked credibility, but they themselves. Towards the end of 2014 a loose coalition of opposition groups named 'Sudan Call' came together in Addis Ababa, including representatives from the rebel Sudanese Revolutionary Forces of Darfur, the Umma party and the Alliance of Sudanese Civil Society Organizations. They stridently declared that Sudan was 'sliding towards an abyss as a result of the policies of the regime', prompting the Khartoum government to denounce them as 'traitors'. But, as yet, Sudan Call has failed to transform its rhetoric into anything very much more substantial on the ground in Sudan.

It was in this context that the general election took place in April 2015, despite international calls (including from the African Union) for it to be postponed until there was more evidence that a genuine national dialogue could take place. The election was a dull and empty affair, with none of the sense of expectation that had marked the previous election five years earlier. There was an almost total boycott of the election by the opposition, lacking any of the hesitations and soul-searching that had characterized the partial boycotts of 2010, and the turnout even among NCP supporters was remarkably low, perhaps about 30 per cent. Unsurprisingly, Bashir officially won 94 per cent of the vote and the NCP won 323 of 426 National Assembly seats. It was a hollow victory for the NCP but, nonetheless, it proved sufficient for the regime's purposes as Bashir had secured another 'democratic' mandate from the people. This marked the end of any serious attempts arising from the social and political forces unleashed by the Arab Spring to unseat him. The great survivor had survived again.

OUR FRIENDS IN THE GULF, AND EUROPE

Just as Bashir played his dangerously weak hand in domestic politics extraordinarily well, so too did he hold the trump card in foreign affairs. His manoeuvrings in the world of Middle Eastern and regional diplomacy were essential to shoring up the regime's precarious position at home.

Again, at the time of the break-up of Sudan, Bashir's international position seemed distinctly perilous. His ICC indictment made him a pariah in the West, and as all signatory states to the ICC are obliged to act on the arrest warrants if in a position to do so, Bashir had to take great care as to which other countries he could fly over, or touch down in, as well. Furthermore, the regime's close friendship with Shia-

Muslim Iran, a country which had supplied much of Sudan's military capacity over the years, continued to irritate a good deal of the majority Sunni Arab world, straining relations with the Gulf states, Saudi Arabia and others. The lingering strain of Islamism within the regime, a leftover from Turabi's days as the ideologue-in-chief, also continued to estrange countries doing battle with their own Muslim Brotherhoods, especially Egypt.

With Sudan's economy teetering on the brink of disaster after the secession of South Sudan, however, Bashir acknowledged that he could no longer afford to alienate most of the very rich Arab world for the sake of an alliance with relatively impecunious Iran, a country which, exactly like Sudan, was then subject to a range of Western economic sanctions due to its pursuit of nuclear weapons. From 2013, therefore, Sudan started to pivot away from Iran and towards Saudi Arabia in particular. Sudan, also a majority Sunni country, could give the Saudis land and, later, soldiers, in exchange for desperately needed financial support. Doubtless, also, Saudi Arabia played an active role in the rapprochement: it was desperate to isolate Iran in the region, and detaching Sudan from Tehran's orbit was always going to be something of a coup for the kingdom.

The first signs of a Sudanese pivot came in September 2014 when Sudanese officials ordered the closure of several Iranian cultural centres in Khartoum and elsewhere, accusing their employees of preaching Shiism. In October 2015 came a much more concrete sign of Sudan's realignment when it committed troops to the Saudi-led coalition fighting the Iran-backed Houthi rebels in Yemen; it is thought that, to date, Sudan has sent about 8,000 troops there. This was followed in January 2016 by Sudan breaking off diplomatic relations entirely with Iran at Riyadh's request after the Saudi embassy in Tehran was attacked by a mob following the Saudi execution of the Shia cleric Nimr al-Nimr. Apparently Bashir barely hesitated when he was urged to take this extreme step by the Saudis.

So Sudan cast its lot firmly with the Saudis in the great Shia–Sunni divide, and it has been well rewarded for its wise choice. At the beginning of 2016 the Sudanese investment minister told parliament that Saudi investments in Sudan now totalled $11 billion. This included, according to reports in the *Sudan Tribune*, $1.7 billion for dam projects alone.[11] Saudi Arabia was also promising to invest in the Sudanese armed forces. As well as this, millions of acres of Sudanese land has been leased or purchased by Gulf and Saudi investors in recent years, mainly for agricultural purposes – a mass sell-off of land that has been characterized as a neo-colonial land-grab by its critics. This phenomenon is not confined to Sudan, but the country has probably been selling off more land at cheaper prices than anywhere else in Africa. The Chinese have been involved in some of these projects, lending technical and other kinds of support, but Saudi Arabia, Qatar, Kuwait and Abu Dhabi have provided most of the investment. It is unclear how much (if any) of the profits from these agricultural projects and land speculations are captured by Bashir's regime for the benefit of the Sudanese people.

Sudan's very pragmatic pivot towards the Saudis and the Gulf states probably angered some of the NCP's core supporters who still hankered for the good old days of the Islamist revolution, but if so there has been little sign of it. More to the point, the Sudanese regime's newfound commitment to the mainstream of Sunni-Arabic Islamic identity for financial gain has further reduced any incentives it may once have had to seek solutions to the country's various internal conflicts, such as in Darfur or the east. As the International Crisis Group concluded in a report in March 2016, the regime's 'recourse to an internationalised Arab nationalism, historically adopted by the riverine elite but rejected by many others . . . further reduces the vestiges of a political and ethnic pluralism already severely tested by the South's secession and those conflicts'.[12]

As well as finding succour in the Sunni world of Saudi Arabia and the Gulf states, more surprisingly still, by 2015–16 President Bashir had also managed something of a rapprochement with his erstwhile critics in Europe. Taking advantage of the Mediterranean refugee crisis, when hundreds of thousands of desperate people tried to cross from Africa and the Middle East into Europe, all too often dying in the process,

President Bashir managed to sell himself to the Europeans as the man who could help them solve the crisis. His government promised to provide intelligence on the people-smuggling gangs and also to prohibit the flows of refugees streaming across Sudan's vast open spaces from countries such as Eritrea. In return, eager to be seen to be doing something to tackle the refugee crisis at its source, the EU pledged an aid package of around $100 million to Sudan. This deal was enshrined at a ministerial conference in Rome in November 2014, with the launch of the EU–Horn of Africa Migration Route Initiative, which became known at the Khartoum Process.

Ostensibly, this $100 million was to be used to better tackle the causes of irregular migration, in the hope that fewer desperate people would then arrive at the southern shore of the Mediterranean seeking to make the perilous journey to Italy or Greece and ultimately to Germany, Britain, Holland and Scandinavia. In reality, this was mainly a move to appease hostile global opinion appalled at the sight of a very disunited Europe squabbling over how to shore up some very porous borders. The main beneficiary of this rapprochement, however, was undoubtedly the government of Sudan, for it once again lifted the pressure put upon it over Darfur and its other civil wars. As PAX, an NGO, put it in a damning report on the Khartoum Process, treating Sudan 'primarily as a transit country for refugees ignores the extensive role of the government in producing refugees and IDPs, not least through its brutal counter-insurgency attacks, through its exacerbation of the catastrophic humanitarian situation of refugees and IDPs'. For instance, in the first six months of 2016 alone, it was estimated that a further 130,000 refugees had been created in Darfur due to the fighting there, mainly the result of the Sudanese army's assaults on rebel groups. Moreover, the report noted: 'Stabilising the regime is not likely to contribute to regional stability, judging by its history as a destabilising actor, only most recently in Libya and the Central African Republic, as well as in South Sudan.'[13] Quite apart from these criticisms, there was also plenty of evidence that Sudanese security officials colluded with the people traffickers.

In America, one official told me, the Khartoum Process had also become important as a means of tracking would-be Islamic State (IS) terrorists across North Africa, reminiscent of the early 2000s when Sudan's security apparatus had sold itself to the West as an essential source of knowledge about al-Qaeda. Consequently, as far as the late Obama administration was concerned, Sudan had once again become a security rather than a human-rights issue in Washington, which is exactly how Khartoum preferred it. All this, despite evidence that small-arms weapons made in Sudan were ending up in the hands of IS terrorists. President Bashir had again proved himself an adroit and sophisticated master of international politics, taking advantage of the slightest turn to sell his regime as an indispensable partner to many who should have known better.

DARFUR: THE ENDGAME

If by 2016, then, Europe, the US and the Gulf states were inclined to treat Sudan virtually as a partner rather than a pariah, enlisting its help in fighting IS and stemming the flow of refugees to Europe at source, the main people to suffer from this near normalization of Sudan's status were the people of Darfur. After the upsurge of international interest in Sudan's hitherto obscure western region during the mid-2000s, it was only natural, perhaps, that concern should fade as new crises came along (such as that of the refugees fleeing the civil war in Syria). However, Sudan's government also played this to its advantage, again. Aware of the relatively short attention spans of Western governments, leaders in Khartoum knew that if they could just ride out the first years of Darfur-fever, eventually they could achieve most of their aims in the region while still claiming that nothing serious had ever happened there in the first place. Unfortunately, by 2016 it was looking very much as if the Sudanese government had succeeded and that it was getting very close to the endgame in Darfur.

Broadly, from 2010 onwards the Sudanese government pursued twin policies in Darfur. On the one hand, they participated in a peace process sponsored by the Gulf state of Qatar, and on the other, Bashir and his military commanders continued the campaign of relentless aggression that they had started in earnest in 2003, albeit changing their tactics a bit. By and large, however, the latter was of more importance than the former in shaping the eventual outcome in Darfur.

Qatar assumed control of attempts to broker a peace deal after the repeated failures of the Western and UN-led efforts, the assumption being that an Arab country might be able to make a better fist of it. Indeed, the Qatari efforts did occasionally score small advances, backed by the deep pockets of an oil-rich government seeking a role as a regional diplomatic power. In 2011, for instance, Qatar brokered a peace deal between the Sudanese government and the small Liberation and Justice Movement, an alliance of Darfur rebel splinter parties. Both sides signed the grandly named Doha Document for Peace in Darfur, which unlocked large-scale funding from Qatar and its allies to 'develop' Darfur, and thereby, hopefully, end the conflicts there. In the following years, indeed, hundreds of millions of dollars were released for spending on projects in Darfur.

But the Doha peace process, however promising at the beginning, never succeeded in drawing in all the rebel groups, let alone the main ones such as the Sudan Revolutionary Front (SRF), a relatively new alliance founded in 2011 that included the Justice and Equality Movement (JEM). The SRF remained too suspicious of the government to accept the Doha process at face value; consequently the Qatari efforts, though doubtless well-intentioned, never came to fruition.

The government, for its part, accused the rebel groups of being too stubborn to take any risks with the peace process, while the rebels accused the government of maintaining its assault on their villages and peoples throughout the negotiations. They had a point, and the government's policy of keeping up the military pressure on the rebels and the civilian population of Darfur was accompanied also by a determined attempt to isolate Darfur from the outside world, to draw a veil over what was really going on there. This reversed the previous policy of letting journalists into Darfur; from now on it became extremely rare for reporters (as well as diplomats, NGOs and the UN) to gain access to the region, cutting off the flow of news and effectively obscuring it from public gaze. For those who did manage to get in, it now became very hard to travel much beyond the main cities and the most frequently visited IDP camps. By this time, Western audiences were probably suffering from Darfur-fatigue anyway, but the news blackout ensured that Darfur (and Sudan in general) once again dropped towards the bottom of international news agendas, helped also by the spike in interest in South Sudan and the new country's bloody civil war.

Meanwhile the Sudanese military continued in its previous strategy to defeat the rebel groups, namely attacking villages in order to deprive the rebels of their bases of support. Hundreds of thousands of new refugees were consequently driven into IDP camps, and thousands of people continued to be killed. There were two new elements to the fighting as well. Instead of the *janjaweed*, the army now deployed a new force, the Special Reaction Force, as their proxy killers, and, with promises of gold, Arab tribes were also drawn into the conflict. Gold began to be mined on a relatively large scale in Darfur as Sudan's other sources of income started to dry up after the separation of the country. According to the Enough Project, by 2012 the country's annual gold production of over forty tons yielded around US$2.2 billion. Sudan's gold industry was the third biggest on the continent after Ghana and South Arica, and gold accounted for almost 60 per cent of the country's overall exports.[14]

Tragically, the force that had been sent to keep the peace in Darfur, UNAMID, also became deeply embroiled in the government's determined attempts to deceive the world into believing that it was genuinely searching for peace in Darfur while at same time pursuing its original aim of ethnic cleansing. From its initial deployment in 2008, UNAMID had never been very effective at protecting civilians and refugees, but its presence in Darfur was rolled over every year by the UN Security Council, principally for want of a better alternative. The Sudanese government went through the ritual of protesting against its presence in Darfur as an egregious intrusion upon the country's sovereignty, but in fact UNAMID came to be rather useful to President Bashir as it regularly under-reported, or censored, the news of government attacks on civilians, thus helping to perpetuate the myth pedalled by Bashir that in Darfur everything was returning to 'normal'. Indeed, as early as 2009 the outgoing head of UNAMID, General Martin Luther Agwai, declared that the war in Darfur was over, attributing any lingering violence to banditry and robberies, despite the clear evidence of ongoing attacks – and sometimes mass rapes – of the civilian population by the Sudanese Armed Forces and its proxies, amongst others.

How did this awful state of affairs come about? The world would have known little of the story had it not been for the courageous decision by UNAMID's chief spokesperson to 'blow the whistle', much as Mukesh Kapila had done to first bring the killings in Darfur to the world's attention in 2003. Aicha Elbasri had previously worked with the UN Development Programme in Khartoum (where I had got to know her) in the mid-2000s, but with her excellent Arabic, English and French she was appointed as the UNAMID spokesperson in August 2012. She resigned from her post in disgust in April 2013.

What she saw during her time in Darfur was a systematic campaign by the mission to under-report the Sudanese army's assaults on civilians there, making the UN essentially complicit in what the International Criminal Court, in its indictment of President Bashir, had described as war crimes and even genocide. In a démarche to her former employers after she resigned, Elbasri chronicled, in great detail, sixteen cases in which UNAMID had, so she claimed, deliberately 'concealed from the Security Council, the media, the Sudanese people and the public in general' attacks on Darfur civilians and even UNAMID's own peacekeepers, mostly by the Sudanese army or their proxy militia. These attacks sometimes involved rapes; in one incident a hundred unarmed persons were massacred in a village called Hashaba.

UNAMID connived in these deceptions because the African nature of the mission meant that it naturally tried to protect one of its own, namely President Bashir, and because in the end UNAMID was there at the behest of the Sudanese government and had to 'maintain the consent and goodwill of the host government', as the UN put it, to survive at all.[15] All UN missions, to varying degrees, have to accept the same operating parameters, but UNAMID took these to the extreme; in the words of one long-time Sudan expert, UNAMID was 'a mission paralysed by fear of the government'.[16] There was a geopolitical aspect to UNAMID's mendacity as well. The Russians, who as one of the permanent members of the Security Council had sanctioned the deployment of UNAMID in the first place, nonetheless saw the mission in Darfur very much as a Western initiative. In the era of President Putin's confrontation with the West over Libya, Syria, Ukraine and elsewhere, it suited the Russians to sabotage UNAMID's effectiveness and cultivate President Bashir's Sudan as an ally, another point of pushback against the perfidious West.

Aicha Elbasri's outspoken criticism of UNAMID was unprecedented and forced the UN to undertake its own review of her very serious allegations. This review was circulated in October 2014, and even though it treated UNAMID as sympathetically as it could, nonetheless the secretary-general of the UN Ban Ki-moon still wrote in a covering letter that the 'lapses in the reporting standards of the Mission and its tendency not to report fully on incidents involving attacks on civilians and United Nation peacekeepers are very troubling'.[17] Indeed, the UN's internal investigation found that in five of the sixteen cases, Elbasri's strictures were fully justified.

But did this lead to any heads rolling at the UN? Or within UNAMID? Not at all. Everything just carried on as before, and the mission has been rolled over twice more since Aicha Elbasri resigned. The whole saga encapsulated how poorly the people of Darfur have been served by the international community, which had contrived to spend almost $1 billion a year on a UN force that was effectively covering up the violence visited upon the very people it was supposed to protect.

President Bashir spent a couple of days in the region in April 2016 to campaign in a referendum to decide Darfur's future administrative status. Now the conflict was 'over', he argued, the last stage of the

Doha peace process could be implemented: a people's vote on whether to keep Darfur as five distinct states, or to unite it into one single region. This seemed a rather arcane point to the millions of Darfuri refugees, the majority of whom were not allowed to vote, or to many of the local Darfuri politicians who boycotted the vote entirely. But to Bashir, it was important to put on a good show as it maintained the fiction of a peace process successfully coming to its conclusion. He impatiently batted away irritating questions from the few international journalists about a recent spike in violence that had made around 130,000 more people homeless in the previous months.

For what it's worth, 98 per cent of Darfuris were recorded as having voted Yes to the five states option, provoking howls of derision from opposition politicians, civil society groups and Darfur's numerous refugee groups. No matter: in the government's eyes, the process is what counted, in that it took another step to 'normalization'. Next, Bashir has declared, UNAMID must leave, and then many of the IDPs will depart their camps, although exactly where they are to go has not been made clear. What is certain is that millions more will live in the camps that have been their homes since 2003–04, permanent victims of the Darfur conflict. Remarkably, it seems that Bashir will have ultimately faced down the combined might of the US, Europe, much of the UN, the ICC and most of the world's human rights groups over the course of a decade. The endgame in Darfur is of his choosing rather than anybody else's.

* * *

On Friday 9 July 2016, South Sudan's two old rivals Riek Machar and President Salva Kiir were making yet another attempt to patch up their differences inside the presidential compound in Juba. Enough, at least, to maintain the semblance of a unity government mandated by regional peace negotiators and the UN. Beyond the walls of the compound, however, the two leaders' entourages of bodyguards were plainly not in a peace-making mood; a firefight kicked off, and within hours over a hundred people were dead. It's unclear how the shooting started, and who pulled the first trigger, but that hardly matters anymore. Unfortunately, by that point such a deadly confrontation was almost inevitable.

Over the subsequent weekend a further 250 people or so were killed as the fighting spread beyond Juba to other parts of the country, and about 40,000 civilians, according to the UN, were made homeless. So worrying was the fighting in Juba that some foreign nationals started to leave, although the airport was closed temporarily. Germany pulled a hundred of its people out: some NGOs suspended their work. The UN Security Council urged an immediate ceasefire, and Riek Machar asked for UN peacekeepers to establish a buffer zone between his troops and those of the official South Sudanese army controlled by Salva Kiir, a proposal rejected by Kiir's supporters. But the damage had already been done: another outflow of foreign support for the South Sudanese people, hundreds more killed and made homeless, and a little more trust drained out of the inaptly named peace process, if there was any left by that point.

Given the record of the past five years, it is difficult to be anything but deeply pessimistic about the future of South Sudan. The day after the latest round of shooting started, 10 July, was the nation's fifth birthday, yet few had the chance to celebrate as they took cover from bullets and rocket-propelled grenades, all fired by their own countrymen. As I argued in the first edition of this book, South Sudan will only be able to find a measure of peace and reconciliation when a new generation of leaders take over, but the prospect of that happening looks as far off as ever. Furthermore, as the two sides sink ever deeper into the bog of sectarian violence, so it becomes less and less likely that anyone, on either side, whatever their age, won't be consumed by the same myopic hatreds that for decades now have apparently driven the likes of Riek Machar and Salva Kiir. With hindsight, the untimely death of John Garang looks ever more tragic with every passing year.

The only real beneficiary of the civil war in the south is President Bashir in the north. As the UN, the West and East African nations have had to focus on the mess in South Sudan, so the regime in

Khartoum has had more of a free hand to continue its policies in Darfur and elsewhere largely unhindered. That is a tragedy for the people of Sudan, particularly those inhabitants of South Kordofan and the Blue Nile states, and Darfur. As in South Sudan, the conflicts in these areas continue, both politically and militarily, with little end in sight. Sudan also deserves new leadership, but, again, it is hard to see now from which direction this is going to emerge. That will certainly have to wait for a third edition, and probably more.

NOTES

CHAPTER ONE: THE ONE-CITY STATE

1. Fergus Nicoll, *The Mahdi of Sudan and the Death of General Gordon*, Sutton Publishing, 2005, p. 26.
2. There are dozens of books about General Gordon, Omdurman and Sudan: two of the best most recent ones are by Fergus Nicoll (above) and by Michael Asher, *Khartoum: The Ultimate Imperial Adventure*, Penguin, 2007.
3. See Robert Collins, *A History of Modern Sudan*, Cambridge University Press, 2008, p. 239.
4. M.W. Daly, *Imperial Sudan: The Anglo-Egyptian Condominium 1934–56*, Cambridge University Press, 1991, p. 14.
5. See the prologue of Wilfred Thesiger's *Desert, Marsh and Mountain*, Flamingo, 1995, for a snapshot of a district commissioner's life in Sudan before the war.
6. See John Paden, *Faith and Politics in Nigeria*, United States Institute of Peace Press, 2008, pp. 40–42, for more on these important links between northern Nigeria and Sudan.
7. Alex de Waal, *War in Darfur and the Search for Peace*, Justice Africa, 2007, p. 8.
8. See Collins, p. 277, for a discussion of this.
9. Mohamed Omer Beshir, *The Southern Sudan*, Khartoum University Press, 1968, p. 36. See Chapters 4 and 5 for a good discussion of these issues.
10. Francis Deng, *War of Visions: Conflict of Identities in the Sudan*, The Brookings Institution, 1995, p. 64.
11. Deng, pp. 72–7.
12. Daly, p. 383.
13. Deng, p. 137.
14. See John Young's two papers for the Small Arms Survey for the whole story of the wars between Sudan, Eritrea and Ethiopia in east Sudan: 'Armed groups

along Sudan's eastern frontier: an overview and analysis', 2007 and 'The eastern front and the struggle against marginalisation', 2007.

15. Daly, p. 398.

CHAPTER TWO: POPULISTS AND CIVIL WAR, 1956–89

1. Douglas Johnson, *The Root Causes of Sudan's Civil Wars*, Indiana University Press, p. 34.
2. Alex de Waal (ed.), *Islamism and its Enemies in the Horn of Africa*, Shama Books, Addis Ababa, 2003, p. 112.
3. De Waal, *War in Darfur and the Search for Peace*, p. 79.
4. For a longer exposition of this point of view, see Deng, Chapter 5.
5. Jago Salmon, 'The paramilitary revolution: the Popular Defence Forces', Small Arms Survey, 2007, p. 12.
6. For an excellent recent account of the Misseriyya, see Sarah Pantuliano, Omer Egemi, Babo Fadlalla and Mohammed Farah, 'Put out to pasture: War, oil and the decline of Misseriyya pastoralism in Sudan', Overseas Development Institute, London, 2009.
7. See also Deng, Chapter 7, for more on the issue of slaving and racism in the confrontation between the Misseriyya and Dinka.

CHAPTER THREE: THE NATIONAL ISLAMIC FRONT AND TURABI IN POWER, 1989–2000

1. Collins, p. 186.
2. See Jago Salmon, 'A paramilitary revolution: the Popular Defence Forces'.
3. For a graphic description of life as an aspiring child soldier in these camps, see the account by the guerrilla turned rap star Emmanuel Jal in *Warchild: A Boy Soldier's Story*, Abacus, 2009.
4. For a full account of the splits within the SPLA ranks, see Douglas H. Johnson, *The Root Causes of Sudan's Civil Wars*, African Issues, Indiana University Press, 2003, Chapters 7–8.
5. Amnesty International, 'The Tears of Orphans', p. 28.
6. De Waal, *Islamism and its Enemies*, p. 73.
7. Judith Miller, *God Has Ninety-Nine Lives*, Touchstone, 1997, p. 162.
8. Collins, p. 195.
9. Peter Bergen, *The Osama Bin Laden I Know*, Free Press, 2005, p. 124.
10. Abdel Bari Atwan, *The Secret History of al-Qaeda*, Abacus, 2006, p. 48.
11. Mansour Khalid, *War and Peace in Sudan*, Kegan and Paul, 2003.
12. Quoted by John Young, 'Armed groups along Sudan's eastern frontier', Small Arms Survey, 2007, p. 24.
13. Quoted in Don Petterson, *Inside Sudan: Political Islam, Conflict and Catastrophe*, Westview Press, 2003, p. 217.
14. For an excellent account of the spread of Sufism in Sudan, see Deng, Chapter 2.
15. Jack Mendelson, quoted in Deng.
16. See Paden, pp. 42–3.
17. For various discussions of these events, see Bergen pp. 87–8, Collins pp. 220–1.
18. See Sondra Hale's essay 'Ideology and identity; Islam, gender and the state in Sudan', in Haideh Moghissi (ed.), *Women and Islam: Critical Concepts in Sociology*, Routledge, 2005.
19. For a fuller account of women during the Islamic revolution see the three volumes of *Women and Law in Sudan*, (1997) by the Women and Law Project in Sudan.
20. Ministry of Foreign Affairs, Personnel Department.

CHAPTER FOUR: SUDAN AND THE WEST: SLAVERY, CONSCIENCE AND AL-QAEDA

1. See Steve Coll, *Ghost Wars*, Penguin, 2004, pp. 270–1.
2. Don Petterson, *Inside Sudan: Political Islam, Conflict and Catastrophe*, Westview Press, 2003, p. 15.
3. Walter Waihenya, *The Mediator: General Lazaro Sumbeiyo and the Southern Sudan Peace Process*, Kenway Publications, 2006.

CHAPTER FIVE: DARFUR: HOW THE KILLING WAS ALLOWED TO HAPPEN

1. See Chapter 2.
2. M.W. Daly, *Darfur's Sorrow: A History of Destruction and Genocide*, Cambridge University Press, 2007, pp. 209–11.
3. See de Waal and Flint, *Darfur: A Short History of a Long War*, p. 33.
4. See Adam Lebor, *Complicity with Evil: The United Nations in the Age of Modern Genocide*, Yale University Press, 2006, pp. 150–60 for a discussion of this point.
5. Samantha Power, *A Problem from Hell: America and the Age of Genocide*, Harper Perennial, 2007, p. 385.
6. Power, p. 389.

CHAPTER SIX: DARFUR, THE VORTEX

1. Samantha Power, p. xviii.
2. There are now several books that devote long discussions to the designation of Darfur as a 'genocide'. See, for instance, Gérard Prunier, *Darfur: The Ambiguous Genocide*; Hurst and Company, 2005; Totten and Markus (eds), *Genocide in Darfur*, Routledge, 2006; Mahmood Mamdami, *Saviours and Sinners*, Pantheon Books, 2009.
3. For a fuller analysis of Darfur and the dangers of celebrity activism see Alex de Waal, 'The humanitarian carnival: A celebrity vogue', in *World Affairs Journal*, Fall 2008.
4. See, for instance, the WHO Collaborating Centre for Research on the Epiemiology of Disasters, report of 24 April 2008: 'Although the conflict [in Darfur] is still very active, several surveys have shown that mortality rates are probably lower than the emergency level'. The 'emergency' level is taken to be 36 deaths per thousand of people a year; by late 2007 that level had fallen to around 30 per thousand per year in Darfur.
5. 'Investing in Tragedy', *Human Rights First*, p. 17.
6. www.securitycouncilreport.org
7. Alex de Waal, 'Darfur and the failure of the responsibility to protect', in *International Affairs*, vol. 83, no. 6, November 2007.
8. See Opheera McDoom interview on Reuters, 18 October 2004.
9. See, for instance, de Waal and Flint, *Darfur: A Short History of a Long War.*

CHAPTER SEVEN: SURVIVING IN THE NORTH, FAILING IN THE SOUTH, 2005–10

1. See *Africa Confidential*, vol. 50, no. 18, for a discussion of this. For more detail, see *Rescuing the Peace in Southern Sudan*, a Joint NGO Briefing Paper, 2010, available at www.oxfam.org
2. Human Rights Watch, 'The Way Forward: Ending Human Rights Abuses and Repression across Sudan' (2009).
3. See the UNDP's excellent *Situation Analyses* on Kassala State and Red Sea State, both published in 2009, for a comprehensive look at the poverty and health indicators for two states.

4. Munzoul A.M. Assal, 'Is it the Fault of NGOs Alone? Aid and Dependency in Eastern Sudan', paper for the Chr. Michelsen Institute (Norway) and the University of Khartoum, 2008.

5. See International Crisis Group, Africa Briefing No. 72, 'Rigged Elections in Darfur and the Consequences of a Probable NCP victory in Sudan,' 30 March 2010.

6. For a full discussion of the Sudan–China commercial links, see Sharath Srinivasan, Chapter 4 entitled, 'A Marriage Less Convenient; China, Sudan and Darfur', in Kweku Ampiah and Sanusha Naidu (eds), *Crouching Tiger, Hidden Dragon? Africa and China*, University of KwaZulu-Natal Press, 2008.

CHAPTER EIGHT: NEW NATIONS, OLD WAYS

1. Jeremy Astill-Brown, 'South Sudan's Slide into Conflict: Revisiting the Past and Reassessing Partnerships', Chatham House Research Paper, December 2014, p. 6.

2. UNDP, 'Search for a New Beginning: Perceptions of Truth, Justice, Reconciliation and Healing in South Sudan', October 2015.

3. Astill-Brown, p. 9.

4. Alex de Waal, 'When kleptocracy becomes insolvent: Brute causes of the civil war in South Sudan', *African Affairs*, April 2016.

5. Astill-Brown.

6. These paragraphs are largely drawn from The Sentry's report, 'The Nexus of Corruption and Conflict in South Sudan', July 2015, available at https://thesentry.org/reports/south-sudan/

7. The Enough Project, 'Addressing South Sudan's Economic and Fiscal Crisis', February 2016.

8. www.hrw.org/sites/default/files/reports/sudan0414_ForUpload.pdf

9. Eddie Thomas, 'The Future of Sudanese Health Care and the Wealth-Sharing Protocol of Sudan's 2005 Comprehensive Peace Agreement', paper delivered 2015.

10. Ibid., p. 11.

11. *Sudan Tribune*, 5 November 2015.

12. International Crisis Group, 'Sudan's Islamists: From Salvation to Survival', March 2016, p. 2.

13. PAX, 'Sudan Alert: The EU's Policy Options for Sudan', 2016, p. 27.

14. Omer Ismail and Akshaya Kumar, 'Darfur's Gold Rush: State-Sponsored Atrocities 10 Years After the Genocide', Enough Project, May 2013.

15. Ban Ki-moon, 'Letter dated 29 October 2014 from the Secretary-General addressed to the President of the Security Council', United Nations Security Council, S/2014/771, available at www.securitycouncilreport.org/atf/cf/%7B65BFCF9B-6D27-4E9C-8CD3-CF6E4FF96FF9%7D/s_2014_771.pdf

16. The Sentry.

17. Ban Ki-moon.

SELECT BIBLIOGRAPHY

The following is a list of the books, articles, reports and a blog that I found most useful for writing this book. It is by no means a comprehensive survey of the literature on Sudan – that would now run to many pages!

Everything below is listed alphabetically, but I would like to recommend, in particular, two books that I found essential for understanding the often bewildering complexities and paradoxes of Sudan's past and present. *A History of Modern Sudan* (Cambridge, 2008) is the best straightforward narrative history of Sudan, written by Robert O. Collins, an American academic who died in 2008. *War of Visions* (Brookings Institution, 1995) is the indispensable guide to the sociology, religion and anthropology of Sudan, written by Francis Deng, a southern Sudanese who held several positions in Sudan's government during the 1970s and 1980s.

The dates of the publications refer to the editions that I used; they do not necessarily indicate when the book was first published.

BOOKS

Alden, Chris, *China in Africa*, Zed Books, 2007

Ali, Abdalla Ali, *The Sudanese–Chinese Relations Before and After Oil*, Sudan Currency Printing Press, 2006

Ampiah, Kweku and Sanusha Naidu (eds), *Crouching Tiger, Hidden Dragon? Africa and China*, University of KwaZulu-Natal Press, 2008

Asher, Michael, *Khartoum: The Ultimate Imperial Adventure*, Penguin, 2006

Bergen, Peter L., *The Osama bin Laden I Know*, Free Press, 2005

Beshir, Mohamed Omer, *The Southern Sudan: Background to Conflict*, Khartoum University Press, 1970

— *The Southern Sudan: From Conflict to Peace*, The Khartoum Bookshop, 1975

Bin Laden, Najwa, Omar bin Laden and Jean Sasson, *Growing Up bin Laden*, St. Martin's Press, 2009

Burr, J. Millard and Robert O. Collins, *Darfur: The Long Road to Disaster*, Markus Wiener Publishers, 2006

Clarke, Richard A., *Against All Enemies: Inside America's War on Terror*, Free Press, 2004

Coll, Steve, *Ghost Wars: The Secret History of the CIA, Afghanistan, and Bin Laden, from the Soviet Invasion to September 10, 2001*, Penguin, 2005

Collins, Robert O., *A History of Modern Sudan*, Cambridge, 2008

Copnall, James, *A Poisonous Thorn in Our Hearts: Sudan and South Sudan's Bitter and Incomplete Divorce*, C. Hurst & Co., 2014

Daly, M.W., *Empire on the Nile: The Anglo-Egyptian Sudan, 1898–1934*, Cambridge, 1986

— *Darfur's Sorrow: A History of Destruction and Genocide*, Cambridge, 2007

Deng, Francis, *War of Visions*, Brookings Institution, 1995

Gilbert, Lela, *Baroness Cox: Eyewitness to a Broken World*, Monarch Books, 2007

Hari, Daoud, *The Translator: A Tribesman's Memoir of Darfur*, Random House, 2008

Hoile, David, *Darfur in Perspective*, European–Sudanese Public Affairs Council, 2005

Holt, P.M., *A Modern History of the Sudan*, Weidenfeld and Nicolson, 1961

Jal, Emmanuel, *Warchild: A Boy Soldier's Story*, Abacus, 2009

Johnson, Douglas H., *The Root Causes of Sudan's Civil Wars*, James Curry, African Issues, 2003

Khalid, Mansour, *War and Peace in Sudan: A Tale of Two Countries*, Kegan Paul, 2003

Lebor, Adam, *Complicity with Evil: The United Nations in the Age of Modern Genocide*, Yale University Press, 2006

Mamdani, Mahmood, *Saviours and Survivors: Darfur, Politics and the War on Terror*, Pantheon Books, 2009

Miller, Judith, *God Has Ninety-Nine Names: Reporting from a Militant Middle East*, Touchstone, 1997

Natsios, Andrew S., *Sudan, South Sudan and Darfur: What Everyone Needs to Know*, Oxford University Press, 2012

Nazar, Mende, *Slave*, Charnwood, 2005

Nicoll, Fergus, *The Mahdi of Sudan and the Death of General Gordon*, Sutton Publishing, 2005

Paden, John N., *Faith and Politics in Nigeria*, United States Institute of Peace Press, 2008

Petterson, Don, *Inside Sudan: Political Islam, Conflict and Catastrophe*, Westview Press, 2003

Power, Samantha, *A Problem from Hell: America and the Age of Genocide*, Harper Perennial, 2007

Prunier, Gérard, *Darfur: The Ambiguous Genocide*, Hurst and Company, 2005

Salih, Tayeb, *Season of Migration to the North*, Penguin, 2003

Thomas, Edward, *South Sudan: A Slow Liberation*, Zed Books, 2015

Totten, Samuel and Eric Markusen (eds), *Genocide in Darfur: Investigating the Atrocities in the Sudan*, Routledge, 2006

Waal, Alex de, (ed.), *Islamism and its Enemies in the Horn of Africa*, Shama Books, Addis Ababa, 2003

— *War in Darfur and the Search for Peace*, Justice Africa, Harvard University, 2007

Waal, Alex de, and Julie Flint, *Darfur: A New History of a Long War*, Zed Books, 2008

Waihenya, Waithaka, *The Mediator: Gen. Lazaro Sumbeiywo and the Southern Sudan Peace Process*, Kenway Publications, 2006

Wright, Lawrence, *The Looming Tower*, Allen Lane, 2006

Yousif, Galal Mahmoud, *The Gezira Scheme: The Greatest on Earth*, Africa University House for Printing, Khartoum, 1997

ARTICLES

Assal, Munzoul A.M., 'Is it the fault of NGOs alone? Aid and dependency in Eastern Sudan', Chr. Michelsen Institute, Norway, 2008

Astill-Brown, Jeremy, 'South Sudan's slide into conflict: Revisiting the past and reassessing partnerships', Chatham House Research Paper, December 2014

Hale, Sondra, 'Ideology and identity: Islam, gender and the state in Sudan', in Haideh Moghissi (ed.) *Women and Islam: Critical Concepts in Sociology*, Routledge, 2005

Manger, Leif, 'Pastoralist-state relationships among the Hadendowa Beja of Eastern Sudan', *Nomadic Peoples*, vol. 5, issue 2, 2001

Pantuliano, Sarah, Omer Egemi, Babo Fadlalla and Farah Mohammed, 'Put out to pasture: war, oil and the decline of Misseriyya pastoralism in Sudan', Overseas Development Institute, March 2009

Salmon, Jago, 'A paramilitary revolution: the Popular Defence Forces', Small Arms Survey, 2007

Slim, Hugo, 'Dithering over Darfur? A preliminary review of the International Response', *International Affairs*, vol. 80, no. 5, 2004, pp. 811–33

Waal, Alex de, 'The humanitarian carnival: A celebrity vogue', *World Affairs*, Fall, 2008

Young, John, 'The eastern front and the struggle against marginalisation', Small Arms Survey, 2007

— 'Armed groups along Sudan's eastern frontier: an overview and analysis', Small Arms Survey, 2007

REPORTS AND OTHER DOCUMENTS

Amnesty International, 'The Tears of Orphans: No Future without Rights – Sudan', 1995

Human Rights First, 'Investing in Tragedy: China's Money, Arms, and Politics in Sudan', March 2008

Human Rights Watch, 'Sudan, Oil and Human Rights', November 2003

— 'Entrenching Impunity: Government Responsibility for International Crimes in Darfur', December 2005

— 'Soudan: les plus petits temoins: la crise du Darfour au travers du regard des enfants', 2005

— ' "They Came Here to Kill Us": Militia Attacks and Ethnic Targeting of Civilians in Eastern Chad', January 2007

— 'Child Soldiers in the Chad Conflict', July 2007

— 'Darfur 2007: Chaos by Design', September 2007

— 'The Way Forward: Ending Human Rights Abuses and Repression across Sudan', October 2009

International Crisis Group, 'God, Oil and Country: Changing the Logic of War in Sudan', 2002

— 'Sudan's Islamists: From Salvation to Survival', March 2016

Sudan HIV/AIDS Working Group, 'Tackling the HIV Challenge in Sudan: The Way Forward', November 2008

Waging Peace, 'China in Africa; the Human Rights Impact', February 2008

BLOG

SSRC Blog, 'Particularly Julie Flint, Examining the Rebels – At Last', 23 May 2008

INDEX